D1052851

Fat China

How Expanding Waistlines are Changing a Nation

Paul French and Matthew Crabbe

ANTHEM PRESS
LONDON · NEW YORK · DELHI

Anthem Press
An imprint of Wimbledon Publishing Company
www.anthempress.com

This edition first published in UK and USA 2010
by ANTHEM PRESS
75-76 Blackfriars Road, London SE1 8HA, UK
or PO Box 9779, London SW19 7ZG, UK
and
244 Madison Ave. #116, New York, NY 10016, USA

Cover image 'Zuguo chuchu chuan xixun' by Liu Shumao
courtesy of the International Institute of Social History
IISH Stefan R. Landsberger Collection
available at http://chineseposters.net/.

British Library Cataloguing in Publication Data
A catalogue record for this book is available from the British Library.

Library of Congress Cataloging in Publication Data
A catalog record for this book has been requested.

ISBN-13: 978 0 85728 978 0 (Hbk)
ISBN-10: 0 85728 978 0 (Hbk)

ISBN-13: 978 0 85728 965 0 (Pbk)
ISBN-10: 0 85728 965 9 (Pbk)

ISBN-13: 978 0 85728 986 5 (eBook)
ISBN-10: 0 85728 986 1 (eBook)

'China has entered the era of obesity.'

Ji Chengye, of the Child and Adolescent Health Section
of the China Preventive Medicine Association

'China's first week-long campaign against obesity was launched in Beijing on Monday by the Chinese Preventive Medical Association. In the four cities of Beijing, Shanghai, Guangzhou and Shenzhen, experts will give lectures and provide free examinations to help more people understand the dangers of obesity. Shi Yifan, a professor of endocrinology with Peking Union Medical College Hospital, said that obesity was a growing threat to the population's health, which most people failed to realize. The campaign aims to inform people that obesity can lead to many diseases, and losing weight is imperative, though only under a doctor's supervision.'

China Daily, 7 May 2002

'The obesity problems are all due to a 21st-century lifestyle high technology, high calories, high anxiety we have to change all these things...'

Ma Guansheng, a nutritionist with the Chinese Centre
for Disease Control and Prevention

'Obesity is more of a threat than avian flu and much more difficult to treat.'

Dr. Henk Bekedam, former WHO Chief China
representative in Beijing

TABLE OF CONTENTS

LIST OF TABLES

PREFACE

While China's economy booms, its pollution and social problems have been commented on, researched and worried over, both inside and outside China. Commentators are divided between (1) those who think that eventually, as China grows more prosperous, it will be able to solve all these immense challenges, and (2) those who are more pessimistic and feel that the good years are coming to an end. As one expert put it, China will be the first country in history to grow old from its demographic problems and poison itself from environmental degradation before it gets rich.

Less commented on has been China's looming healthcare crisis. In 2003, during the Severe Acute Respiratory Syndrome (SARS) outbreak, when migrant workers were sent back to the countryside, it became clear that for large parts of China, the healthcare system had broken down. Since then, more investment has gone into hospitals, preventive healthcare, and medical research. In 2009, as part of China's RMB4 trillion (about US$586 billion) fiscal stimulus package, the central government budgeted for billions more to go into the healthcare system, in the countryside and cities.

But as Paul French and Matthew Crabbe show in this fact-filled, hard-hitting study of obesity in contemporary China, the real killer is only just emerging. The US, Europe and other developed countries suffer from huge – and soaring – rates of obesity, something attributed to the lifestyles, diets and educational systems which have developed over the last century. As an industrializing country, with vast epidemics of famine in living memory (China lost over 30 million in the famines of the early 1960s), it might seem strange to argue that obesity has so quickly become as much a problem in China as in the West. But French and Crabbe summon the evidence. And more importantly, they explain why this is happening and where it might be heading if nothing is done.

Food and drink is the most basic human need. In the space of a generation, the dietary behaviour of the Chinese people has changed radically. Patterns of buying food, of rising meat consumption, of huge increases in fast-food consumption, urbanization and more sedentary, pressurized lifestyles have all given rise to the same issues as in the West. Things have been made worse by the phenomenon of the one-child modern family, where parents, grandparents and extended family grant every wish and need of their 'young emperors and empresses'. The ancient Chinese tradition of snacking and eating the staple diet of rice, supplemented by plentiful vegetables, has been merged with a meat-and-potato diet, with meals and snacks taking place throughout the day. This has ended up being the worst of both worlds, with calorie intake soaring in cities that lack adequate recreational and sporting facilities. Beer drinking, which has risen enormously in the last decade, hasn't helped things, and smoking rates remain extremely high.

French and Crabbe have devoted many years to looking at consumer and lifestyle trends in modern China. Few are better placed to draw out the bigger picture of what is happening at the most fundamental level of people's lives. Obesity runs alongside the processes of urbanization, new-found consumer wealth, and the creation of modern office-centred working lives, where time is in short demand, and disposable income rising.

The illnesses that arise from this are already quantifiable in terms of rising rates of heart disease, diabetes and hepatitis. Diabetes in particular has become a huge problem, exacerbating other underlying ailments. The key question that the authors pose is how an overstretched system will be able to cope with the increased need from younger Chinese who are eating themselves into obesity and illness.

Modern China is a bewildering place, not only to those looking at it from outside, but also to those who are within. No government has lifted more people out of poverty, more quickly, than the Communist Party of China. In chapters on the changes in diet to chicken, beef, seafood, much of it exotic and more often than not, imported, and bought in vast new hypermarkets rather than the old-style wet markets that used to dominate China, the authors look at the willing complicity of mostly foreign fast-food companies in this change of lifestyle. Kentucky Fried Chicken and McDonald's have sprung up across the country, delivering some of their most profitable business in the world. This has run alongside the same fetishization of slim models and thinness that exists in the West. Staggering numbers of cosmetic surgeries are performed. In one remarkable example, a girl in the impoverished southwest almost forced her father to donate a kidney to fund her own body enhancement. Backstreet surgeries sometimes do such a bad job on patients that they suffer years of pain and undergo remedial surgery to try to put things right again – if they ever can be.

Chinese people deserve to realize the dream of a good life as much as anyone else. Their recent history has been marked by tragedy, poverty (there are still over 20 million people living below the poverty line in China, suffering from malnourishment) and conflict. From what surveys have been taken, it is clear that they want, and enjoy, prosperity. The ancient rural patterns of land distribution are being replaced by the same agribusinesses that have revolutionized food production in the West. Hundreds of millions more will move to cities in the coming decades. By the middle of this century, China will want to look, act – and eat – much like people in Europe and North America. The environmental and economic impact of this is bound to be profound.

But China can also look at the lamentable state of the West, where as many as half of all Americans are obese, and most of the healthcare budget is spent dealing with the impact of people's lifestyle and diet choices, and reflect. They have little time to get things right. 'Fat China' is an important contribution to the understanding of a little noticed, but critical aspect of modern China. It says a great deal about the kind of country China is becoming, and about the challenges that face it in the future. It reveals much about the mysterious, extremely important new middle class that is growing up, mostly in the eastern part of China, in the great modern cities – cities like Shenzhen, which the authors use as an illustration of the chaotic results of fast, often unplanned development (ironically in a country where central economic planning is still partially maintained). This middle class will hold the fate of the country, and of the Communist Party itself, in their hands as the years and decades move on. As this book shows, in order to do that they will have to start being more careful about how they eat and what they eat, and a little more sceptical about the claims of advertisers and multinational companies. The battle has only just begun. And with French and Crabbe's comprehensive analysis and compelling data, they – and we – cannot say we haven't been warned.

Kerry Brown
Senior Fellow, Asia Programme
Royal Institute of International Affairs
Chatham House, UK

INTRODUCTION

How Expanding Waistlines are Changing a Nation

Obesity has become an issue of global concern. Despite the fact that most of the world remains short of food and that large portions of the planet periodically fall into either climate-generated or politically engendered famines resulting in severe food shortages, obesity rates have grown globally – a clear sign of the uneven division of resources across the world. The growth in obesity is essentially due to two major reasons: Firstly, the countries of the developed world, primarily North America and Western Europe, have seen obesity become a widespread phenomenon with significant growth rates among lower-income and less diet-aware sections of society where the causes are primarily poor levels of dietary knowledge and bad food choices, compounded by increasingly sedentary lifestyles. Secondly, emerging nations, especially those in Asia, have seen obesity become a new problem that has emerged as a spin-off of their rapid economic growth and newfound wealth for increasingly sizeable sections of their societies.

In the past, the debate about weight and obesity has largely centred on two possible factors: (1) obesity as a disease that requires medical treatment and understanding,[1] so as not to ostracize the obese, or (2) as a failure of will, due to the pressures of human life requiring intervention by either the state, parents or individuals in their own increasingly sedentary and glutinous lifestyles. But as we think China shows, fat can also be a developmental issue, and in China, obesity is a problem for the wealthy, newly emergent middle-class consumers – a rapidly growing number of people – that have benefited most from the last thirty years of openness and reform. Obesity is therefore one "wealth deficit" among a long list of "wealth benefits" in China over the last two decades of change.

Excess weight and obesity has become a real issue in the developed world, though consensus on the causes is far from unanimous, and strategies to combat obesity rates are fragmented and championed by points of view ranging from fad dieticians, daytime TV hosts and tabloid newspapers to the American surgeon general, presidents and prime ministers. While some have argued that the new generation of extremely overweight people should be made more aware of their condition, others have called for more radical, interventionist steps – similar to those suggested for diehard smokers – with surgery postponed or refused if the patient makes no effort to shed the excess pounds. Advocates for levying "fat taxes" on high-sugar and high-fat foods, those that believe weight should be a factor in charging tariffs for airline tickets or charging overweight people for treatment for weight-related illnesses and other ways of bringing home the issue to the obese, are numerous and found from Baltimore to Beijing. However, others argue that too radical a campaign against fatness will lead to a furtherance of the supermodel, heroin-chic, size-zero skinniness that has also meant, conversely, that at a time of rising obesity levels in the developed world, we have also seen rising levels and growing awareness of eating disorders, notably anorexia.

Obesity, like gout, was historically a condition of the wealthy until fairly recently.[2] Kublai Khan managed to control most of China and the world's largest land empire despite suffering terrible gout and being notoriously obese. Now the West has started to get concerned; unsurprisingly, with some estimates claiming that 61 per cent of American adults are either overweight or obese. Dr David Satcher, President Clinton's campaigning Surgeon General claimed that obesity had reached 'epidemic proportions' in America and in 2002 openly equated obesity with cigarette smoking as major preventable causes of disease and death.[3] Satcher sparked a major debate that involved giant food conglomerates, political representatives of the major food-producing states, television channels that accept advertising, fast food chains, supermarket multiples and not a few concerned consumers. We have seen fast food giants sued by the obese and the success of movies such as *Supersize Me* and books such as *Fatland* and *Fast Food Nation*.[4] Canada and Australia have seen overweight and obesity rates rise steeply. Concern has also spread to Western Europe where first the British got concerned about rising rates of obesity – again largely among the lower income groups in society – and then other European countries such as Germany. Even the traditionally slim French were amazed at their own national obesity rates; Mireille Guiliano's (CEO of Veuve Clicquot) best-selling book, *French Women Don't Get Fat*, was clearly not a book about all French women.[5]

China Gets Fat

For China, the simple fact is that the rapid economic growth of the country in the last fifteen to twenty years has meant that for many people, overwhelmingly based in the major coastal urban centres of the country, but elsewhere too, incomes have grown and disposable income is far higher than ever before.

This has meant a growth in social inequality too, with a significantly wealthier urban population than rural, meaning that the so-called "spirit level" effect occurs where obesity rates grow rapidly as inequality accentuates.

This shift has occurred at a time of dizzying change in terms of the range of products and brands available to Chinese consumers and the channels through which they can access them from neighbourhood convenience stores to giant edge-of-town hypermarkets. The ability to consume – in terms of choice, range and affordability – has meant a significant change in lifestyles. Fast food, a culture of snacking, fizzy drinks and more confectionery have all added to China's waistlines as have increased car ownership, more white collar jobs (an increasingly desk-bound nation) and hectic work hours that do not allow time for exercise. Additionally, urban planning, the growth of supermarket retailing and other issues have not necessarily helped. China's major cities have an alarming lack of parks and open spaces available to the public. When parks are built, it is invariably against the rules to actually go on the grass. At school, the intense pressure to succeed academically has reduced the space for sports on the curriculum. Urban China has a highly organized retail sector, but wet markets are disappearing and the range and availability of prepared, processed and other high-fat, high-sugar food is growing compared to fresh food.

None of these reasons for the fattening of China are original to the country. We have seen them all in other places, from the promotion of unhealthy foods to the privatization of public space. However, most of these causes have specific Chinese characteristics, and Chinese culture and society have traditionally had different attitudes towards fatness and weight. There are also specifics unique to China that influence the increasing weight of children, notably the One-Child Policy that has been in force since the late 1970s.

The intent of this book is to examine all these causes, trying to understand just how urban China got so fat so fast, then to assess the scale of the problem now, the factors contributing to its spread and what this 'healthcare time bomb' will mean for China's welfare and health service provision in the future and perhaps what can be done about it.[6] China has gone through a sea change of tremendous proportions – and portions – in the last three decades since Deng Xiaoping started the 'reform and openness' movement. Little more than 20 years ago many people, even in China's richest cities, were struggling to feed themselves; now they are struggling to lose weight – Weight Watchers is now open for business and recruiting in China.

The initial outlook for China's fat statistics is not good. Several years ago in Shanghai a new upscale retail mall development opened. Raffles City is adjacent to Shanghai's showpiece People's Square, which contains the city's grand theatre, museums of urban planning, Chinese history and art. The new mall could be in almost any major developed city in the world – retailers, both independent and chain brands known the world over, a multiplex cinema alongside, of course, a food court. However, although the Raffles City food court is one of the latest in China, it sells hardly any Chinese food. You can get hot dogs, kebabs, very large burgers, premium brand ice cream and chocolate chip cookies. And the place is full at lunchtime with Shanghai's legions of *bai ling* – white-collar office workers – eager to chow down and get back to the office.

A combination of greater personal independence and choice combined with more entrepreneurial opportunities in China's cities has led to a greater individual level of freedom, though obviously in China still highly circumscribed. It was also a clearly highly aspirational culture that sought to 'catch up' with the rest of the world, gain respect and have what everybody else had; the initial way to do this in politically restricted China was to buy things, to consume – Coca-Cola, Marlboro cigarettes, Budweiser beer, McDonald's. All these products were Western, new, aspirational, often slightly more expensive than local equivalents and so, popular in a culture where showing wealth was becoming acceptable and offered status. As China's markets have liberalized, so the range of goods has grown from Prada bags to BMW SUVs to Scotch whisky. For many ordinary urbanites, Big Macs, Dove chocolate, Magnum ice cream bars, 250 ml bottles of Pepsi, Whoppers and Chicken Zingers became easily available and affordable.

Lifestyles changed in ways that benefited the sellers of goods. People had more disposable and discretionary income to spend on themselves, their families, children and friends. The combination of rising incomes, greater longevity and the one-child policy meant that the 'six pocket' phenomenon appeared with each child having richer parents, grandparents, aunts and uncles – all keen to spoil them. At the same time, careers and education became more important to a new generation and couples started marrying later, taking a few holidays, buying an apartment and a car before they got hitched. People dated more, ate out more, went to nightclubs more, drank, smoked and worked out in the country's new gym culture; many decided to postpone kids for a while or indefinitely, leading to a growing Dual Income, No Kids (DINK) culture. Li Jie, 33, a sales manager in Beijing is one-half of a typical DINK couple: 'We can't afford the time at present. We've got to invest our time in a more profitable way.' Personal fulfilment was in; traditional filial obligations were put on the back shelf by many, and the state retreated significantly from people's personal lives and consumption choices. It was all pretty good for retail sales and restaurant receipts and those linking their brands to aspirational lifestyles.

However, there has been a downside to all this. Just as China's coastal economy grew rapidly and many of the social traits seen in Western society emerged, so did some of the other factors that tend to leave people neglecting their diet and forgetting their weight and health – China's urban professionals became 'cash rich and time poor'. With work and career pressures increasing, they wanted things *now*; gratification had to be instant. Consequently, the fast-food chains, those that fuelled the snacking culture in the rash of new convenience stores and *xiaomaibu* (neighbourhood mom n' pop outlets) saw greater profits while the emergent Chinese middle class, always in a rush to get somewhere, stopped walking, dumped their bikes and started buying motorcycles and cars and began taking taxis. The amount of time they spent on their rear ends increased. When they did get to relax, they headed back to the restaurants or got home so exhausted they couldn't work up the energy for much else than slapping on a pirated DVD, cracking open a Tsingtao beer and ordering in junk food. All of a sudden the pizza delivery bike became a regular sight on the streets of China's cities.

With cars and supermarkets growing and free time shrinking, the Chinese middle class took to the supermarket aisles. The government helped by encouraging supermarket multiples and closing down wet markets. Most food shopping may remain a daily activity in China, but a large proportion of food is now bought in supermarkets. Foreigners like the French supermarket chain Carrefour, America's mighty Walmart and the UK's Tesco joined local chains like Lianhua, WuMart and Hualian with supermarkets and hypermarkets springing up across the country – many extremely large and often open 24 hours a day. Basket counts may remain stubbornly low by international developed-nation standards, but they are growing. Carrefour has been particularly successful and many of their branches come with a McDonald's, a Häagen-Dazs or a SUBWAY on the ground floor. In the new supermarkets were rows of freezer cabinets, aisles of fizzy drinks and an unprecedented range of product lines. These stores became a major way to introduce new products. No visit to a supermarket was complete without being asked to taste test a new range of crisp or soda, biscuit or sweet of some kind.

So clearly, China's diet has changed with the introduction of previously unavailable foods, a more cosmopolitan range of cuisines and foodstuffs, growing disposable incomes and greater access to foods through a variety of retail channels. Add to this the end of chronic food shortages, the reduction of crop failures, improved logistics and distribution systems and the opening up of the food production and manufacturing sector, and things are radically different from pre-1979.

However, it should be noted that the Maoist period from 1949 to 1979 was a unique period in modern Chinese history; imports were reduced to below pre-revolutionary levels, food production was standardized and "blandished" by being concentrated in large state-owned enterprises (SOEs), choices were limited, retail channels drastically reduced (and all state controlled), rationing was introduced at various periods, prices were subject to strict controls and private enterprise in the food economy was virtually wiped out. The collectivization of land and the imposition of a command economy severely reduced both the range of fruits, vegetables and other foods produced and, due to its economic inefficiency, ultimately led to drastically reduced yields, shortages and periodic famines. The same was true of restaurants, where the socialist canteen or the state-run dining hall replaced entrepreneur-run eateries.

But this was not always how it was, despite the Communist Party 'Big Myth' that rural China was impoverished and backward before 1949, that food choice was limited and that farmers were exploited in a wholesale manner by the Republican government of 1911–1949. More recent research indicates that this is far from the complete picture, though life in China's rural areas has always been far from a pastoral idyll. In both the major coastal cities and many inland areas in the Republican period, the introduction of industrial production methods significantly expanded food choice and availability – rice, sugar and wheat were produced industrially, while widespread innovations such as Primus stoves, Thermos flasks and ice machines revolutionized food storage. Food hygiene was a major target of the Republican government's 'New Life Movement' and independent restaurants opened across the country (to be closed wholesale after 1949). This was the period when dishes now seen as quintessentially Chinese, such as scrambled egg and tomato, made their appearance.

Historian Frank Dikötter has noted, 'Bread, ice cream and yoghurt became popular, sold by peddlers on the street, while "[W]estern" restaurants could be found in most cities by the start of World War Two. Several hundred emerged in Shanghai alone, more than thirty vied for customers in Canton *(Guangzhou)* and a dozen catered for the social and political elites in Tianjin. In Chongqing, foreign food could be found all over the city.'[7] As the revolution consolidated and the Maoist economic model was enforced, this variety and choice to be found in China's cities vanished to be replaced by mass-produced, non-variable basic foods. This situation was not to fundamentally change until the 1980s.

Alarm Bells

What China consumes will change the world. An old adage among analysts is that if China is selling it, the price is cheap; if China is buying it, the price is high. This has been true for many commodities from steel to soybeans over the decades. However, selling to the Chinese consumer has never been an easy proposition and this difficulty is not a new one; in 1937 the American businessman, writer and advertising entrepreneur Carl Crow wrote that clients regularly opined to him, "I suppose the Chinese will buy anything, provided the price is cheap enough.' That is an idea held by most people, even by some foreigners who live in China and should know better.'[8] But it was never that simplistic, as so many companies discovered for themselves between the Wars and, more recently, in the last few decades since China's opening up to the world.

Chinese society is changing in myriad ways – indeed, Chinese people are physically changing. The Chinese body shape is changing; clothing retailers now have to order additional larger sizes, for instance. Urban Chinese people are getting bigger. How much bigger have urban Chinese gotten?

- In 20 years, urban boys have grown by an average of 6 cm (2.4 in) and girls by 4.8 cm (1.9 in) in height.
- The average Chinese child is 3 kg (6.6 lb) heavier than 30 years ago.
- The average urban shoe size is up by two in 30 years.
- Sales of C-, D- and even E-cup bras are rising rapidly in China's cities – even to women under 20; A- and B-cup bra sales are down, indicating larger chest sizes and hence larger skeletal frames.
- The average urban female's chest circumference is now 83.53 cm (32.9 in), a growth of 1 cm (0.4 in) since 1992, according to the Beijing College of Clothing Technology.
- The average waist of an urban male was 25 in (63.5 cm) in 1985; it is now closer to 30 in (76.2 cm) on average. For males in the 40–50 age group, waistlines have reached an average of 82.6 cm (32.5 in), extending by 7.9 cm (3.1 in) compared with the national average in 1987; the waistline of men aged between 30 and 40 extended by 5 cm (1.9 in) and that of those between 20 and 30 years old by 0.1 cm (0.03 in).
- Collar sizes are increasing – leading Chinese shirt maker PPG now features large collar shirts in its catalogues distributed to office workers in Shanghai.

When considering the changing size of Chinese people in recent years, it is worth noting that this is a trend that was interrupted, rather than commenced, by the revolution of 1949. The Communist Party's 'Big Myth' that China prior to 1949 was a completely impoverished, economically stagnant and backward-moving society is being challenged in myriad ways as academics (mostly outside China due to the problems of framing this argument in the People's Republic) reassess the late Qing and Republican periods in the first half of the twentieth century. Stephen L. Morgan's research on height as an indicator of net nutrition in Republican China is indicative of this reassessment. Morgan's data indicates that most Chinese people grew taller from the 1890s until the 1930s, but that there was hardly any material gain in height in those born in the 1920s (and measured in the 1940s) and those born in the late 1970s (and measured in the 1990s).[9] What this indicates is that during the period of the Second World War and the entire Maoist period, height growth stagnated in China. Since 1979 and the onset of Deng Xiaoping's reform and openness policies, it appears that height growth has restarted and has been gathering pace, increasingly so in the last decade.

Clearly Chinese people are now richer, better fed and generally healthier than they ever have been. However, despite the overall benefit to China of getting richer, and the existence of two generations of urban Chinese who have not known shortage, war or famine, there is still the 'wealth deficit' of rising levels of overweight and obese Chinese, a growing group of citizens that indicates just the start of a trend towards more widespread obesity as China's middle class expands, placing new and considerable strain on the country's fragile and underfunded healthcare system.

Consequently, it is important to note that there is a very real monetary cost to obesity for the Chinese Party-State. Obesity is increasing to levels that are alarming the country's healthcare authorities and the number of overweight is growing to ever-higher percentages. The situation is particularly worrying among children. It's showing in their waistlines and their health with the full range of obesity-related metabolic syndromes. Primary among these is diabetes (known in Chinese as *xiaoke zhi ji*, or the thirsty illness, as diabetes can make you thirsty, hungry and tired as well as inducing frequent urination), which, among the young, is rising dramatically; for many school kids, sport is something to be watched and followed rather than participated in (a trend that actually accelerated in 2008 – China's Olympics year), cooking is something done by chefs in restaurants, walking is to be avoided. At the same time, Chinese society is in a periodic obsession with beauty. The contrast between the image of Chinese beauty shown constantly in televised beauty pageants, taxicab cosmetic-surgery ads and fashion magazines is clearly at odds with China's expanding waistline.

But most crucially, the question arises of what this may all mean for China's healthcare system. The severe acute respiratory syndrome (SARS) crisis of 2003 showed how fragile the system was. The diseases and afflictions associated with fatness and obesity will only add to this load on the system as lifestyle-induced diseases become major killers. China's population is ageing and longevity is increasing, indicating that long-term care and provision for the aged and their age-related diseases will also place strains on the system, while rising levels of pollution will also lead to high instances of pollution-related disease. Obesity and weight will play a key role in this mix – respiratory illnesses, type 2 diabetes, hypertension, heart disease, stroke – the list is long. Take an overweight person, assume they are one of China's 350 million smokers, assume they are overworked, prone to stress and lacking in exercise and all the time subject to high levels of pollution and a poor diet, and you have a healthcare nightmare. The system, like the waistline, may be stretched to breaking point.

China's healthcare system has already faced several severe challenges including SARS, and other epidemics could strike at any time, while new strains on the system have materialized from a significant rise in cancer diagnoses (often related to obesity) to at least 700,000 people with HIV requiring treatment. Illnesses caused by pollution are rising sharply, while people are living longer and requiring health service for more years, for more ailments (and all more intensively). In 1995 just 17 per cent of China's population was over 50 years of age, but by 2025 this percentage will reach 35 per cent and by 2050, 42 per cent. Already, increased longevity means that Beijing and Shanghai are among the 'oldest' cities in Asia after Japan's. Of course, increased longevity is good news, but will inevitably place more burdens on the healthcare system. Along with ageing, lifestyle diseases such as obesity will be among the new challenges for the system. Quality of life is the true measure of the benefits of economic growth and increasing wealth and prosperity; however, for many Chinese these benefits will ultimately lead to years of illness, discomfort and an early death – death by affluence.

The rise of obesity and lifestyle diseases could ultimately inhibit economic growth and affluence. The establishment of a healthcare system with a low level of basic coverage, followed by a pay-on-the-door charges system beyond the basic coverage provided, is already under great strain – three-quarters of rural Chinese cannot afford anything beyond the very basic; China's newspapers regularly report of people across the country who are unable to afford treatment; corruption and under-the-table payments to doctors, specialists and hospitals is rife. All this combines to force people to save for a rainy day and accounts, in part, for China's high savings rate that averages 30 per cent of household income – effectively better understood as a form of self-taxation. Lifestyle diseases will merely accentuate this problem.

The Wider Implications

In terms of the wider implications for studying obesity in China, there are several points of interest:

(1) The ticking time bomb of obesity in terms of deteriorating health for a key constituency of the Chinese population and the inevitable rise in the rates of type 2 diabetes and other obesity- and weight-related diseases will put further pressures upon two of the major Achilles heels of the Chinese social system: the healthcare system and pensions provision.

(2) Economists trying to divine the future of China have basically two tools at their disposal: hard metrics and soft metrics. The main difference between the two is that hard metrics can be measured while soft metrics are more amorphous. When it comes to forecasting most economic statistics (GDP, inflation, trade flows, etc.), economists deal with soft metrics – what if commodity prices and inflation pushes up the 'China price' slowing exports? What if America and the EU hit a severe depression, simultaneously slowing orders from China? Obesity is, in the sense of forecasting, a hard metric. For instance, scientists and healthcare professionals agree that obese people are 40 times more likely to develop diabetes. Given the obesity rate there will be a severely rising rate of diagnosis of diabetes over the coming years in China and this will add significant costs to the national healthcare system. It is not a supposition, nor a modelled projection for the future, but a fact that China's healthcare planners will have to face up to.

(3) As a form of political economy, the obesity issue indicates how China's changing social economics – greater wealth, choice, spending power, access to goods and services – are causing a range of benefits and deficits for China's people that have longer-term implications for the stability of Chinese society, a stability the ruling Communist Party has pledged to maintain.

But first – just how severe is the obesity problem in China?

Chapter 1

CHINA GETS ON THE SCALES

Quantifying the Size of the Problem

Quantifying the potential size of China's obesity problem naturally requires measuring the growing size of the Chinese waistline. So first a technical note: Firstly, this book differentiates between being overweight and being obese. Literally, obesity means a condition characterized by excessive body fat. The body cannot store protein or carbohydrates, so the excess is converted to fat and stored. One pound of fat represents approximately 3,500 excess calories. Being overweight is nothing new and certainly not in any way specific to China – about 25 per cent of the world's population is overweight – that's over 1.2 billion people, according to the World Health Organization's (WHO) classification system, and 300 million of them are clinically obese. More alarmingly perhaps, the WHO estimates that worldwide, 22 million children under five are overweight.

Secondly, being obese is different from being overweight. An individual is considered obese when their weight is 20 per cent (25 per cent for women) or more over the maximum desirable for their height. When the excess weight begins to interfere with vital functions such as breathing, it is considered morbid obesity. Again, China is far from alone in seeing rising rates of obesity; indeed, in many ways the country severely lags the obesity rates of North America and Western Europe. Globally, approximately 5–10 per cent of children are obese; between 13 per cent and 23 per cent of all adolescents are obese. However, child obesity is an indication of longer-term trends – surveys have found that around 80 per cent of obese teenagers are likely to grow into obese adults.

Thirdly, most definitions of overweight and obesity rely on the Body Mass Index (BMI) calculation. There are problems with this as discussed below, but it is an internationally used measure of obesity, with some adaptations. The BMI formula was developed by the Belgium statistician Adolphe Quetelet (1796–1874), and was previously known as the Quetelet Index. BMI is also referred to as 'body mass indicator'.

However, it should, once again, be noted that the BMI is controversial for a number of reasons including that it is designed primarily for people aged between 25 and 65; it does not take into account muscle mass or overall body type ('apple' vs. 'pear' body types); and, perhaps most controversially of all,

Table 1: **BMI – The Maths**

Calculating BMI is straightforward and requires only two measurements, height and weight.

Metric Formula: weight (kg)/height (m)^2

With the metric system, the formula for BMI is weight in kilograms divided by height in meters squared. Since height is commonly measured in centimetres, divide height in centimetres by 100 to obtain height in meters.

Example: Weight = 68 kg, Height = 165 cm (1.65 m)

Calculation: $68 \div (1.65)^2 = 24.98$

Imperial Formula: weight (lb)/(height (in))^2 x 703

Calculate BMI by dividing weight in pounds (lbs) by height in inches (in) squared and multiplying by a conversion factor of 703.

Example: Weight = 150 lbs, Height = 5' 5" (65")
Calculation: $(150 \div (65)^2) \times 703 = 24.96$

Though there are variations, the US Department of Health and Human Services weight status categories are as follows:

BMI	Weight Status
Below 18.5	Underweight
18.5–24.9	Normal
25.0–29.9	Overweight
30 and above	Obese

---

until recently it was generally considered a measure applicable to all racial types, while some in the fashion industry (who talk of 'silhouettes' rather than 'shapes') have called for variable BMIs for men and women and for age, too.

There are several alternative measures of weight that are occasionally used to determine obesity. Waist-to-hip ratios can provide an indication of whether an individual has too much body fat. Generally, the waist-to-hip ratio should not exceed about 0.9 for men and 0.8 for women. Higher ratios indicate an increased risk of stroke, diabetes and heart attack. There are also skinfold tests and Bioelectrical Impedance Analysis (BIA) that measures the total amount of body weight from fat. This method is considered far more accurate by some, though BMI remains the major, most widely used and popular global calculator of weight.

Weighing the Nation

At the start of Deng Xiaoping's 'Reform and Opening Up' movement in 1979 there was no data on weight in China available. In 1980 Charlotte

Ikels, a regular visitor to Guangzhou, reported that hardly anyone appeared overweight, but this was about to change and by the end of the decade, obesity would be declared a national health issue in China's large cities.[1]

The question of China seriously gaining weight first came to light in a series of partially comprehensive surveys on diet and nutrition that were conducted in the 1980s and early 1990s. However, none of these reports really focussed specifically on the prevalence of weight gain and obesity, but rather concentrated on how the more pressing issue, at the time, of China's successful reduction of the incidence of malnutrition across the country was progressing.

As a side effect of these studies, some findings relating to weight were published; figures compiled in 1982 reported that the number of overweight people in China accounted for approximately 7 per cent of the population (by way of contrast, in 1980 it was claimed that 26 per cent of American adults were obese). A decade later, a 1992 survey suggested that 15 per cent of Chinese were overweight and approximately thirty million were clinically obese. In other words, the number of overweight Chinese had doubled in percentage terms in a decade. Even compared to a slightly later survey conducted in 1996, the massed ranks of overweight Chinese had grown by 23 per cent. A trend was beginning to appear, but needed closer scrutiny. What was immediately becoming evident was that China was sharply divided between urban and rural on the question of weight, just as it was in terms of income, living standards, material well-being, lifestyle and access to services such as healthcare. In short, the cities were becoming richer and life for urbanites was dramatically improving compared to those residing in the countryside; one side effect of this was urban weight gain. The weight profile of the typical urbanite and the typical rural dweller was starting to significantly diverge.

China officially got on the scales as a nation and weighed itself in June 2002 when the country's State-associated China Academy of Medical Science (CAMS) issued its first-ever Obesity Index for Chinese Adults as part of CAMS' Fourth Nutrition and Health Survey. The Index was based on various data that had been gathered in the 1990s and Professor Zhou Beifan published the key findings in the journal *Popular Medicine*. The survey used the WHO standard index references of BMI – body weight divided by body height squared, as outlined above.

Since this was launched, there have been arguments about how applicable the traditional measurement of BMI is to Asians, being worked out largely on the basis of more wide-ranging and thorough studies conducted in the West on Europeans. In the West, a BMI of 25 to 29.9 is considered overweight; while 30 and above is categorized as clinically obese, indicating an abnormally high proportion of body fat. There is also the category of morbid obesity, a severe form of obesity in which a person is 100 or more pounds overweight. However, research in the US had suggested that the BMI normal threshold for Asians should be lowered to 23 or 24, with 25 or over being defined as obese. Asian researchers largely agreed with the American findings and China started revising its definitions of BMI in line with these calculations in 2001. Since then most researchers have used them, with some arguing that a BMI of as low as 20 should be considered overweight for Asians, while other researchers have suggested still lower thresholds. This naturally had inflationary ramifications for China's fat statistics.

The *Beijing Chenbao*, a daily newspaper in the Chinese capital, claimed that 50 per cent of the population in China would be classified as overweight under the new Asian weight index compiled by the WHO. Even under less stringent criteria, the *Beijing Chenbao* estimated that 40 per cent of the Chinese people would still be classified as overweight, and one-eighth of the overweight would be classified as obese.[2] When Singapore's Health Ministry conducted a survey of the island state's population, they found that 60 per cent of Singaporean adults could be classified as overweight using the revised Asian BMI calculation. These findings and recalculations radically changed the discussion of obesity in China and other majority ethnic-Chinese nations such as Singapore and Taiwan. All agreed that this revealed a problem that had been partially hidden by the former European-standard BMI calculations, which had given false indications.

Despite this, according to these BMI standards, individuals were deemed overweight when their BMI surpassed or equalled 24, and obese when the index surpassed or equalled 28. Further, a male gets abdominally obese when his waistline reaches or surpasses 85 cm, and females, 80 cm. Waistline is considered an important measurement for abdominal obesity, because it reflects a person's abdominal adiposity (defined clinically as central obesity, or more commonly perhaps as 'belly fat') which has a lot to do with the onset of a series of metabolic disorders.

BMI also gives some indication of the potential future strains a country's healthcare service may have to suffer – when the BMI increases by two, the risks of coronary heart disease and stroke increases by 15.4 per cent and 6.1 per cent respectively, according to CAMS. When an individual reaches 24 on the index, then their likelihood of suffering high blood pressure, diabetes (which the WHO categorizes as a chronic non-communicable disease) and hyperlipidemia (excess levels of fats in the blood) at the same time exceeds 90 per cent. The key is abdominal fat, where the alarming-sounding 'red-line' is a level of 100 cm^2 for males in the visceral fat area – the amount of fat inside the peritoneal cavity, packed in between the internal organs in the abdomen. With a high level of abdominal fat, patients are at risk of developing diseases such as hypertension (defined as a blood pressure of over 140/90 mmHg in adults) and diabetes.[3] Indeed, those with elevated levels of visceral fat are three times more likely to suffer from diabetes (which can also be inherited) and have twice the risk of hypertension, stroke and heart attack. Since 2001 most Chinese research studies have used the designation of a BMI of 25 as indicating obesity.

It took another 18 months, though, before China's first comprehensive national survey on diet, nutrition and disease was released. China's then Vice Minister of Health Wang Longde announced the disturbing findings at a Beijing press conference.[4] The survey had discovered that 22.8 per cent of Chinese adults were overweight and that 7.1 per cent were clinically obese (amounting to 60 million people). Twenty years after the first published surveys, there were now as many people defined as clinically obese in China as had been previously designated as simply overweight in 1982. Over the intervening two decades, the number of overweight people across the country had risen to an estimated 200 million out of a total population of around 1.3 billion, according to Vice Minister Wang. These were significant advances over Professor Zhou's earlier surveys, which had concentrated more on nutritional intake and the incidence of malnutrition than excess weight problems. However, Vice Minister Wang was forthright in the conclusions that had been drawn concerning the nation's growing obesity problem commenting, 'Compared with the nutrition survey results of 1992, the prevalence of being overweight has increased 39 per cent and the prevalence of obesity has increased by 97 per cent.'

In light of these findings, if the earlier surveys from the 1980s are looked at again the contrast becomes stark – by 2005 the official *Xinhua* news agency was reporting that 70 to 90 million Chinese were clinically obese. Though this number appears high, and is not substantiated scientifically, it would mean that China, due in part to its highly populous nature, could account for nearly one-third of the total number of obese people worldwide, which is rising, given the WHO's estimate in 2000 that obesity affected 300 million people globally and that approximately 1.2 billion people were overweight. Even if *Xinhua's* number was a little high, others didn't radically disagree; Pan Beilei, deputy director of the government-affiliated State Food and Nutrition Consultant Committee (SFNCC), estimated that 60 million Chinese were obese in 2006, while Chen Chaogang, a university doctor in southern China's Guangdong province who was studying obesity rates across China, predicted that as many as 200 million Chinese people would be dangerously overweight by 2015.

Vice Minister Wang continued to be quite frank and publicly warned that the problem was only going to get worse in China, his open comments on the subject indicating that the ruling Communist Party was now aware of a growing urban obesity problem and the long-term impact this could have on the nation's healthcare system. The rising obesity figures had immediately alerted the central government that chronic non-infectious disease rates were likely to start rising steeply. Lifestyle diseases had arrived in China's cities and the problem had already got noticeably worse. The 2002 survey had taken some time to be published – approximately two years – as it was far larger than any previous study on the nation's diet; 270,000 people were surveyed across a wide range of municipalities, cities, towns and counties nationwide. By the time it was released, there were already a lot more obese people around.

The adverse effects on health in China were already starting to show: 260 million individuals were considered either overweight or obese; hypertension rates among adults had reached 18.8 per cent, increasing by 31 per cent, or 70 million cases, since 1991; 160 million people, or 18.6 per cent of the population, were suffering from high blood pressure (which can be caused by a high salt intake, common in many traditional Chinese dishes) and abnormal blood lipid levels (hyperlipidemia), while a further 160 million were suffering from arteriosclerosis (hardening of the arteries); over 20 million Chinese were diagnosed with diabetes, fully 2.6 per cent of the total population, while a further 20 million Chinese had poor blood sugar levels, according to China's Ministry of Health. But it was diabetes that most worried health professionals. Compared with the data collected in the 1996 survey, the prevalence of diabetes among adults over the age of 20 in China's major cities had increased from 4.6 per cent to 6.4 per cent and in small- and medium-sized cities the rate had risen from 3.4 per cent to 3.9 per cent.

By mid-decade things were looking increasingly worrying. A survey jointly conducted by Ministry of Health and the National Bureau of Statistics (NBS), China's primary statistical gathering and dissemination organization, indicated that 30 per cent of the total population in China's big cities were overweight, compared with 21 per cent in 1992. Fully 12.3 per cent were considered to be obese, approximately double the 6.2 per cent recorded in 1992. The China Preventive Medicine Association (CPMA) issued a press release arguing that the number of overweight people in China's cities had reached the 100 million mark. Again, it seemed clear that as the urban economy was growing, so were 'prosperity induced' waistlines.

Back in the 1990s the figures had indicated that obesity was becoming a worrying factor, but only in China's largest and most advanced cities – the tertiary cities of Shanghai and Beijing in particular. But as wealth and changing lifestyles rippled out across the country, so did weight-related problems, as reported by tier-two and tier-three cities. In 2007 the 'Report on Sichuan Residents' Nutrition and Health' released by the Sichuan Provincial Disease Control and Prevention Centre (part of the fourth national nutrition and health investigation sponsored by the Ministry of Health, the Ministry of Science and Technology and the National Bureau of Statistics) disclosed that about 10 million of Sichuan's 87 million population, predominantly in the increasingly prosperous city of Chengdu, were suffering from hypertension as salt intake rose and fruit and vegetable intake fell. The report noted that the average Sichuan resident's salt intake had risen to 10 g a day, 4 g more than the recommended amount by nutritionists and dieticians. The report also noted that diabetes was becoming a more worrying problem and that approximately 2.5 million people in Sichuan Province were diagnosed as diabetic. Deng Ying, a leading official at the Sichuan Provincial Disease Control and Prevention Centre, explained the problem succinctly: 'The higher a family's income, the higher the incidence of diabetes.'[5] Similar reports were starting to come in from other tier-two and tier-three cities in China – for instance, a study in the city of Wuhan, the capital of Hubei province, found that 8.9 per cent of 10–12-year-olds could now be classified as obese.

And, of course, obesity is related to a far wider range of problems that have been noticed in Chinese society in recent years. A 2007 report from the Shanghai Disease Prevention and Control Centre (SDPCC) noted bad diet, obesity and a lack of physical exercise among the causes of the startling finding that the number of female cancer patients in the Shanghai urban area had almost doubled in 20 years and that younger women were contracting the disease in increasing numbers. The Centre's figures revealed that women accounted for 56 per cent of the city's total cancer patients. Cancer diagnoses rates in Shanghai had reached levels comparable to the European Union (EU).

In addition to problems over lack of concentration, sleep apnoea (where the accumulated fat presses on the upper respiratory tract and causes the throat to become narrower disturbing sleep), constipation, osteoarthritis (for which the most important modifiable risk factor is obesity), slipped discs, bad backs and pulled muscles, a 2007 survey from Shanghai's Jiaotong University found that urban China was suffering lower fertility rates with up to 10 per cent of urban Chinese couples unable to conceive without some form of medical help. One of the causes of the average Shanghai infertility rate of 7–10 per cent among married couples was, as well as delayed childbirth, infertility or low sperm count, related to obesity.

Women seemed to be suffering especially badly. When the SDPCC released the startling findings of its 2007 survey in Shanghai regarding female cancer, it also found that 27 per cent of the 13,000 women surveyed had an irregular diet, 23 per cent were overweight and 29 per cent never took any exercise. That breast, cervical and ovary cancers were all becoming increasingly common was shocking enough before the survey found that over 50 per cent of Shanghai's cancer patients were women. Clearly, the survey concluded that lifestyle, in particular the growth of sedentary lifestyles, was a contributing factor. It seems stress and obesity are all part of China's new fast-paced urban lifestyle; in 2006 more than 160 million Chinese were registered with high blood pressure, over 70 million more than the figure five years previously.

Overall productivity was being adversely affected too. *Food at Work*, a review commissioned by the United Nations International Labour Office, found that overweight and obese employees are twice as likely as fit workers to miss work due to weight-related illnesses and conditions ranging from diabetes to sleep deprivation or breathing difficulties (both accentuated by noise and air pollution in many Chinese cities). China's urban residents were certainly richer and eating more, but they were also getting sick more often and missing work more frequently.

From Famine to Feast

As with its red-hot economy, China has once again been outstripping growth rates elsewhere in the developing world. Research commissioned by the International Food Policy Research Institute (IFPRI) for the 2020 Vision initiative and carried out by David Pelletier of Cornell University and Timothy Gage of the State University of New York at Albany, examined increases in obesity and changes in death rates due to diet-related diseases in developing countries over three decades. The study found significant increases in obesity since 1957 in all regions of the developing world. However, while the overall prevalence of obesity increased by 8.4 per cent since 1957 regionwide, the percentage growth had been even higher in China. Indeed, according to the IFPRI research, obesity rose rapidly in both rural and urban China during the 1980s, marking '…a significant trend due to China's influence on world food supply and demand'.

In this sense, China's urban dwellers were gaining weight at an incredibly rapid rate just as China was expanding in other areas such as annual economic growth and urbanization. Stephen Green, the Chief China Economist with Standard Chartered Bank based in Shanghai, has tried to calculate the speed of this expansion. In 2007, Green calculated that one American year was equivalent to one quarter of a 'China year', or 2.8 months, while one British year was equivalent to 3.1 China months. As Green puts it, 'In other words, an American or a Brit will experience as much change in China in the space of three months as he or she would at home in a year. Life here really is four times quicker.' Green simply took per capita local currency gross domestic product (GDP) data in constant prices and calculated the average rate of growth over 1980–2007 for 60 or so countries. Using constant prices means the numbers reflect real change (without the effects of inflation or exchange rate fluctuations). He then compared these average annual growth rates with China's to calculate 'China years'.[6] Green admits his calculations are ultimately a 'bit of fun', however, they do indicate the pertinent point that just as life changes rapidly for the positive in China, so do growth-related problems such as rising rates of obesity and the growth of lifestyle-related diseases. Similarly, people could draw a comparison to the fact that as Chinese people had enough money to buy themselves cars, they did so in large numbers, although over the same time, the number of road fatalities also tragically soared skywards.

The original CAMS survey is the official one used by the Beijing government, but others have also been conducted that shed further light on the scale of the problem. A study by America's Tulane University argued that by 2000, just under a third of all Chinese urban adults were overweight, and further revealed a sharp rise in the levels of blood cholesterol and diagnoses of high blood pressure and diabetes over the previous decade, even in children. Meanwhile, a separate study by the central government-funded Shanghai Children's Health Care Institute (SCHI) found that 8 per cent of children between three and six years of age, living and being educated within the Shanghai Municipality, were clinically obese.

What was clear from the 2002 CAMS survey and others is that as China, its major cities at least, became richer, so people were getting fatter. Vice Minister Wang believed that one of the reasons that the situation wasn't going to change was that Chinese consumer's knowledge levels regarding diet, nutrition and health were generally low. People were increasingly enjoying their food, able to afford it without thinking, eating increasingly often both at home and outside the home and simply eating more (as is typical of any economically advancing nation from Industrial Revolution England to modern China), but not necessarily better. China had successfully moved from shortages and rationing to widespread availability in two generations. For urban citizens at least, it was literally famine to feast in a relatively short time frame.

Due to rising availability and incomes, urban Chinese were now consuming excessive amounts of meat, oils and fats, but not enough cereals, while there was insufficient intake of calcium, iron and vitamin A as well as other essential nutrients as their diet changed. Approximately 21 per cent of children in Chinese cities (and 34 per cent in the countryside) were reported as suffering from iron deficiency by the WHO and therefore at risk of anaemia. The WHO has also reported that many people, both rural and urban, were lacking sufficient calcium, their average daily intake being only 391 milligrams, just 41 per cent of the WHO's recommended intake. These mineral and vitamin deficiencies also affected rural China, but for different reasons, mostly linked to continuing poverty and unavailability, but in the increasingly wealthy coastal cities, Beijing and a growing number of inland cities, food availability and access wasn't the problem, but rather what people were choosing to eat and in what amounts.

The Beijing central government, though somewhat alarmed at the potential for a future healthcare crisis, saw the trend as generally positive. Some people were eating too much and becoming obese, imperilling their health, but in general, the ordinary urban citizen's living standards were improving – famine to gluttony in two generations is quite an achievement, and the latter is arguably a better position to be in as an individual than the former. Overall, the prevalence of malnutrition and nutritional deficiencies and related problems of birth defects and disease had declined substantially; people had a higher protein intake, especially of meat, eggs and poultry and dairy consumption was also rising. For urban China at least, the issue was not supply but choice – a new problem for China and one many citizens were not able to recognize and were little prepared for.

Obesity and Children

A particularly worrying issue raised once again by the 2002 CAMS survey, but already acknowledged in China at central government level, was the rising number of clinically obese children. Very overweight children had appeared as an issue in the mid- to late-1990s when China saw its first 'kiddie fat farms' set up in Beijing and covered in the news media extensively, as well as a growing number of debates over doting parents spoiling their single 'Little Emperors' with fast food and charges that mums and dads were effectively 'killing with kindness'.

Rachel DeWoskin, an American who lived in Beijing in the mid-1990s and starred in a hit TV series, deciphered the fat issue for herself. In her memoir of that time, *Foreign Babes in Beijing* (the English translation of the TV show she appeared in, *Yang Nu Zai Beijing*), DeWoskin describes the typical approach to fat in mid-1990s '*pang* boom' (fat boom) China: 'It's not rude in China to suggest that someone is *pang* or has *pangqilai*, gotten a little fatter. *Pang* is a cute word, one that suggests a chubby prosperity. But "too" *pang* is rude…Early in the *pang* boom, people wanted to be plump enough to suggest prosperity, but then ideals became increasingly emaciated. As China beefed up, its billboards and magazines sported razor-thin models of beauty. Diet products, herbal remedies, and fat reduction farms spread across the country.'[7]

DeWoskin had hit on a point of contradiction that had emerged in Chinese society: fat was good, fat indicated prosperity but increasingly thin was the body image being presented in China's burgeoning media of fashion magazines, beauty pageants, model shows and advertising. A highly conflicted national body image was emerging and people could be forgiven for being somewhat confused.

The initial concerns about overweight kids led to calls for more parental awareness and responsibility as well as more trained dieticians and nutritionists (calls which had been made for over a decade already by health professionals). TV programmes discussed the issue of severely overweight children, newspaper editorials raised the problem of the damage it was doing to children's health and the government appealed to parents not to spoil their one child. But resources were short. Dr Zhai Fengying, an academic and senior official at China's National Institute of Nutrition and Food Hygiene in Beijing, claimed that China had just 2,000 qualified nutritionists nationwide in 2002, but needed at least four million, based on international standards of one nutritionist for every 300 people.

Still more surveys appeared confirming the trend. In 2004 China's Ministry of Education reported that almost 16 per cent of urban kids and young adults aged between 7 and 22 were considered clinically obese. Further, according to Chen Chaogang, the Chief Doctor at Zhongshan University Second Hospital in the southern city of Guangzhou, who had long studied weight in China, by 2005, 10 per cent of China's children were suffering from clinical obesity and the number was increasing by 8 per cent a year; once again the growth was especially and noticeably rapid – the 'China years' effect was evidenced once more. One survey revealed that 14.8 per cent of boys in primary school (*xiaoxue*) were clinically obese, and some 13.2 per cent of them overweight. Girls were fairing slightly better with 9 per cent being clinically obese and 11 per cent overweight at primary school level, but it was still a worrying trend. In big cities like Beijing and Shanghai there was a recorded average of one obese child in every five. The situation was reportedly even worse in northern China where child obesity rates were hitting 13.2 per cent, compared to around 12.2 per cent in eastern China and down to 10 per cent in southern China. By comparison, according to a study published in the American policy journal *Health Affairs*, 15 per cent of US schoolchildren were estimated to be obese and 30 per cent were believed to be overweight.

All the symptoms and problems to be expected with child obesity were being evidenced in China in the late 1990s and onwards – weariness and lapse of concentration at school, a growing incidence of autistic personalities, unhealthy sexual development (for instance, the early onset of menstruation and puberty, in general, in girls) and a growing incidence of chronic diseases like arteriosclerosis, hepatocirrhosis (cirrhosis of the liver), diabetes and hypertension as well as a rise in the incidence of fatty liver (steatorrhoeic hepatosis or steatosis hepatitis) and hyperlipidemia, both major risk factors for cardiovascular disease. This was aside from increasing rates of diagnoses of depression and reported incidences of bullying and taunting affecting overweight children.

Most worrying perhaps, is the fact that childhood obesity is not usually a temporary state; overweight children invariably become overweight adults (on average, two-thirds of overweight children will become overweight adults, according to the American Center for Disease Control) and that is the point when typically chronic health problems really start to show up, as most studies reveal that for those people for whom obesity starts in childhood, health problems are greatly compounded in later life.

These conclusions are reinforced by the latest surveys available, not just internationally, but also in China. Recent research conducted in China by the Nutrition School of Massachusetts's Tufts University found that Shanghai newborns often weighed 4 kg or more while the national standard ranges from between 2.5 kg to 4 kg. The same survey found that approximately 16 per cent of children in Shanghai aged between seven and 17 years old were overweight, while another 12.5 per cent were obese. In the 18 years and above age group the figures were, respectively, 29 per cent and 4 per cent. This means that the percentage of obese kids in Shanghai is nearly three times the national average, and compares to a median of just 3 per cent in rural areas, while also adversely affecting younger children, i.e., more children are becoming obese at an ever younger age, and the problem is accentuating not dissipating.

Partly as a consequence of being overweight, 30 per cent of Shanghai residents now suffer from hypertension, while the national average is approximately 18 per cent. The reasons for the severe rise in obesity in Shanghai seem clear and are evidenced by research conducted in 2004 by the Shanghai Statistics Bureau (SSB) and the city's Women and Children's Welfare Committee, that basically concluded that the city's kids were spending more time on computers and eating junk food than playing sports, meaning that they were simply not burning off the calories at a fast enough rate. According to SSB's survey, 50 per cent of Shanghai's primary and high school (zhongxue) students now spend less than one hour in the playground or doing sports activities and at least 60 per cent of kids eat junk food regularly.

These findings were borne out as typical of most Chinese cities in 2006 when it was reported that approximately 60 per cent of school headmasters in Beijing admitted that the mandated one hour of outdoor physical exercises per day was not always followed.[8] This also means that while the height, weight and chest measurements of school kids in China's cities keep expanding, certain physical indices, such as lung capacity, speed, stamina and strength, are actually falling. A physical manifestation of this is the findings that the blood pressure of half the secondary school students surveyed was above normal.

Naturally, this has played out in the urban healthcare statistics – babies are born bigger, kids are more likely to become clinically obese and the percentage of people with hypertension is nearly twice the national average. According to the latest survey undertaken by the Children's Hospital of Shanghai's Fudan University, the number of Chinese children under 14 suffering from diabetes is growing fast and has almost tripled over the past 25 years representing a significant rise in Maturity Onset Diabetes of the Young (MODY). They are mostly suffering from type 2 diabetes, which is mainly caused by obesity and lack of exercise, though means that they do not need to take insulin as opposed to type 1, a rarer form often called 'juvenile diabetes', which occurs when the immune system destroys insulin-producing cells in the pancreas. Of course, both types of diabetes can lead to complications such as heart disease, kidney damage and blindness. MODY leads to more type 2 diabetes, caused by the wearing out of insulin-producing cells normally associated with the natural ageing process, in younger and younger patients. As well as more incidences of type 2 diabetes in the young, it also means that more cases of heart disease, strokes and kidney failure – problems caused by diabetes – will develop in ever younger people. Put quite simply, what was once a chronic disease of midlife in China is now a paediatric problem occurring in children as young as ten years of age.

China's Obesity Epidemic[9]

By 2008 – China's Olympic year – the number of obese and overweight people in the country topped more than a fifth of China's adult population and the related economic costs represent 4–8 per cent of the economy, according to the health policy journal *Health Affairs*.[10]

How did this happen? It seems clear that obesity is a product of a developing and generally improving society. The causes are many – changing diet, increased salaries, additional disposable income, changing lifestyles and changing environments – but all are linked as part of China's overall and ongoing development. In this sense, an indication of how wealth and economic growth affect weight and China can be seen from studies on obesity in Hong Kong where diet, lifestyles and the rise of white-collar sedentary jobs indicates where mainland Chinese cities like Shanghai and Beijing are rapidly headed.

In 2005 Hong Kong's Department of Health issued a report (for which the research was conducted in 2003) indicating that waistlines were expanding alarmingly with nearly 40 per cent of the city's 6.8 million population considered overweight (based on a BMI of 23 or above to indicate overweight and 25 or more to indicate obesity), with 18 per cent classified as overweight and 21 per cent clinically obese. As in mainland China, the ratio between men and women was fairly evenly balanced – 22 per cent of males and 20 per cent of females interviewed were obese. Hong Kong also provided an indication of the continued likely growth in childhood obesity; the Health Department's Student Health Service noted a rising trend of obesity among primary school pupils, from 16.4 per cent in 1997/1998 to 18.7 per cent in 2003/2004 – nearly one in five kids. Ho Mei-lin, the Senior Medical Officer of the Department's Central Health and Education Unit (CHEU) told the local press that obesity was now a 'serious problem' in Hong Kong.[11]

A further concern regarding China is underdiagnosis. Diabetes, both type 1 and 2, are believed to be significantly underdiagnosed, while according to the Ministry of Health, only 30.2 per cent of China's population is aware of hypertension as a clinical condition (and to many, this seems a high estimate). Most alarmingly, a 2004 forum convened in the city of Chongqing to discuss the prevention and treatment of diabetes was to hear claims from some delegates that due to underdiagnosis, China could potentially be home to not the official 20 million, but in excess of 50 million diabetics and that their number was rising by an average of 1.5 million to 2 million new sufferers a year. In 2010 the Chinese and international media reported a study that set further alarm bells ringing concerning the spread of diabetes. In March 2010 the prestigious *New England Journal of Medicine* published a report by the China National Diabetes and Metabolic Disorders Study Group, *Prevalence of Diabetes Among Men and Women in China*. The study, conducted in 2007 and 2008, found that '…because of the rapid change in lifestyle in China, there is concern that diabetes may become epidemic.' The report disclosed that the prevalence of total diabetes (which included both previously diagnosed diabetes and previously undiagnosed diabetes) and pre-diabetes was 9.7 per cent (10.6 per cent among men and 8.8 per cent among women) and 15.5 per cent (16.1 per cent among men and 14.9 per cent among women), respectively, accounting for 92.4 million adults with diabetes (50.2 million men and 42.2 million women) and 148.2 million adults with pre-diabetes (76.1 million men and 72.1 million women). The report concluded that, 'These results

Table 2: **China's Prosperity-Induced Waistline – Timeline**

1982 – Three years after its initiation, a partial survey on diet and nutrition finds 7 per cent of China is overweight.

1992 – A national nutrition survey clocks 15 per cent of the country as overweight – double the figure of a decade ago. Some 30 million Chinese are now clinically obese.

2002 – The China Academy of Medical Science conducts the most comprehensive national diet study to date, surveying 270,000 people countrywide. Some 22.8 per cent of Chinese adults are found to be overweight (200 million people) while 7.1 per cent are clinically obese (60 million). Within a decade, the prevalence of the overweight has increased by 39 per cent and the obese by 97 per cent.

2005 – *Xinhua* reports that 70 to 90 million Chinese are now clinically obese – one-third of the total number of obese people worldwide. Between 6 and 10 million adult Chinese become obese each year.

2008 – China's largest and most shocking survey of obesity and diabetes to date finds that the prevalence of diabetes and pre-diabetes to be nearly 10 per cent and 16 per cent, respectively, across China, accounting for 92.4 million adults with diabetes and 148.2 million adults with pre-diabetes.

2015 – Predictions indicate that as many as 200 million Chinese will be morbidly obese within five years. China's heavyweights still lag behind the US, where two out of three people are overweight or obese, but China is on course to be exactly like the US in approximately 10 to 20 years.

indicate that diabetes has become a major public health problem in China and that strategies aimed at the prevention and treatment of diabetes are needed.'[12]

The global obesity epidemic has now reached China's cities and is spreading swiftly as wealth spreads from the primary cities to the second and third tiers of the country. It is fair to say that on the question of rising obesity, the Beijing government has been more proactive than with certain other new or sudden health-related issues such as SARS, H5N1 avian influenza (bird flu) or, indeed, tobacco smoking. The Beijing authorities have recognized that the problem exists and have generally been transparent in terms of statistics and the government has requested the help of the WHO and other international bodies to look at ways of tackling the problem. Yet, the obesity crisis in China's cities is fundamentally different from an outbreak such as SARS or bird flu or even the periodic outbreaks of diseases such as encephalitis or, in 2008, hand, foot and mouth disease (HFMD) – which particularly affected children – or even the rash of serious and tragic food scares in recent years, notably those around milk and infant formula. Obesity cannot be quarantined or cured simply with the distribution of vaccines; obesity cannot be simply recalled as is the case with tainted or dangerous products; waves of inspectors and new testing procedures cannot rapidly be sent in and legislated to correct the problem; instead, the fight against obesity requires long-term education, awareness raising and, ultimately, governmental and community intervention to change and improve patterns of behaviour, diet and consumption. In a very real sense, this is a new challenge for China's medical community and health authorities.

Obesity has become part of the everyday language of urban China as people worry about their weight, are bombarded with advertising for weight-reduction products (genuine and spurious), join weight-loss programmes, are diagnosed with obesity and weight-related illnesses and conditions, and commit to bariatric medicine (the branch of medicine that deals with the prevention and treatment of obesity), which is rapidly becoming a growing discipline for China's medical community, from local healthcare workers in China's schools to the arrival of Weight Watchers in China in 2008 to the legion of private cosmetic surgeons catering to the newly rich and their desire to shed weight fast.

The following chapters examine some of the causes of China's rising obesity levels in more detail – who is suffering most from obesity? What role is changing diet playing? and how are food retailing and marketing exacerbating the situation? However, having established that obesity is largely affecting the wealthier new middle class of urban China, it might be useful to ascertain exactly how many of them there are and how wide the obesity epidemic could spread.

Chapter 2

CHINA'S FAT CLASS

Defining China's Middle Class?

Since the early 1990s the growing body of statistical evidence about weight and obesity in China indicates that overweight and obesity is an urban issue – it is proliferating in the cities. It is also a problem largely affecting the newly wealthy, a group that has grown in the last quarter of a decade, forming China's rapidly expanding urban middle class, living in the newly expanding cities.

Much has been made of this new Chinese middle class as consumers, as the agents of job creation and entrepreneurism and also, possibly, as the social class that will most vociferously demand political change at some point. It is also, of course, the social class that most government and party functionaries belong to as well as those in the legal, medical and media professions – it is an influential, connected and educated group.

So before we discuss the more specific causes of obesity in China – changing lifestyles and diet – it is necessary to recognize that this is a key middle-class issue – it is the middle class that are getting fat, the middle class that is most radically changing its traditional diet and the middle class that is at the forefront of new lifestyles that are contributing to China's rising rate of obesity. This is perhaps the inverse of the thrust of the obesity debate in the more-developed West, where obesity is increasingly seen as a disease of the poor rather than the middle class. But how do we define the Chinese middle class? How big is it? How rich is it? And, perhaps most importantly for predicting how obesity will grow as a health problem in China, how fast is the middle class growing?

Defining a middle class is essentially all about income brackets, and naturally it is impossible to apply those used elsewhere. The middle classes of North America and Western Europe became affluent earlier, and have already developed a certain cultural history that further alters the way people behave as consumers, so economics cannot be the only measure of what a middle class is. However, it is really the only one that can quantify the difference between middle classes in different countries, without getting into some very complex social studies metrics.

So, economics it is, and dealing with consumer groups, the best metric is what they earn. According to the US Census Bureau, in 2003 the overall median household income in the US was US\$45,016, while the median household income by level of educational achievement went from US\$100,000 for those with a professional degree down to US\$18,787 for households where people quit school after the ninth grade. By comparison, in China the top income bracket starts at only US\$15,000 per annum, meaning that even the top earners, the so-called 'Golden Collars', within the middle class in China are earning less than the average for US households with the lowest level of educational attainment.

In short, the middle class in China are those people with an annual household income of RMB40,000–120,000 (US\$5,000–15,000); upper income earners are those over RMB120,000 (US\$15,000) in 2003.

There are three caveats before we jump to any conclusion from this stark statistical comparison. First, purchasing power (the money you, need, relative to income, to buy stuff). Many prices, especially food prices, are lower in China, because incomes are lower. Average incomes are much lower than they are for the middle class, who form a smaller section of the society than in the West, so many basic goods are priced for those with lower spending power who comprise, by far, the majority of the country, and consequently, middle class spending power would be imagined as being much stronger than the absolute average annual income figure would have you think. But, there is a weakness in the argument that Chinese consumers have stronger purchasing power, as this assumes that products and services in China are equivalent to those in developed countries, and that Chinese consumers get the same products and services at a lower price. The reality is that the quality of many products and services in China is still lower than those demanded in developed countries, and so the price paid by Chinese consumers reflects the value of those goods in any market, not just in China.

Next, it is important not to forget that the Chinese middle class is still putting a lot of its cash into savings, paying a relatively low rate of income tax (and getting very little in social security from the government). Chinese consumers are effectively taxing themselves to provide for key life needs such as healthcare and education; they pay this 'tax' into their savings accounts rather than to their national treasury. If they paid more in taxes, and received a better social safety net (including healthcare, unemployment benefits, pension or state education), then the likelihood is that they would spend more of their income, after the requisite taxes, which would almost certainly have to increase as a proportion. The need to save, therefore, suppresses potential consumer spending by this income group and most others in China, and is likely to continue to do so for the foreseeable future.

Growth is the final caveat. In 2003, the median American per capita income was, as mentioned above, US\$45,016. But, by 2005, that had actually fallen to US\$44,389. In the same period however, the national average income (not the middle class average), grew from RMB14,040 (US$2,057) in 2003, to RMB18,364 (US$2,690) in 2005, a rise of 30.8 per cent; middle class incomes will have grown at least at that pace. It is not so much that Chinese middle-class consumers are catching up with the Americans as it is that they are getting wealthier within their own economic context, are experiencing faster social and economic change than their US peers, are living in a country that feels that it is still striving to achieve its potential and is therefore much more optimistic in outlook.

How Big is China's Middle Class?

Another crucial problem in the sizing of the consumer market in China, beyond the valuation of the market, is the insistence of certain China-watchers that China somehow has a huge (and rapidly growing) middle class which will somehow overtake the US, Europe and Japan as a driver of the world economy. The problem with this view is that it is misleading.

In 2006 research company Access Asia worked with the *China Economic Quarterly* to come up with a realistic measure of how large the urban 'middle- and upper-income groups' in China actually were and what the level of income and expenditure (total and per household) really is.[1]

Based on the findings of that research, only 7.4 per cent of China's households in 2005 could be classed as middle income (having an annual household income of between RMB40,000 and RMB200,000, or US$5,000 to US$15,000) and that by 2010, this would grow to about 11.3 per cent. Again, from this study, household earnings above this annual income represented only 0.8 per cent of total households in 2005, and would grow to about 1.4 per cent by 2010. This gives a likely current significant consumer market in China in the region of only 11 per cent to 12 per cent. As such, this significant consumer market in China is still way below what are termed 'middle class' in developed countries.

However, this consuming class is more significant, based on its spending, than its demographic numbers suggest. Again drawing upon the Access Asia/*China Economic Quarterly* study, by 2015 the middle-to-upper-income consuming classes in China are forecast to represent approximately 44 per cent of consumer spending, and over the 2005 to 2015 period, total household consumer spending is forecast to grow by 73 per cent, middle-income household spending by 194 per cent and upper-income household spending by 406 per cent. Likewise, over this same period the number of middle- and upper-income households is forecast to grow by approximately 168 per cent, compared with total household numbers growing by about 29 per cent.

The number of these significant consuming households is therefore estimated to be around 37 million in 2005, rising to approximately 70 million by 2010 and up to about 102 million households by 2015. But these households do not form some kind of homogenous middle class, with broad consumer trend similarities. These households are clustered across China in key regions of development, and are culturally and economically diverse. For instance, middle income households in Guangdong, Shanghai and Beijing will each have their own separate levels of income, differences in housing stock available, widely different climates, be served by different retail and, often, catering chains, have access to different ranges and brands of products across many sectors and have different cultural influences, both native and from abroad (e.g., Guangdong is heavily influenced by Hong Kong, Shanghai is more influenced by Japan, Fujian has strong influences from Taiwan, while Korean influences are much more significant in Dalian).

Something that is also very significant to the consideration of who the middle and upper income consumers are is location. Based on various research studies, it is clear that the majority (approximately 75 per cent) of significant consuming households live in or close to the main urban centres of eastern and central China, such as the cities of Beijing, Tianjin and Shanghai and the provinces of Hebei, Shandong, Jiangsu, Zhejiang, Fujian and Guangdong.

Additionally, a third factor boosting the potential size of the Chinese urban middle class is the significant growth of the services sector, employing a wider range of white-collar employees. Fully one-third of China's workforce is now employed in services of one sort or another, up from 28 per cent in 2000 and just 19 per cent in 1990. Between 2000 and 2008, services (the tertiary sector) accounted for 109 per cent of total employment growth in China, compared to 91 per cent for industry and construction. In contrast, the number of people working in agriculture fell by 54 million, while total employment rose by about the same amount. Another factor mitigating the impact of fewer manufacturing jobs is the shrinking size of China's working-age population. The size of the 15–34 age group, those most likely to work in factories, fell to 374 million in 2008 from 451 million in 2000, a drop of 17 per cent in just eight years. This age cohort accounted for 28 per cent of China's total population in 2008, down from 36 per cent in 2000, and demographers expect it to continue shrinking.

Based on all of this evidence, it is clear that the bulk of consumer spending power remains, and will likely continue to remain, generally focused on a minority of China's population, and located in a smaller percentage of the

Table 3: **Where China's Fat Class Works:**
China's Growing Service Sector, 1980–2008

	% of Total Workforce		
	Agriculture	Industry	Service
1980	68.7	18.2	13.1
1990	60.1	21.4	18.5
2000	50.0	22.5	27.5
2008	39.6	27.2	33.2

Source: Access Asia from national statistics.

country's geographical area. It should also be noted that the social and cultural influence of this income group is also dominant. People in this income group work in key government positions, or key jobs within key companies. They are the also target market of most media marketing and much of the creative media content.

However, this is not to say that there are not rural middle-income and higher-income households, but they are less common and therefore harder to target as a market. Yet, the rural consumer market is now growing faster than the urban one in many regions of the country, and new middle-income households will begin to appear much faster than before in the rural areas. Again, the Chinese market continues to rapidly reinvent itself!

Meanwhile, new evidence on urban incomes shows that official data tends to exclude generally lower-level private-sector wages from its average, and so average urban incomes could well be lower than previously assumed, meaning the middle income group would be smaller than estimated above. But this is just one point of view among many, and there are other sources citing other data that would indicate that the middle-income household numbers are actually larger than the estimates given above.

In this sense, it is clear to see why hailing the Chinese 'middle classes' as the future saviours of the global economy based on such weak data is very rash indeed.

What About the Rest of China?

The rest of China is rapidly shifting into becoming an urban population. Based on official government data, between 1999 and 2008 China's rural population went from about 65 per cent of the total down to 60 per cent. Not only have many rural workers headed to the towns and cities in search of work, but many rural areas have become new towns, new cities or extensions of existing urban areas. Quite simply, fewer people are working the land in China. This huge

Table 4: **A Wealthier China – Growth of Average Salaries per Workforce Sector in China, 1997–2008**

Sector	% Growth, 1997–2008
Banking, insurance & other financial	415.8
NATIONAL AVERAGE	***346.6***
Wholesale, retail & catering trade	344.3
Culture, sports & leisure	342.2
Scientific research	341.9
Mining & quarrying	328.1
Government & social agencies	309.9
Utilities (water, gas & electricity)	309.6
Transport, storage, post & telecoms	303.5
Education	302.7
Leasing & business services	296.9
Health, social security & welfare	290.0
Manufacturing	279.2
Hotels & catering	267.9
Service sector	260.0
IT, computer & software	259.3
Agriculture, forestry & fisheries	237.1
Construction	236.8
Real estate	229.2
Water conservancy	226.5

Source: Access Asia from National Statistics.

demographic shift has been created by the disparity in incomes attainable in these different regions.

The problem is that income levels have been rising much more slowly in rural areas than in urban ones, and even those rural workers moving into urban environments to find work have done so by entering mostly low-cost export manufacturing jobs, many of which have now been lost to the global economic downturn, or working as construction labour on very low incomes.

Average incomes in the agricultural sector grew by 237 per cent between 1997 and 2008, but over the same period the national average grew by 346.6 per cent, largely driven by the emerging massive retail and distribution trade and services. Construction pay has seen even less growth than in agriculture (236.8 per cent over the same period), but the average construction worker was earning RMB21,043 (US$3,082) in 2008, compared to only RMB12,740 (US$1,866) in agriculture.

This leads neatly to the growing concern about the widening income gap between the two Chinas, and the social, political and environmental implications. With consumption being increasingly concentrated in the main urban areas, the logistics of consumption will develop apace in these regions, and less so in regions outside these consumption hotspots.

Solving this widening disparity in incomes and economies has become the central policy focus of the current Chinese leadership's political platform, by which it must deliver results or face serious political challenge. It is worth remembering that the Communist Party of China was put into power in 1949 by the rural peasantry, not by the urban working classes, and its main constituency remains that rural labouring class.

Part of helping to narrow the economic gap between rich, eastern and urban China and the rest has been to pour investment cash into rural development. This has gone alongside creating rebate schemes to allow rural families to be able to afford to buy household appliances and vehicles, promoting rural retail chains that supply goods to rural communities and create distribution networks to allow for improved distribution of rural produce, increased investment in rural healthcare provision (so rural consumers need save less to cover healthcare expenses themselves) and land reform.

The latter has changed how the leases for agricultural land can be traded. Previously, the government leased land to those living in rural areas so they could have their own income and feed themselves from what they grew. But the system did not allow these farmers to sublet their land if they wanted to leave and find work in the cities. Many farmers did sublet anyway, in order to get income from land they themselves did not tend. The new legislation now legalizes this, and has helped those still involved in agriculture to buy leases to many tracts of land in one area, thus creating larger tracts of land for more efficient and larger-scale farming under the control of local farmers' cooperatives. These cooperatives are now becoming much more efficient and significant, and are even negotiating directly with large supermarket chains for their goods.

All of this has allowed an increasing number of rural people to either set up local businesses or to migrate, untying them from the land and allowing them to seek better-paying jobs. This will, therefore, only accelerate the pace of urbanization in China. Meanwhile, the greater efficiency and economies of scale in farming should help to produce more food and keep prices down.

More Money – More Temptation to Eat

Between 2000 and 2007, the total average salary in China grew by 110 per cent, while the average in urban areas grew even more. Average retail food prices grew by about 115 per cent over the same period. However, food was already relatively inexpensive, especially for urban consumers who are on much higher levels of income than their rural compatriots. So, if anything, the sharp rise in food prices in 2007/2008 (since dampened) was arguably a good thing for those working in agriculture, as it meant they got a better price for the food they were producing, something the Chinese government is keen to promote as part of their national campaign for a Harmonious Society (*hexie shehui*), and food is not now really a major budget concern for the majority of Chinese households.

The relative cheapness of food for urban Chinese means that they do not need to think too hard about what food they purchase. In fact, most urban Chinese can eat out most nights of the week, even at the more 'expensive' restaurants. Before the economic boom in China, people tended to eat out only occasionally, and at low-cost outlets. But with the sharp growth in incomes, which food prices have just begun to catch up with, the ability to eat more expensively has given rise to a widespread eating-out culture in China's cities and elsewhere.

Banquets are now common, and increasingly lavish. More is being spent on cuts of meat and types of seafood that only a few years ago were well beyond the pockets of most Chinese, but which are now eminently affordable. People are making the most of their new pocket power. Though still relatively exclusive, salmon from Scotland, lobster from Australia and soft shell crab from Sri Lanka are all available and affordable to an increasingly large group of consumers.

Likewise, buying the more expensive branded, packaged foods that have become more common in the supermarkets (which increasingly include the aspiration-attracting 'IMPORTED' shelf) is also now not that much of a financial issue; when milk went up by RMB1 (US$0.14) per litre overnight in 2006, sales were unaffected, while Starbucks' sales remained constant after they raised prices for the first time in five years that year.

Although Chinese consumers are generally quite cautious in their spending habits, they will quite happily pay more for a product that they perceive to be of good quality. And what defines quality to a Chinese consumer? Often, it is as simple as good quality packaging. If the product is basically of a good standard (even if the ingredients are not expensive), uses high quality packaging and strong brand imagery, this creates the impression of a product that is more expensive than it really is. So long as your product's price is well above the cost of production, but just below the perceived value of the finished article, in all its packaged finery, consumers will believe they are getting a good price for such finery. Back this up with slick blanket advertising, key celebrity endorsements, prominent in-store positions, in-store sampling and other promotions, and you can persuade the consumer to buy – at least once.

Loyalty is significant in the marketing game in China. Brand loyalty is often overrated, but there is a sense that Chinese consumers, if they trust a brand, will tend to stick with it. Once you have a strong brand following, you can begin to use brand extensions to persuade more of your core consumers to come along for the ride up the value-added ladder, step by step. As your loyal consumer group earns more money and they can afford to trade up to better things, if you are already there with the better things they want, you will increase that brand loyalty, or so the theory goes. And it is a theory that seems to work. Recent history shows that Chinese consumers have developed a taste for expensive food, which creates a realm of expectation. Meeting that expectation is what keeps food manufacturers busy.

A prime example comes from the humble instant noodle. Even instant noodles, the ubiquitous, low-cost snack of the masses with approximately 245 companies competing in a market where the vast majority of the product is priced on average between RMB3 and RMB6 (US$0.43–US$0.86) per pack, can be turned into a 'premium' product, using more expensive packaging, advertising, a celebrity slurping the noodles, a few more sauce packets and the right promotion. This is how noodle manufacturers are managing to continue to make profits on such a cheap and competitive staple product. The other key consumer expectation that instant noodles live up to is that of convenience. So it is increasing convenience that drives the creation of new niche-product sectors, or allows for products sectors to be pushed towards the creation of a 'premium end', the likes of which have not existed before in China.

Consider also the jars of cook-in sauces and tin trays of ready meals that now crowd the shelves and chill cabinets of China's supermarkets. Such products simply did not exist in China until very recently, and only now are they becoming more sophisticated. Take frozen dumplings, for example: Five years ago the taste and quality was considered generally poor, sales were few and most consumers preferred freshly made products. However, quality gains and growing demand for convenience as well as widespread freezer ownership have meant that sales of frozen dumplings have grown remarkably – by an average of 15 per cent a year.

These products fit the demand for convenience by the consumer. To the shopper, they also represent an improvement in product quality and variety – something that adds value to their lives – and so they will pay that little bit extra for. This means that such products also fit the profit margin targets of retailers. Likewise, products such as bread, spreads, jam, breakfast cereals, pizzas and dairy products are now common in Chinese stores, whereas before, they did not exist. These have all worked their way into the Chinese diet because they are now readily available, relatively cheap, really convenient and rather heavily advertised. They also make more money for the retailers and manufacturers.

There is a plus side to the rise in consumer spending power, though. Chinese consumers, as already stated, are very thrifty with their money and very choosy about quality. Fears about fake food products containing banned ingredients (such as high rates of growth hormones and steroids), pesticides on fruit and vegetables, dangerous and easily contaminated packaging, fish full of zinc and lead deposits from polluted rivers and other newspaper-headline issues have raised consumer concerns about the food they eat. Many urban Chinese consumers are much more aware of these issues than perhaps is the case in even the 'developed' world. Food contamination scares, tainted produce and mass poisonings get wide coverage in China's media, raising awareness and fears among the public, as well as severely damaging many a major company's reputation. According to the Asian Development Bank (ADB), approximately 300 million Chinese people annually are affected directly in some way by tainted food that could be costing the country around US$5 billion a year. The ADB fears that this situation could exacerbate China's risk of major disease outbreaks.[2]

Such issues have given rise to a strong consumer protection lobby, which has forced improvements in legislation on manufacturing processes and packaging, as well as leading to the growth in demand for 'organic' food. There are now a range of 'green food marques (brands)', the validity of which is variable, which are often the deciding factor in a consumer's choice in food products. However, there is a distinct lack of 'joined up' government here; China has at least nine state-level ministries independently issuing food safety and hygiene regulations and when the number of provincial and lower level departments involved is added in, the numbers become legion. Rules and regulations overlap and contradict each other and are often just plain confusing. Consumer protection has also spawned a growing litigation culture, which has been perhaps even more successful in changing food manufacturer activities than any official enforcement of government legislation.

A growing constituent of the Chinese consumer population is also using their increased wealth to consciously buy healthier products. This is a particularly strong trend among urban, upwardly mobile women – the so-called 'Office Ladies', or 'OLs'. Their newfound wealth is being spent on self-improvement in many ways including gym memberships, spa treatments, relaxation therapies, dieting pills and cosmetic surgery. It is one of the odd contradictions in modern consumer society that while China's urban population has been rapidly getting obese, the value of the market for gym membership in China grew by over 1,000 per cent between 2001and 2007! The OLs are very media literate, and consume the plethora of new women's magazines now available. Apart from fashion and makeup tips (and the inevitable celebrity gossip), these magazines also cover many aspects of how to live more healthfully, including articles on eating healthier foods and the new buzz acronym on everything from magazines to spas – LOHAS (Lifestyles of Health and Sustainability).

Such media articles have a consumer effect; many Chinese women are increasingly changing their eating habits. For example, there has been a significant rise in people becoming vegetarians, attested to by the rise in the number of vegetarian restaurants in China's main cities. It has also been media attention to issues like the use of pesticides on farm products that has created demand for 'organic' foods, much of the demand coming from women, who are traditionally more in control of household spending than their husbands or boyfriends. Security sells!

Consumption pattern changes among Chinese women are also being reflected in what retailers are stocking on their shelves, giving some balance – if only limited –between the amounts of products being promoted that are healthy, as opposed to those that are less so. There is healthy food within China's shops, but it isn't very easy to find.

China's new middle class is real and growing; it's richer and more confident and keen to consume, and is the group most susceptible to obesity. It is also totally urban and so it is to the cities that we must look for one possible answer to Fat China.

Chapter 3

FAT CITY – OBESITY AND URBANISATION

Living an Obeseogenic Life

Urbanization appears to be a key factor in rising obesity rates in China. The country's cities have rapidly become 'obeseogenic' locations, places that encourage obesity through encouraging sedentary lifestyles and bad diet as well as being the places where China's new middle class is clustered and consuming at historically new levels.

China's rapid urbanization over the last 20 years has been unmatched anywhere else on the planet – and it's not over yet. In the next 12 years, at least another 320 million people will migrate from China's rural areas to the cities. Naturally, this incredible internal migration has led to the expansion of cities, radical urban planning and the need for more urban infrastructure. And yet, it has often simply meant more high-rise apartment buildings and roads without a concomitant growth in the number of parks, green spaces or public transport. Cities have gotten larger and sprawled out into vast overspill suburbs, while parks are more ornamental than useful and increasing swaths of public space become privatized and out of bounds to ordinary people.

People in China, like people pretty much anywhere, move to cities for one basic reason – to escape poverty and earn more. Whether they be securing good jobs or merely moving from subsistence farming to a factory or construction site, this aim is invariably achieved. And so the truism that as soon as people get to the cities they start eating more protein is substantiated. Almost immediately upon entering urban life, Chinese migrants' diet changes: protein intake increases; they consume less wheat and grains as they 'upgrade' to pork and other meats, while finding themselves almost instantly surrounded by high-calorie, high-fat processed foods to a greater extent. This increase in calorie intake nationally is partly the result of China's rise from poverty in the last quarter century, but also of the massive urbanization and internal migration into the cities that has occurred. In 1976 China had a population of 948.6 million people and the per capita daily calorie consumption was 2,051. By 2000 China's population had officially grown to 1.282 billion people and the per capita calorie consumption had risen to 3,029. Over those 25 years,

China's gross food calorie consumption grew from 1.945 billion kilocalories a day to 3.884 billion kilocalories a day. That's a 35 per cent increase in population and a 48 per cent increase in total calories consumed. Calorie consumption is outstripping population growth as wealth and urbanization increase.

Unsurprisingly, and perhaps understandably, the Chinese government and local authorities across the country's major cities have been stretched thin in coping with this internal migratory pressure that while contributing to China's economic rise by manning the factories and providing the services has placed incredible strains not just on housing, job creation, infrastructure such as roads, water and power supply and resources, but also on the social infrastructure of China's cities – schools, hospitals and welfare facilities. It's notable that most of the debate on China, particularly when led by the boosters, tends to focus on the incredible number of skyscrapers, airports and expressways built in the last two decades and decidedly less on the expansion of the healthcare, welfare and education system; the latter tells a far less compelling story about China's development than the former. The overwhelming focus on growth without any appreciation of the unbalanced nature of this growth reflects both the party-state's priorities over the last two decades and the prism in which the international media and most commentators have framed the debate around China. That unbalanced growth can eventually become a destructive force has been far less talked about, but is now a growing priority for Beijing and a question of increasing concern to commentators. Pollution, environmental degradation, the large areas of depopulated countryside where only very old people and very young children still live and the alarming decline in arable land as well as rising urban obesity and associated ailments, are just some of the side effects of this period of unbalanced growth.

Fat-Creating Cities

Whatever your weight, China's cities are not the healthiest to live in. More than 400,000 people in China die prematurely each year due to air pollution, according to a widely reported but unpublished study by the Chinese Academy on Environmental Planning (CAEP). The study found that 300,000 people died annually as a result of outdoor pollution and 111,000 due to indoor pollution. This will come as no surprise to many residents of cities such as Beijing and Linfen (China's coal production centre) among others that regularly appear on the government's charts of the most polluted with the worst air quality. Even as the government closes down factories in cities, new pollutants replace the filth in the air; vehicle exhausts now account for 79 per cent per cent of total air pollution in China's cities.

Table 5: **China's Cities Ranked by Per Capita Food Sales, 2008**

	Total Population (m)	Total Food Sales (RMB bn)	Per Capita Food Sales (RMB/Capita)
Ten Highest Food Consuming Cities			
Guangzhou (Guangdong)	10.18	91.27	8,963.97
Xiamen (Fujian)	1.69	13.46	7,964.67
Nanjing (Jiangsu)	6.23	48.40	7,768.27
Beijing SAM* Shenzhen	15.62	117.85	7,544.62
(Guangdong)	8.77	65.46	7,465.81
Shanghai SAM*	18.88	135.78	7,190.01
Wuhan (Hubei) Shenyang	8.37	59.47	7,105.21
(Liaoning)	7.17	48.06	6,703.06
Dalian (Liaoning) Hangzhou	5.84	38.36	6,568.85
(Zhejiang)	6.79	42.58	6,270.68
	6.11	37.42	6,124.09
The Next Ten Highest Food Consuming Cities			
Jinan (Shandong)			
Ningbo (Zhejiang)	5.71	34.01	5,956.25
Changsha (Hunan)	6.54	38.51	5,888.44
Haikou (Hainan)	1.55	8.82	5,690.45
Tianjin SAM* Qingdao	10.78	59.61	5,529.70
(Shandong) Nanchang	7.66	40.41	5,275.61
(Jiangxi)	4.96	27.40	5,525.13
Fuzhou (Jiangxi) Kunming	6.37	35.16	5,520.06
(Yunnan) Zhengzhou	5.23	26.92	5,147.33
(Henan)	7.14	36.50	5,112.22
All Cities total/average	**261.36**	**1,375.07**	**5,261.19**
National total/average	**1,355.64**	**3,683.41**	**2,717.10**

Source: Access Asia from National Bureau of Statistics.
*SAM = Self Administered Municipality.

Current obesity levels in China are below 5 per cent across the entire population, a relatively low prevalence level according to the WHO. However, in China's cities this rate can rise as high as 20 per cent. China's cities, particularly the coastal belt from the Hong Kong border up the eastern coast of China to Shanghai and then north inland somewhat to Beijing and then into northeast China, are the centres of Fat China. Clearly, a large amount of this discrepancy between China's fat cities and lean countryside is due to simple economics. The majority of China's 900 million rural dwellers are peasants and still subsist on an annual average salary of US$100. It is tough to get fat on that amount of money. Similarly, the inland cities, where wealth and investment have been slow to arrive also do not demonstrate the levels of clinical obesity and general fatness that the coastal cities do. But as they get that investment, as they get richer, all indications are that they also get fatter.

The coastal cities are where most white-collar workers live, the new rich and the expanding middle class of car-owning, office-working urbanites. These are the cities where trends start and where the foreign multinationals first arrive – McDonald's, KFC, Coca-Cola and the rest. These are the cities where, for a growing number of people, affording these products regularly is no longer a financial problem and they are consuming more of most food groups. They are also where time is of the essence and competition for career, money and success are most intense. They are incubators of wine consumption, speed dating, nightclubs and cosmetic surgery as much as of fast food, snacking and convenience lifestyles. At the same time, people in cities still smoke as much as anyone in a society where cigarettes still have something of the 'modern' about them. They are also expanding rapidly; Shanghai alone has perhaps 19 million citizens – nobody is absolutely sure – with maybe three million being migrant workers. They are increasingly impersonal, fragmented cities and it can be hard to find a social life. Often consigned to the ever-expanding suburbs, new arrivals can find themselves lonely, out of contact with their traditional social networks of family and community and perhaps increasingly alienated. They are also increasingly divided between rich and poor, those with some personal space and those without any, those with jobs and those unemployed. Life in China's cities is getting more and more stressful by any number of measures: traffic jams (the number of cars on Beijing's roads is growing by 10 per cent per annum, but the amount of road by only 2 per cent), personal relationships (Shanghai has one divorce for every three marriages. A total of 20,225 Shanghai couples negotiated divorces in the period from January to September 2007, up 30 per cent from the same period the previous year); longer commutes, cost of living, etc. All of this is taking a toll on stomachs, wallets, relationships, tempers and stress levels.

However, it is also the case that China's richest cities have also been those most exposed to China's urban planning regime and the grand planner's ideas. These have largely not been helpful to China's cardiac health or waistline.

Beijing is probably China's fattest fat city.[1] A 2004 survey by the Beijing Health Bureau found that approximately 60 per cent of adults in the capital were overweight and that obesity was becoming increasingly common among Beijing children. Liang Wannian, Vice Director of the Bureau, believes that part of the reason was that Beijingers were eating less rice and more fatty and high-cholesterol food, and the growth of Western-style fast-food outlets was not helping the situation. Mr Liang is an interventionist, believing that 'The result of the survey shows it's quite crucial to intervene to guide the citizens to a rational style of eating.' His beliefs are powered by the fact that the statistics gathered by the Bureau on obesity were alarming; Beijing boys of 11 and girls of 9 suffered the highest rate of obesity in Beijing, boding ill for the future.[2]

However, Beijing's top ranking doesn't mean that other Chinese cities can be smug. China's continuing urbanization is far from over...

Instant Noodles, Instant Cities

Not only will urbanization increase in pace, but it will also change in nature. By the authors' own estimates, China's population split between urban and rural could reach parity in the next decade or just a bit beyond that. This will be a major cultural, social, political and economic marker for China, representing a fundamental shift in the constitution of a domestic population that has remained largely rural and agrarian for the past 5,000 years. It is easy to underestimate the significance of this shift culturally. Chinese people take much of their identity from their long ancestry, and the limited number of Chinese surnames (about 200) is indicative of how well preserved those long ancestries have been. These ancestral lineages are closely linked to ancestral village homes, all of which are set in the Chinese countryside. Urbanization is slowly (but, indeed, increasingly rapidly) eroding this cultural and psychological link with this rural root identity. The impact this is having, or will have, is not always clear, but there is a good historical illustration of the social problems that such displacement can cause, and this example is called Shenzhen.

Shenzhen grew from a small village into a large city on the border with Hong Kong with a population of over 2 million (9 million if you include the 'floating' population of migrant workers) since its inception in the late 1970s. Its rapid growth was created by central government policy and its population is largely from elsewhere in China, with it being the only city in Guangdong province where the majority of the population speak *Putonghua* (Mandarin Chinese) rather than the local Cantonese dialect. For most of the people who moved to Shenzhen, even the local subtropical climate was alien.

The speed of growth, and the fact that its population was built very rapidly from migrants who moved there from elsewhere in the country, meant that early on, the city was very much a boomtown full of displaced people. None of the usual social networks and communities was in place, and there was a strong sense of the place being full of lonely individuals simply doing what they could to get rich quick. The result was a society of transience and individual self-preservation. This soon degenerated into a high level of lawlessness and displacement.

The staggering amount of wealth generated in the city drew in thousands of people, mostly migrant workers who lived and worked in appalling conditions right on the porous border with rich Hong Kong. Drugs, prostitution, smuggling and criminal gangs flourished. Shenzhen in the late 1980s and early 1990s felt like the Wild West, and the city had a palpable seediness and criminality. Shenzhen has improved, and much of the problems created by such rapid growth, accumulation of wealth and concentration of displaced people have largely been shunted onto other growth hotspots in the region. But Shenzhen was a model for how traditional Chinese society evaporates into a new form of social structure, based not on familial ties and social networks, but instead on professional acquaintances. This fundamental change creates an environment where traditional moral values and lifestyles are more easily replaced with a new set of morals and lifestyle aspirations. Shenzhen still retains a reputation for lawlessness.

So it is that rapid urbanization elsewhere in China is creating exactly the kind of environment where social structures and personal lifestyles are undergoing fundamental change.

The increasing urbanization of rural China, or the rural Chinese, and the increased suburbanization of the middle-income class in urban China is having a profound effect on how people live. Consumer lifestyles adapt to fit in with the new environments. Those urban Chinese moving away from city centres into the new suburbs and satellite towns are undergoing just as fundamental a change in lifestyles as are rural people moving into the cities. The continued speed of change in the cities means that even long-established cities are changing so rapidly that local people do not recognize parts of the city that they do not frequent often, and so, even their own localities become unfamiliar, with unfamiliar people speaking dialects they do not fully understand.

Fat Flats

Undoubtedly, China has made massive strides in improving its overall housing stock. Until recently, apartments averaged 40 m²; now Beijing and Shanghai apartments' average 80 m². This feels palatial to anyone moving from a dimly lit older property where they may have had to share facilities such as bathrooms and kitchens. It's a massive achievement supported by what was undoubtedly the largest single transfer of wealth in human history when the Chinese government began to privatize the nation's housing stock. Chinese urbanites snapped up apartments and took to home ownership like ducks to water. Still, flats are generally small by the standards of most of Europe or North America. The vast majority of apartments have two bedrooms, meaning that the standard young family of two adults and one child has no spare rooms. You can ease the One-Child Policy but where would you put the additional kids?

Some interior designers have argued that the typical design of flats and apartments in China's cities has further encouraged a lifestyle of convenience foods and/or eating out. Most flats are too small to make live-in kitchens practical or feasible; even in the large edge-of-town villas built for the newly rich, kitchen areas are often ridiculously small. Interiors superstore IKEA, which has five branches spread across the Chinese cities of Beijing, Shanghai, Chengdu, Dalian and Guangzhou (and is planning 10 branches by 2010), reports that Chinese consumers are looking at issues of space maximization and saving rather than buying opulent kitchens or designing open-plan areas. Additionally, the prevalence of wok cooking makes open-plan kitchens impractical and smaller spaces are better to contain the smoke – the wealthier often have two kitchens, one Asian-style (cramped and used) and one Western (open plan and rarely used) – but this is hardly the norm.

This seems to be borne out by a survey of white-collar women in several Chinese cities that found that less than 5 per cent of Shanghai women cook at home after work, compared to nearly half of respondents in Beijing and Guangzhou. Fully 10 per cent of the respondents said they never cooked at all.

An ISOPUBLIC poll for IKEA found that compared to 64 per cent of Canadian families and over 50 per cent of American families, only 20 per cent of Chinese families eat in their tiny kitchens, another contributing factor to people eating out – it is simply easier and less cramped.[3] Yet IKEA's customers, in a country where it is seen as relatively expensive, are the very core group suffering most from the rise of obesity and lifestyle diseases. According to Ulf Smedberg, the marketing manager of IKEA China, most of the ubiquitous Swedish chain's customers are, '…20 to 35 years old…families with children or are double-income, well-educated couples with no children…generally better educated, earn higher incomes, and travel more than the average Chinese.'[4]

China's cities have by and large opted for high-rise as the way to create additional living space. However, while tall apartment buildings on their own are not necessarily a problem, few of these developments have incorporated more than miniscule areas of greenery or common areas within them or adjacent to them. A small patch of ornamental grass is the best most high-rise apartment owners can hope for (despite the lavish greenery usually featured in the pre-build sales brochure), as developers have sought to maximize the land by building on every inch of it. Any leftover is used for parking, a persistent demand from the increasingly car-owning residents. Older developments, originally largely built by the state, often have exercise areas supplied with sturdy exercise machines and used regularly by older people. However, it has been noticeable that many of these have been removed to create additional parking spaces and, anyway, while often good for senior citizen's cardiovascular health and circulation, they're not addressing the core problem of obesity. It is rare to see an adult under 40 or a child using these machines any more than they join in with early morning *tai chi* sessions. These traditional activities are the preserve of the old and are just not cool for younger people.

Hard-working lifestyles, career dedication and long commutes may mark parents' lives and lead them to simply collapse when they get home, but this doesn't explain why children, young people and the elderly are not out exercising more. Living in high-rises they may be, but these are not the rundown council estates, *banlieue* or housing projects of inner-city North America or Europe with high crime rates and broken elevators. China's urban areas are not no-go areas for children or the elderly; it's just a question of where would they go? The park? The public square? Not so easy, it seems.

Parks and Privatized Space

'Greening' has been a major aim of China's cities for some time now. Beijing is not the greenest city in the world, to say the least; densely packed Shanghai arguably even less so. The Shanghai Municipal Government has sought to create new green spaces across the city in recent years. However, many of these parks are effectively off limits and many have been built adjacent to major roads and expressways meaning that strolling in the park may actually be even worse for your lungs than walking along a city-centre street.

In many urban parks you can walk across them along concrete paths or around the edges of them, but step on the grass and a man with a whistle will bear down on you pretty quickly. 'Keep of the Grass' is a general rule in China's parks with few exceptions. This means that parks make useful and decorative shortcuts, but are not useable as playgrounds for children. Some have exercise equipment, but few with the sort of playgrounds seen in other countries; this is a curious omission for a country famed for its fondness for the young. By and large, swings, roundabouts, sandpits and climbing frames are all absent from China's parks; even benches can be few and far between, though patrolling whistle-bearing security guards appear never to be in short supply and the list of 'don'ts' posted by any park entrance always swamps the negligible list of 'do's'.

Occasionally, a few basketball courts are included, but rarely any grass football pitches or other sports facilities. Many parks close early, meaning after-school/work games are impossible to organize. It is noticeable that parks never seem to get larger in China, but do quite often get smaller as property developers nip away at the edges of valuable urban land for more high-rises.

Despite being a People's Republic, it is startling just how privatized urban space has become in China's cities. The areas around shopping malls and adjacent to large-scale private housing developments have become particular areas of forced privatization as developers and property owners seek to extend their remit of control as far as possible. Most privately owned public spaces in China's cities purposely lack facilities such as seating, and are often also under CCTV camera control or the ubiquitous quasi-legal hordes of 'security' personnel that roam constantly and whose actual remit seems unknown to anyone – least of all them.

While no studies of the abuse of privately owned public space have been conducted in China (it is a sensitive topic following the deaths of several people at the hands of so called 'security guards' in shops, malls and other spaces), this has become a major issue of public concern in neighbouring Hong Kong. Given that many of the malls and property developments in China's cities are actually owned and/or operated by Hong Kong companies, or Chinese companies who have used the Hong Kong system as a model, their findings are instructive. A study by researchers at the University of Hong Kong in late 2007 covered 43 privately owned public spaces (mostly large retail mall developments) in Hong Kong and found that people were generally not encouraged to use them, concluding in the study that 'The public spaces are highly commercialized… the public piazza of Times Square *(a major retail mall in Hong Kong's Causeway Bay district)* is like an outdoor shopping mall promoting the enjoyment of consumption.'

That study found that 40 per cent of these spaces were not open 24 hours a day, 65 per cent had installed CCTV cameras, 58 per cent of the sites had no greenery and 19 per cent of the supposedly public open spaces had been partly occupied by outdoor restaurants and cafes with tables and chairs (for which to sit at, of course, you had to purchase something). Additionally, only 35 per cent of these spaces provided any form of public seating (which included those who had grudgingly included bottom-busting rails they considered seating) and only 14 per cent had installed proper benches for seating.

Clearly, developers in Hong Kong, as too-increasingly in mainland China, didn't like the idea of anyone just using the spaces for recreation or exercise. The paper's author, Dr Ken Too Wing-tak was told by one Hong Kong property developer in no uncertain terms that 'no sitting was allowed in the open space because the image of the development would deteriorate if people gathered there.'[5] *The South China Morning Post* got to the heart of the developer's concerns about undesirable interlopers, quoting the managers of one mall development who didn't like the idea of, '…undesirable behaviour, like someone taking their shoes off to rub their feet.' A small victory was achieved in 2009 when the Hong Kong government forced some property developers to open up the public space they had been granted by the government to more overt public use. The property developers were clearly unhappy, and the battle to reclaim public space goes on.

And so the space around numerous malls, residential buildings and other premises has become increasingly privatized and used as an extension of the attached developments, but with people discouraged, or often outright banned, from using the space. Consider the much-praised (by some) Xintiandi development in central Shanghai, whose website proclaims 'Xintiandi is The City's Living-Room, a place to unwind and relax after a long day…'[6] However, bicycles are banned and anyone straying into the area with a bicycle will have it confiscated. Security guards roam the complex and there is not a single, solitary seat a member of the public can 'unwind and relax' on without purchasing and consuming something. Many Chinese local officials see Xintiandi as the model for inner-city development, akin to London's Covent Garden or New York's South Street Seaport, but don't even think of lingering without getting your wallet out. As with so many of China's urban parks, these spaces are regarded by the government and the property developers as showcase spaces where behaviour and activities are to be extremely controlled and regulated. Parks where you can't walk on the grass, city 'living rooms' where you cannot sit down, apartment buildings with no green communal space, mall and other developments that seek to control and modify public land around them – all examples of the massive privatization of public space in China's cities and all leading to an overall significant reduction in space for leisure, exercise or relaxation.

The Rise of the Chinese Suburb

The growth of suburbs adjacent to major cities has come on much faster than most people predicted, and evidence now shows that the suburbs are starting to yield some very strong retail sales figures. New suburban stores are outperforming downtown stores – in terms of growth rates at least. Beijing, Shanghai, Tianjin, Chengdu and others are cities where the local governments (to differing degrees of success, admittedly) have wooed retailers to move in – McDonald's, KFC, Starbucks, department stores, hypermarkets and then the

Table 6: **Populations of Selected Major Developing Suburbs in China, 2010**

Population as a % of Total City/Municipality Population

	City Population	% of Total Population
Shanghai		
Xinzhuang	720,000	5.3
Wujiaochang	1,100,000	8.8
Jinqiao	375,000	2.7
Qingpu	456,300	3.3
Songjiang	604,560	4.4
Beijing		
Wangjing	330,000	2.2
Chengdu		
Wenjiang	326,700	3.1
Ningbo		
Zhoushan	969,800	17.5
Suzhou		
Suzhou New District	260,000	4.3

Source: Access Asia from government data.

mid- and upper-mid-level brands. The rise of the suburban consumer and the development of retail infrastructure in the suburbs is driving an expansion of retailers into new areas, and with downtown areas close to saturation, retailers are taking this opportunity to expand into new spaces, targeting the white-collar workers living away from the centre of town. These are new spaces with new client bases, instead of the too-numerous 'copy-and-repeat' developments of downtown.

There are a number of things worth noting about China's new suburbs. Some have argued that they are just composed of gated, self-contained communities. Some are, but most aren't. The suburbs are also often either (a) mini-factory towns, (b) dormitory-sleeper locations or (c) places of white-collar flight from high downtown property prices, with (c) obviously preferred by retailers and the category more and more suburbs fall into.

What is now emerging is the early genesis of an American-style, 'Starbucks-and-Saks' style suburban culture. It's early – less picket fence and more urban sprawl – but it's moving fast, much faster than anyone predicted, thanks to high downtown rents and saturation, offset by better wages inland and decent rent deals. The white collars moving out to the suburbs don't come downtown on the weekends as much anymore, so everything from supermarkets to coffee shops to clothing stores are going out to meet them on Saturdays. Understanding the rapidity of this 'burb' emergence is crucial in trying to evaluate the expansion claims of brands from Tesco to KFC. Their projected store numbers look far more plausible when you 'get' the rise of China's suburb culture. And, as the table above shows, these are hardly small suburbs!

And it's not a cheap fix. Consider the newly suburbanized Shanghainese in somewhere like Xinzhuang. They don't have the time or particularly the inclination anymore, to travel downtown of a weekend, but they do have money. The retail infrastructure now being established in suburbs such as Xinzhuang is premium, it is close to full-priced retail, chain-dominated rather than allowing space for independent retailers and restaurants, and this is something that is happening all over the country.

The government is, of course, very pleased by all this. Firstly, it goes a long way in bolstering their stated policy aim of boosting consumption. Secondly, it supports their urban planning goals, such as they are, by encouraging the move to the suburbs and the satellite cities. However, the problem has been plenty of housing, but not much social infrastructure (government funded) such as schools, hospitals, clinics, etc. The government's desire to provide 'quick fix' infrastructure in the new suburbs – all-night convenience stores, supermarkets, malls, etc. – is being met by the retailers and the chains. Still, shopping alone is not enough; these suburbs will eventually need the other components of social infrastructure – hospitals, clinics, more schools and public transport.

This means that suburban consumers might be able to get a late-night takeaway, or a potted plant to put in their garden on the weekend, but if they need to send their kids to school or get to a doctor for medial treatment, their options are very limited.

The creation of satellite cities and the forced clearance of many of the people living (often it must be admitted in horrendously overcrowded and substandard conditions) in China's urban downtowns has meant that commutes have increased. The distances involved have simply become too great for either walking or cycling, and so buses, trains and cars have replaced feet and pedals. For some people, the commute, not helped by increasing traffic volumes, has become long – two hours and even more each way. That's four hours a day sitting in a car, a bus or on a train which invariably drops you near the office for eight or nine hours more on a seat before repeating the journey in reverse, back to your sofa, which you probably collapse onto. The supposedly 'liberating' trends of self-employment, freelancing and outsourcing remain limited in China. Meanwhile, the move to the suburbs has broken up traditional communities and their support networks of shops, restaurants and teahouses. The traditional evening stroll through the neighbourhood is no longer so pleasant or appealing and so, nights are increasingly spent in front of the TV or the PC. Consequently, exercise rates have plummeted due to changing lifestyles, lack of time and distance from facilities.

Is There a Link between Urbanization and Obesity?

The answer is almost certainly – yes.

Urban lifestyles are, compared to rural ones, much more sedentary, rely more on automotive transport, mean more time sitting at work, rest and play, and mean more discretionary income available to spend on treats. The correlation between urbanization and obesity has been cited often in research conducted on the obesity problem elsewhere in the world. That the Chinese are becoming an increasingly urban people is clear. That urban Chinese are becoming increasingly sedentary in their lifestyles is also clear. What is unclear is the potential effect of urbanization of such speed as is being witnessed in China, and across such a large population.

Taking into account the shifts in government policy directed at raising rural incomes, increased urbanization, development of the domestic consumer market, spread of organized retail and consumer services and the retooling of China's industry away from cheap export manufacturing and towards higher-end, higher-tech manufacturing, the forecasts created by Access Asia and the *China Economic Quarterly* (noted in the previous chapter), as to the potential size of the urban middle-income class, are likely to be conservative.

As has been noted in the first chapter of this book, that the rising obesity levels in China have been most acute in the main urban centres is now well recorded. Likewise, there has also been a strong indication that high levels of obesity are moving towards the so-called tier-two and tier-three cities. It is not just urbanization that is to blame, but the rising levels of income among Chinese people in these cities along with the disruptive effects of such rapid rates of change to more traditional social structures and norms. None of these things on their own might be considered a problem if people were more aware of them.

Based on more recent estimates, it is arguable that urbanization, and the middle-income consumer group, will both grow more rapidly than previously forecast. Previous estimates (such as those conducted by Access Asia/ *China Economic Quarterly* in 2006) put the likely consuming classes (in 2005) at between 37 million and 51 million households (between 110 and 150 million people). Based on these figures, the share of urban population was between 19.5 per cent and 26.7 per cent. A more recent revision of this estimate, carried out

Table 7: **Two Comparative Estimates of the Total Size and Shape of 'Consuming China', 2008**

	Estimate 1 (high)	Estimate 2 (realistic)
Households (m)	81	59
Population (m)	244	178
Share of urban population (%)	44.7	33.4
Expenditure per household (US$)	13, 108	13, 108
Total expenditure (US$ bn)	1, 062	775
Total expenditure % of US consumer expenditure	17.2	12.5

Source: Access Asia from National Bureau of Statistics data.

by Access Asia, concluded that by 2007 the total range was more likely somewhere between 58 million and 80 million households (175 million to 240 million people), or between a third and 46 per cent of total urban households.

With rates of urbanization continuing to increase, the size of the urban consumer class in China is perhaps going to grow more rapidly still, and we will see a further acceleration of growth in the size of that consuming class in the coming years. It is not only the Chinese government that hopes this is so, but many countries outside China are hoping that China's consuming classes will grow exponentially, in both sheer size and in spending power, over the coming years, to take up the slack in the world economy brought about by the global recession that began in 2008. The headlines told it all in 2009 – China's middle-class urban consumers were being expected to save the world!

- Korean Firms Look to Chinese Consumers to Bolster Profits
- Rise of Chinese Consumers Already Making Waves Online
- China's Shanghai is New York on Steroids
- E-Commerce Is Getting Chinese to Loosen Their Purse Strings
- China Spending Spree to Continue Despite Bubble Fears
- China Spending to Continue Despite Fears
- Luxury Goods Seen to Thrive in China Despite Crisis

Although China's consuming classes are very unlikely to replace the key US consumer market, or even really take up the slack created by declines in the US consumer market, China's consumers are going to consume more. The resurgence of the property market again in 2009, following government intervention in early 2008 to slow the market and avoid overheating, should create a better economic environment for more people to buy their own homes. Continued strong retail sales throughout 2009 also indicated that Chinese consumers did not face the same kind of self-imposed austerity as their peers in other countries, especially the developed economies.

China's consuming classes are still growing both in size and in spending power, while the consumer classes in most other countries are facing stasis or a decline in spending power, and certainly less mobility in terms of increasing their incomes. The Chinese are now looking at their current situation, in comparison with the rest of the world, and feeling rather pleased with themselves and their government and are feeling very confident. Such confidence only helps the consumer market to keep on growing rapidly, and for consumers to spend more of their incomes. Such sustained economic fluidity also creates an environment where more people can move up the income scale by finding new jobs, because there are still new jobs out there to get – although admittedly times are tough for those seeking oversubscribed graduate jobs.

Obese City or Healthy City?

The good news is that cities, while the breeding grounds and incubators of obesity in China, are also potentially the solvers of the problem. Cities, messy as they can be, are invariably clusters of the educated, the inventive and the innovative; they are where the early adopters of new ideas congregate and the best equipped to devise solutions congregate. They are where trends, both good and bad, emerge and display themselves first and, invariably, where answers and solutions are found. They are the home to the middle class which even if it doesn't have the vote, is the group most able and educated to use the media, legal system and political lobbying to effect change; the group the Party most wants to keep onside, but also the group most likely to vocalize its anger about everything from the environment to food safety, the healthcare system to education. Whether or not they choose to exercise this latent power is a big question for another book.

However, to date, urban planning in China has ultimately encouraged obesity. Indeed, urban planning strategies and the desire to complete the process in record time has also been bad– if not deadly – for people's health. Constant change, forced relocations, endless round-the-clock construction with few controls on noise reduction or site pollution control, record levels of dust and dirt in the air have adversely affected people's health. Recent research findings in Beijing – one of the epicentres of this hyper-rebuilding – have shown that the average age at death in the city has actually fallen compared to the rest of the country. Urban planning is killing Beijingers. One study of the Zhongguancun district, Beijing's supposedly hi-tech equivalent of Silicon Valley, found that average life expectancy was only 53 – five years less than a decade earlier.[7]

Cities can be health-endangering places and obeseogenic locations – but they are where the middle class lives, eats and shops and no discussion of the rise of obesity in China can ignore the question of China's changing diet. If it's true that 'you are what you eat', then Chinese people are very different these days than just a generation ago.

The simple conclusion from this is that as China increasingly migrates towards urban consumerism, it will naturally see obesity rates continue to rise. Specific among the key changes in lifestyle created by the shift towards urban consumers that are linked to obesity rates is the change in the average diet. In the following chapters, we explore the changes in the average diet, the effects of food retailing and food supply to Chinese consumers, as well as the rise of fast food in the Chinese diet.

Chapter 4

MEGA-WOK – CHINA'S DIET FROM CABBAGE TO CUISINE

Economies of Scale – More, More, More

China's economy has grown from next-to-nothing to being the world's second largest (based on World Bank calculations of purchasing power parity) in just over 30 years, despite its economy having been declared overstated by about 40 per cent at the end of 2007. However you cut the figures, the change over a single generation has been huge, over two generations, gargantuan. It is hard for anyone who has not lived through these immense social and economic changes to imagine how it has fundamentally altered everything about life in China, and how it must feel for the people who have lived amidst that change. Not only is the economy totally different, so are roads, cities, shops, leisure, technologies, neighbourhoods, populations, schools – everything – including food and diet.

To suggest that the Chinese diet and attitudes towards food have not changed, along with everything else in the country, would be folly. There have been huge changes in the way Chinese people perceive food, shop for it, cook it, eat it– even digest it! They can afford to buy amounts and varieties of food that no previous generations of Chinese would have been able to imagine, the previous generation being the one before the present! Food has therefore changed from being dull and repetitive, and reliant on the seasons, to being rather interesting, exotic and full of new possibilities. It can be bought in huge new hypermarkets that are chock full of everything, including some stuff that remains totally alien, for now.

In the mid-1990s there was a vogue for cookbooks in China; recipes that had been largely forgotten by many were recalled and reinterpreted for a new generation. As the variety of vegetables grown and available in China increased, so recipes that included aubergines, shallots and other vegetables that had long been rare were reincarnated for a new generation. Later, cookery programmes on TV became popular, teaching the Chinese how to cook dishes that had been forgotten for centuries and only served at the tables of emperors. Banqueting was back, TV 'super chefs' created, gourmands interviewed in magazines. Chinese people were eating food in restaurants, at home, in the street, at their desks, in cars and on the hoof, bought from fast-food outlets, whilst talking on their mobile phones. Foods that were not traditionally seen by many Chinese as part of their diet were becoming popular, dairy products being the most obvious example.

The major factors fuelling the change in eating habits have been the dropping of import barriers, thanks to China's World Trade Organization (WTO) membership in 2001 (after 15 years of negotiations), the price liberalizations of the late 1980s and early 1990s, the end of rationing, the growth of organized retail chains, stronger harvests and more meat/fish, a rapid rise in consumer incomes and spending power and the increased penetration of imported goods leading to more domestic companies making Western-style products, with a knock-on effect being the growth of a vibrant and private consumer catering and fast food businesses.

The key development has been increasing crop yields in China. Total crop yield grew in volume terms by 67 per cent between 1990 and 2006 (according to official statistics), which is all the more impressive considering that China has only 5 per cent of the world's available arable land from which to feed about one-sixth of the world's population, and that the available land only grew by 10 per cent since 1990 (again according to official statistics). The true amount of arable land in China and its increase or reduction is a topic of intense debate, as some areas are being reclaimed for arable crops while other land is lost to the forces of urbanization, industrialization, pollution, desertification, golf courses and myriad other uses.

The volume growth in the crop yield is actually not as significant as the shift in what that volume consists of, namely, additional higher-value crops. The total value of crops grown, in current value terms, increased by 664 per cent in the period 1990–2006 or 529 per cent at constant 1990 prices. In per capita terms, this amounts to a growth of 447.4 per cent since 1990, to reach a total value of RMB1,245.08 (US$180) per capita in 2006.

Meanwhile, as the output of food has grown rapidly, consumer incomes and spending have grown faster still, with many urban Chinese effectively doubling their wealth every seven years on average. In 1990, the average urban resident in China spent RMB693.77 (US$100) a year on food, out of a total annual disposable income of RMB1,510.16 (US$218), according to China's National Bureau of Statistics (NBS). This meant that urban consumers in China were spending 45.9 per cent – just under half – of their expendable income on food in 1990. However, by 2006 the average per capita urban expendable income had reached RMB11,759.45 (US$1,698), a figure 679 per cent the size of the 1990 income level. Even if you account for inflation, the average urban income still grew by 541.29 per cent over the 1990 to 2006 period.

Also, by 2006 per capita annual urban food spending had grown to RMB3,111.92 (US$449), representing just 26.6 per cent of annual per capita expendable income. Even though per capita food spending among urban Chinese consumers grew by 269 per cent between 1990 and 2006 (at constant 1990 prices), food spending has nearly halved in significance, again according to the NBS. The crucial factor to note here is NOT that food spending has really diminished. Food spending has actually gone up hugely in overall terms. But instead, that average wages have gone through the roof, applying a new level of spending power to the average urban Chinese that previously was inconceivable just a few years ago.

Increasing numbers of urban Chinese consumers can now afford to make discretionary purchases of luxury goods, such as cars and beach holidays in Thailand, but they were still only being asked to pay about 21.4 per cent more for their food than in 1990.[1] So, food spending has not diminished; it has just become ridiculously cheap compared to the growth in spending power. Even with China's consumer market being increasingly supplemented with exotic food imports and more processed and packaged convenience foods, the cost of food has remained comparatively very cheap for urban Chinese consumers.

The price inflation witnessed in China in 2007 that continued into 2008 and which was almost wholly attributable to food price rises (due directly to the rise in pork prices following the 2007 outbreak of Blue Ear disease), certainly hurt the many Chinese still living below the poverty line (some 8–10 per cent of the population, depending upon who's calculations you believe), as well as the many rural Chinese whose incomes, although above the poverty line, are only barely so.

Despite this, for the average urban Chinese resident, the recent inflationary rises in food prices were almost insignificant in terms of their pockets, even if inflation did become a subject of much debate and grumbling among shoppers. If you average food price rises in 2007 at about 30 per cent for the total, this would mean that the average urban consumer would have spent about RMB4,045.50 (US$584) a year on food in that year. That equates to RMB933.58 (US$135) more on food than the previous year, or nearly RMB18 (US$2.60) a week, based on national statistics. But the average wage increased by 10.56 per cent in 2007, according to the NBS (and given the 'greyness' of income statistics in China probably more), which would have made the average annual urban disposable income in the region of approximately RMB13,001.25 (US$1,877) in that year. That means that income was an extra RMB23.88 (US$3.45) per week compared to 2006.

Of course, other costs of living have also gone up, from education fees and taxi fares to subway tokens and petrol; but food was one of the fastest inflators, and even food's growth from 26.5 per cent of average disposable urban income in 2006 to 31.1 per cent did not really hit urban consumers too hard. Continued price inflation during 2008, again mainly in food, continued to hurt the poorer sections of society, but had little effect on overall urban spending at a time when deflation was still apparent in the prices of many non-food goods (electronic appliances, clothing, etc.), but at the same time, Chinese consumers were increasingly discovering the use of credit. Food inflation dwindled in the latter half of 2008 as the Blue Ear disease problem retreated and by 2009 there was food deflation in some sectors.

The main point of all this statistical juggling is to point out that the cost of food for the average urban Chinese shopper has been very low for an awfully long time. Not only has this meant that poor farmers really haven't been getting the income they deserve from the crops they produce (not including those that have done well by exporting food to Japan and other arable land-light and high-paying countries), but that urban China has been able to pig out to its heart's content, in many ways, without really having to worry about the cost. Food has become almost a given, with the exception of exotic and expensive imported trophy foods. That the new middle class and the wealthy urbanites of China knew this, has been seen in the phenomenon of purposefully overordering in restaurants to gain *face* and demonstrate that the bill payer is rich enough and unconcerned enough to be able to leave half the food on the table.

This phenomenon has been observed since the late 1990s. The state-controlled media has regularly run editorials and articles pointing out the stupidity of this practice – one's prestige depending upon how much money one spends on meals – and also pointing out that the worst offenders appear to be officials eating out on the taxpayers' tab. Many diners have become reluctant to ask for uneaten food to be packed up to take home, seeing this as sending a signal they are not wealthy enough. According to the *People's Daily*, as far back as 2001 when the press first start condemning wasteful practices, Shanghai restaurants were forced to dump 1,200 tonnes of leftover dishes every day, and Chinese sociologist Chen Xin of the Chinese Academy of Social Sciences (CASS) estimated that of the more than RMB100 billion of public money spent by officials on eating out in China that year, one-third was wasted in discarded food.[2]

So China's economic growth has created a situation where food for urban consumers is almost so cheap you can ignore the cost. At the same time, the economic growth has also created massively improved food market penetration. This means that a greater volume of an increased number of food products are being shifted more efficiently to more markets, shops, canteens, restaurants and other catering outlets across the country, while the number of those outlets has also increased – massively. This in turn means that the average urban Chinese consumer is, at any given time, physically much closer to a greater range and volume of food products than ever before.

You can literally walk from one block to the next in Shanghai and never be more than a block away from a convenience store, never mind the growing number of supermarkets, hypermarkets and speciality food stores, while, despite their decline, you are rarely that far from a wet market. You could buy a chocolate bar and a can of Coke at one shop, and be standing outside another shop before you finish it. And the same goes for catering outlets. It is almost impossible to open your eyes on a Shanghai street, and not see a restaurant. In China's cities, food is omnipresent.

Moving Up the Food Chain

But it is not just sheer quantity of food that is making urban Chinese people fatter. What has really made the difference is the change in the composition of their diet – the 'share of throat' of the various types of foodstuff that make up what the urban Chinese habitually eats. We use the word 'habitually' consciously, as obesity is not caused by trying new, expensive, exotic foods on rare occasions – one trip to a steak house for a wedding anniversary wouldn't do it –obesity is caused by wholesale diet change, which requires the habitual and regular consumption of certain kinds of food.

Consider the comparative growth in total sales of some key food categories that typically can add to weight gain when consumed frequently:

Percentage growths such as these are not caused by the occasional purchase or the odd treat, but by habitual consumption regularly over a period of time. Many of these product categories were tiny in the early 1980s. Even by the late 1980s there was hardly any chocolate to be found, and most of that was of a pretty low standard and expensive, and consequently, not exactly flying off the shelves! But, during the first six years of this century, chocolate consumption in China doubled – twice. Likewise, chilled ready meals, which were rare until the late 1990s, are now common in convenience stores and supermarkets. Another example is ice cream, long a consumer favourite (Chinese were eating ice cream in growing amounts back in the 1920s, and can claim to have invented it), and so was already a well-established market before the economic reforms of the 1980s, but has still grown at a rapid pace despite its already advanced state of development in China with long-standing and well-known brands and product lines.

However, most of these sectors are not core food items – they are not dietary basics. In order to understand the fundamental changes in diet, we

Table 8: **Total Volume Growth in Retail Sales of Selected Food Products in China, 2003–2009**

Volume Growth, 2003 –2009	
Ice cream	132%
Cakes	124%
Sweet biscuits	124%
Chocolate	78%
Candy	54%
Chilled ready meals	131%
Savoury snacks	113%
Sodas	81%
Alcoholic drinks	62%
And by way of contrast:	
Fresh fruit	123%
Fresh vegetables	73%

Source: Access Asia.

need to consider the shifting proportions within the Chinese diet of food commodities such as fruit, vegetables, meat and poultry, fish and seafood, grains and pulses. It is already clear, from the agricultural output data detailed above, that overall production of food has increased significantly. China has, in the space of 50 years, gone from the national famine caused by the Great Leap Forward (retrospection is always bound to be somewhat ironic) to a situation where obesity is reaching epidemic proportions. Economic reform has done a lot to improve food production and security in China, even though glaring inefficiencies in the agricultural industry remain. But that's another story.

What directly concerns us here is that since the economic reform movement began, China's climb up the food chain has been staggering. Meat not only reappeared as a feature of many people's diets, but it has become a regular feature of everyday meals, and in greater varieties and amounts. For instance, in Shanghai the percentage of meat in the local diet expanded from 10 per cent to just under 26 per cent in the 20 years up to 2008. As consumer incomes rose, the population, largely those benefiting most directly in the urban areas, adjusted their diets to their new living standards.

Remember, 50 years ago it was famine that grabbed the headlines, when people literally lived on weeds and grasshoppers, and Western children were encouraged to eat their greens and think of 'the starving children in China'; now China's consumers (acutely aware of their country's recent past) have access to, and the means to afford as much meat, fish, poultry, eggs, fruit, vegetables, grains and dairy as they can comfortably fit in their bellies, and more.

Pork – The National Meat

Pork has traditionally been the major meat of China. Pigs are relatively easy to rear, feed and provide fertilizer for the soil, while requiring little space and no grazing or herding. By 1994 pork still accounted for three-fourths of all meat consumption in China, and today represents over 60 per cent of total meat consumption, despite the rapid rise in the consumption of other meats. Pork consumption in China is close to Western levels in per capita terms, and grew by 90 per cent in per capita consumption terms between 2001 and 2006. This means the 'average' Chinese has doubled their intake of pork in the last five years. Consider how much this has increased for the 'exceptional' Chinese, those who fit into the urban middle-income bracket!

The hikes in food prices in China most dramatically illustrated the importance of pork to the Chinese diet in 2007. All of the inflation had been caused by pork prices, or rather, the disease that made pigs' ears turn blue. Blue Ear disease is a deadly virus that affects pigs, and in spring 2007 it was spreading out of control among China's swineherd, causing many deaths, both from the disease and the cull instigated to control the disease. The result was that a large portion of China's swineherd was wiped out. The laws of economics kicked in and pork prices went up rapidly and continued rising until new piglets born in 2007 became hogs ready for slaughter in the summer of 2008.

The most significant thing about this whole episode was not that Chinese consumers had to pay more for their pork, but that the pork price rises caused a knock-on effect throughout the food market, pushing up prices across all food sectors in varying degrees. That is how important pork is within the Chinese diet. In fact, pork's share-of-throat per capita increased from 3.5 per cent in 1997 to 4.93 per cent 10 years later, an increase of 1.43 percentage points.

Poultry – Chickens Die Younger in China Now

Carl Crow, the famous journalist and advertising executive who lived in China between the wars, noted in the 1930s that chicken was a poor dish in China, as no chicken would be sacrificed to the pot until its egg-bearing days were over.[3] Consequently, chicken meat was stringy and inferior to other meats. How things have changed since then.

Between 1990 and 2005, output of chicken meat has increased from 2.7 million chickens to 10.7 million, an increase of just under 300 per cent.

This means that overall chicken consumption in China tripled in the space of just 15 years. Chicken has become a staple meat, and is also, of course, popular as a fried food as witnessed by the success of KFC and a host of imitators. The government has encouraged poultry production, as chickens convert grain into meat far more efficiently than either pigs or cattle, reducing feed costs. Western companies found a profitable niche exporting their discarded poultry claws to China, as Chinese consumers ate all the chicken feet available in China and local demand outstripped local supply. It's been a profitable niche as the only other realistic use for the claws in the West is as cat or dog food, which pays only waste-level prices.

But there has been a downside to the rapid growth in chicken rearing and consumption: most notably, Bird Flu – the H5N1 avian influenza virus. The intensive nature of chicken farming in China, as in much of the rest of Asia, lent itself perfectly to the development and spread of an avian virus that managed to mutate very quickly into a killer disease, thanks to the high concentrations of millions of chickens, all of which are transported across regions to supply the voracious consumer market and stored in many wet markets and live elsewhere before being slaughtered for sale to the consumer, rather than the retailer, in many cases.

That chicken provides a cheap and plentiful supply of protein has been a boon to the average Chinese diet, but the widespread use of rapid-growth hormones to get mature chickens out of newly hatched chicks in as short a time as possible is also causing significant problems. Cases have been reported where children have been showing disturbed developmental patterns, including reaching puberty up to two years too early, and these cases have become increasingly common, judging by reports in the domestic Chinese press. Consumers and scientific and medical researchers see the problem as being directly linked to the increased use of rapid-growth hormones in rearing livestock, such as chickens, combined with the increased consumption of those meats.

Poultry consumption, in terms of retail sales, saw an increase in per capita consumption of 77 per cent in the ten years between 1997 and 2006, but non-retail consumption of fresh poultry (including the catering and food processing industry) increased even faster than this, rising from 44 per cent of total consumption in 1997 to 66.5 per cent by 2006. The rise of fast-food chicken in particular has created massive growth in demand for poultry outside the retail sector.

Eggs – Consumption Pattern May Change Due to Lifestyles

By 1990 Chinese urbanites were consuming 100 eggs a year each, according to official figures. The government wanted this to increase to 200 per capita by

2000, and surpassed this target by another 32 eggs per capita. By contrast, in America, according to the United States Department of Agriculture's (USDA) Economic Research Service, consumers eat an average of 259 eggs per annum (actually down from 402 in 1945). The per capita growth in China required a greatly expanded flock and also significantly larger grain consumption by the poultry industry. The flock grew by 265 per cent between 1990 and 2006, and per capita egg consumption among the Chinese now stands at about 414 eggs per year per person, whether consumed 'from the shell', or as an ingredient of prepared foods, and both bought through catering outlets or within packaged processed foods from retail outlets.

In highly developed countries, per capita egg consumption actually falls, as shown above by the USDA figures. China has expended considerable effort to raise egg consumption rates in per capita terms and this was initially successful. However, as the Chinese urban diet changes, so egg consumption may fall due to the trend towards increased consumption of prepared foods and fast foods, where processed eggs are more commonly found, as well as the decline in at-home preparation of meals, which tends to require more eggs.

Beef – Eating Wealth

China is now encouraging both the rearing of cattle for beef as well as importing it; indeed, China is an exporter of beef and about half of China's beef exports are to Hong Kong, followed by exports to Russia, Kuwait, Egypt and other countries.

Beef is a relatively new meat to most Chinese, and only really dates back to 1993, when 2,100 tonnes of Australian beef were brought into the country, primarily for the use of five-star hotels and high-end restaurants. Imports accelerated when, as part of China's accession to the WTO in 2001, the government committed to reducing tariffs on beef.

Since then, beef consumption has become widespread in urban areas, and is no longer just the preserve of the rich. Between 1990 and 2006, beef production rose by 527 per cent, and per capita retail consumption (which just includes beef bought at stores to cook at home and does not include catering sales) rose by 177 per cent between 1999 and 2007. Because of its recent association with opulence, newly moneyed Chinese middle-class consumers are keen to enjoy their ability to eat beef as often as they can, mostly through restaurants. Additionally, beef has noticeably suffered less from the inflationary pressures of 2007–2008 than pork, although beef prices increased by 7 per cent on average to US$2.19 from US$2.04 per kg between January and August 2007;

the change was much smaller compared than the average 74 per cent rise in pork prices over the same period.

In line with this, the market is being supplied at both ends; McDonald's and other burger-type fast-food places are supplying beef in relatively cheap and affordable fashion to many urbanites across the country while upmarket steakhouses are opening apace in major cities, selling beef from grain-fed cattle with marble lines that appeal to upmarket diners. Beef is also being increasingly incorporated into more traditional Chinese cuisine than burgers and steaks. The ever-popular hotpot restaurants are selling increased quantities of frozen beef (as well sheep and goat meat). Additionally, hotpot, which enjoyed a boom and became extremely fashionable across China in the first years of the twenty-first century, increased demand for offal such as the omasum (the third compartment of the stomach in ruminants) that is widely used in both hotpot and cold dishes all over China. As pork prices rose in 2007, bovine offal was increasingly used as a substitute for pork offal in hotpot restaurants.

The major point about beef is that it is seen as a symbol of rising prosperity and aspiration and therefore, as the urban economy and incomes grow, so too will beef sales and consumption.

Rice and Grain – It Ain't What it Used to Be

It is not surprising that survey after survey has found that grain consumption is down in China's cities. The pattern of emerging wealthy societies moving from high grain consumption to less, but with the substitution of meat, is a traditional pattern observed in developing societies the world over. China has not been an exception. It was also not new knowledge that this shift tended to lead to higher rates of obesity and heart disease. A number of surveys in the early part of the new century were confirming what most people already knew: that China's urban grain consumption, while growing in overall terms, was slowing as a component of the overall urban diet.[4]

The same trend had already been seen in Japan and Taiwan, where rice consumption had fallen by 50 per cent in 30 years. The reasons behind these changes were also predictable: wider choice of food, new food cultures (particularly fast food and ready meals), the rise of convenience foods in tandem with changing lifestyles and more sedentary lives for more of the urban population. All meant less grain and more fat.

Between 1997 and 2006, just ten years, the average per capita apparent consumption of grains fell by about 0.3 per cent, from 407.8 kg per capita in 1997 to 406.6 kg per capita by 2006, thus remaining fairly constant. This means that other foods have increased their share of the total Chinese diet, relative to grain. And it seems that the rate of decline of per capita consumption has been just as rapid in rural areas of the country as in urban areas. However, retail sales of grain to be cooked at home declined by 25 per cent over the same period. This means that more of the grains consumed by Chinese people are now, on average, consumed either at restaurants or bought as part of prepared ready meals, snacks or other convenience foods, and not grain as a raw product in itself.

Over two billion people across Asia derive between 60 and 70 per cent of their daily calorific intake from rice; rice is usually the main component of almost all the meals most Asians consume. But such dependence on rice causes chronic micronutrient deficiency in many Asian people. Although rice is able to provide adequate energy, it has only a limited amino acid profile, and therefore offers only limited amounts of micronutrients (dietary minerals needed by the human body in small quantities). Milling, which produces white rice, the most commonly eaten form, removes much of the protein, fibre, fat, iron, zinc, chromium, iodine and vitamin B from the rice. About half of all women in their reproductive ages in Asia suffer from iron deficiency, while vitamin A deficiency affects 10–25 per cent of children and pregnant women. Vitamin A deficiency has been noted specifically by the Chinese government as a key weakness in China's changing diet; lack of vitamin A can cause blindness and even death by diarrheal dehydration.

Potatoes – A Highly Productive Vegetable

The sharp surge in the price of rice and other grains in 2008 led to a sense of alarm among China's leaders and slight concerns among the population. Even fairly well-off consumers noticed price rises in some key areas of household staples such as cooking oil as well as rice. Potatoes, of course, have a high nutritional value and provide a good supply of high-quality protein full of vitamin C and amino acids. Crucially, for China's food-supply planners, potato cultivation is four times more productive than grain in terms of land area and labour input. In a country still in the shadow of food shortages 30 years ago and with limited supplies of arable land (and potatoes, endemic to the Andes, can grow in even poor mountain soils), China's planners turned seriously to potatoes. In the mid-1980s, China started deliberately increasing its potato crop. The central planners in Beijing saw early on that their population growth meant that grain production was not going to meet demand and ordered the planting of more potatoes. The result of this central edict was that China became the world's largest potato producer in 1993 (thanks to the demise and break up of the Soviet Union, the long-running potato kings) and accounted for more than 80 per cent of the increase in global potato production from 1990 to 2002. The *American Journal of Potato Research* estimates that China's potato output should surpass 81 million metric tonnes in 2010.[5]

With rice prices increasing sharply in 2008, the humble potato has risen back up the agenda of importance in China. The country has become an active exporter of fresh potatoes and an importer of the frozen French fry and other pre-prepared potato products. Following the centralized government's decision to grow more potatoes, consumption started to grow (from 11 kg per capita in 1990 to 32 kg per capita in 2001) as, thanks to improved distribution and logistics, people in areas outside of where potatoes are grown started eating them, potato-based dishes started appearing more frequently on restaurant menus and Western-style fast foods like French fries became ubiquitous in China's cities. As well as this, the snacks market has been growing and potatoes have been increasingly processed into a range of high-value products such as potato chips.

Aquatic Produce – All the Fish in the Sea

Food analysts used to quip that if the Chinese population adopted wholesale the typical Japanese diet and consumed as much fish as the Japanese did, then a chain of sushi restaurants in Shanghai would be highly profitable, except for the fact that there wouldn't be enough fish in the world's oceans to meet the demand. It is true that the supply of aquatic produce has improved across more of China as the distribution of such products has become more sophisticated. This has been helped by the spread of organized retail chains, particularly supermarkets and hypermarkets, which not only supply fresh (live) fish and seafood, but also offer a greater variety of frozen, canned and chilled seafood products. Most consumers tend to prefer to buy fresh, though. In most developing countries there has been a trend away from live fish to pre-packed. However, as food safety concerns have risen to prominence in China following a spate of outbreaks and greater press coverage, consumers have continued to demand fresh fish rather than the pre-killed, gutted, filleted and packaged variety.

In terms of overall apparent per capita consumption, aquatic produce increased in volume by 37.7 per cent over the ten years between 1997 and 2006, but a much greater rate of consumption (122.8 per cent) was seen through retail channels during the same decade. The improved availability of fresh fish and seafood through retailers has added strong impetus to consumer purchase of these products to cook at home.

At the same time, away-from-home consumption of fish has also increased. Among wealthier consumers, fish such as salmon and seafood buffets have become increasingly popular, with aquatic produce increasingly flown in from as far afield as Scotland and Alaska. At the lower end of the market, cheap and cheerful sushi restaurants have become popular with many urban young people increasing their fish intake in these establishments.

Fruit and Vegetables – More Choice, More Availability

The greater variety of fruit and vegetables available and on offer, as well as the longer seasonal availability of many products and imports of more exotic produce, has helped to increase consumer interest in them and drive strong growth in purchasing. While vegetables saw a solid 74.6 per cent growth in overall per capita consumption between 1997 and 2006, per capita retail consumption of fresh vegetables actually declined by 1 per cent over the same period. This indicates that while consumers are cooking and eating about the same amount of fresh vegetables at home, they are eating much more through indirect sales through fresh vegetables consumed in restaurants and through prepared ready meals.

A similar trend is seen with fruit. Whereas total apparent per capita consumption of fresh fruit grew by a massive 212 per cent, retail sales only grew by 33.4 per cent over the same 1997 to 2006 period. Again, it seems that more Chinese consumers are eating more fruit, either as part of a meal away from home, or as part of prepared desserts (yoghurts, cakes, etc.) and other packaged products.

Crucial to this rise in fruit consumption has been range and availability. In the late 1970s and 1980s fruits that are now relatively commonplace in urban China, such as kiwi and even oranges, were rare. Apples have become far more common as China's orchards have increased their acreage and yields; China is now a major exporter of apples. Watermelon and lychees, as well as pears and peaches, were the most popular and widely available fruits prior to the 1990s explosion in choice, and remain popular.

Dairy – Breaking Down Taboos

Dairy consumption in China has been little short of revolutionary. For decades, dairy was rejected and still today rarely features as an ingredient in most Chinese dishes. Lactose intolerance is higher than average among ethnic-Chinese, though rates can be reduced significantly through school milk programmes aimed at the gradual reintroduction of dairy into the child's diet. Such programmes have been in place in urban schools in China for nearly a decade now, often jointly sponsored by local authorities and major local dairy companies, and have been successful in reducing the incidence of lactose intolerance and promoting sales and consumption of dairy products.

Thanks to a decrease in lactose intolerance, better marketing, a wider range of products and an increase in at-home refrigeration (few are the apartments without a refrigerator now in urban China) milk consumption has risen significantly, as has that of yoghurt and ice cream, though butter and cheese remain minor segments of the food market and most people's diets. Indeed, most urban Chinese only consume cheese through Western foods such as pizzas and burgers.

The drive to grow the market has also led to a general focus on raising volume rather than improving quality. Raising volume in an environment where, typically, local dairy herds only yield a quarter of the milk that herds in Western Europe do, has meant the continued use of growth hormones and other chemical inputs into the dairy food chain. Recent cases of children reaching puberty at very young ages, due to consuming large levels of growth hormones from foods, especially dairy products, has alerted the Chinese public to the dangers of such poor practice in the agricultural sector. The widespread practice of using growth hormones are only now beginning to show up in effects on consumers, and this issue is likely to come back to haunt the dairy industry, if it does not address this issue soon.

Average per capita consumption of milk in China grew from 5.3 kg in 1999 to 9.2 kg by 2008, representing a 73.1 per cent growth over the decade. Retail sales of milk grew even more rapidly, rising from 0.22 kg per capita in 1999 to 0.62 kg per capita by 2008, a rise of 182.9 per cent over the decade.

Of course, the highly publicized melamine in milk scandal of 2008 forced the dairy industry to rapidly reinvent itself in China. Continued reliance on small-scale farmers, who tend an average of half a dozen cows, and whose low yield led to the temptation to 'bulk out' milk sold to collection stations, often in collusion with those stations, led to the melamine scandal and the illness of tens of thousands of children. A colossal PR catastrophe for the industry, the dairy producers are now busy buying pasture land and building dairy herds of their own, not only to secure their raw milk supply, but also to help restore public trust in their products. By taking over direct production, it is hoped that the use of rapid growth hormones as well as poisonous bulking agents, will be a thing of the past.

The Sectors Compared

Table 9: **Per Capita Food Commodity Consumption and % Growth,
1999–2008**

	Apparent Consumption (KG/Capita)		% Growth
	1999	2008	1999–2008
Grain	192.85	151.23	−21.58
Fresh vegetables	109.59	108.94	−0.59
Edible oil	7.31	7.83	7.15
– Pork	14.54	15.25	4.90
– Beef	1.11	1.31	18.18
– Mutton	0.70	0.82	17.74
– Poultry	3.54	5.79	63.53
Total Meat	20.60	24.30	17.99
Fresh eggs	6.90	7.52	8.92
Aquatic produce	10.54	14.91	41.43
Milk	5.29	9.16	73.06
Fresh fruit	30.77	33.19	7.86
Nuts and kernels	18.41	16.28	−11.57
TOTAL	422.15	396.55	−6.07

Source: Access Asia from Ministry of Health and National Bureau of Statistics.

Sugar – China's Sweet Tooth

By far the largest consumer of sugar in China is the food and beverage
(F&B) processing industry, which consumed 77.7 per cent of total overall
consumption in 2007, although this was down somewhat from 80.6 per cent
in 2001. Taking this into consideration, it is interesting to consider official
data on the size and growth of key food product sectors, where the products
have a significant percentage of sugar as an ingredient.

One thing that is immediately striking from a glance at Table 10, is that
the largest sectoral uses of sugar are for food products that profess to being
rather healthier than others, if you believe the commonly used advertising
strategies. Most dairy products, fruit juices and canned foods contain
significant amounts of sugar, and dairy in particular has grown significantly in
recent times, up by 23.6 per cent in 2007 (January to November), compared to
2006. Indeed, all of the sectors considered high in sugar have grown rapidly
lately, and at faster rates than only a few years ago, testament to the growing
consumer purchasing of such products.

Table 10: **Per Capita Food Commodity Retail Sales, % Share-of-Throat and % Non-Retail Sales, 1999–2008**

	Retail (KG/Capita)		% Growth	% Share-of-Throat		% Non-Retail	
	1999	2008	1999–2008	1999	2008	1999	2008
Grain	7.39	11.64	57.51	11.63	10.87	96.17	92.31
Fresh vegetables	19.80	44.75	125.98	31.18	41.82	81.93	58.92
Edible oil	0.51	1.06	106.39	0.81	0.99	92.98	86.48
– Pork	9.26	9.11	–1.56	14.58	8.52	36.32	40.24
– Beef	0.75	0.77	2.44	1.19	0.72	32.18	41.21
– Mutton	0.46	0.48	3.61	0.73	0.45	34.22	42.12
– Poultry	2.40	3.62	50.54	3.78	3.38	32.19	37.58
Total Meat	12.87	13.98	8.58	20.27	13.06	37.50	42.48
Fresh eggs	2.85	4.42	55.23	4.48	4.13	58.76	41.23
Aquatic produce	1.91	3.53	84.82	3.01	3.30	81.88	76.32
Milk	0.22	0.62	182.90	0.35	0.58	95.85	93.22
Fresh fruit	4.56	12.08	164.92	7.18	11.29	85.18	63.61
Nuts and kernels	0.53	0.95	80.03	0.83	0.89	97.14	94.17
TOTAL	63.52	107.00	68.47	100.00	100.00	84.95	73.02

Source: Access Asia from Ministry of Health and National Bureau of Statistics.

As more processed food fills more supermarket shelves, and inevitably ends up in more consumers' shopping baskets, it is not surprising that per capita sugar consumption is rising fast in China. Chinese government statistics used to have per capita 'table sugar' consumption steadily declining in both urban and rural China until it stopped publishing this set of figures in about 2003 (tellingly, perhaps). In fact, Access Asia's own estimates of per capita retail purchases are lower than the government estimates at that time, but rather than going down, it is almost certain that retail sales are going up.

However, what is most significant is that while the government had per capita retail sales at about 1.5 kg and decreasing, based on total consumption both through retail, catering and processed foods, the average Chinese consumer is now, in fact, getting as much as 10 kg of sugar a year, nearly 83 per cent more than was the case in 2001.

But total per capita consumption is not likely to stay still. Indeed, total per capita consumption of sugar, including both retail sales and sugar added into processed foods, is expected to increase by about another 38 per cent over 2008 to almost 15 kg per capita by 2012, indicating a sharp rise in the overall consumption of sugar in the Chinese diet in general. Based on WHO data,

Table 11: **Total Production of Processed Foods Containing Significant Amounts of Added Sugar in China, January–November, 2006–2007**

Production Volume	1–11, 2006	1–11, 2007	Y-o-Y	2006	2007
	(Tonnes "000)	(Tonnes "000)	growth (%)	break down (%)	break down (%)
Dairy products	13,060.5	16,141.5	23.59	33.53	34.32
Fruit juices and juice drinks	8,080.5	9,851.8	21.92	20.74	20.95
Carbonated soft drinks	8,339.4	9,553.6	14.56	21.41	20.31
Canned food	3,682.1	4,593.4	24.75	9.45	9.77
Frozen food	1,761.0	1,969.1	11.82	4.52	4.19
Biscuits	1,570.0	1,951.0	24.27	4.03	4.15
Chilled convenience foods	1,245.9	1,528.3	22.67	3.20	3.25
Confectionery	724.3	867.9	19.82	1.86	1.85
Cakes & pastries	493.6	579.2	17.35	1.27	1.23
TOTAL	38,957.2	47,035.8	20.74	100.00	100.00

Source: China Sugar Association/Access Asia.

this compares with a decline in per capita consumption in countries like Japan (down from about 23 kg in 1991 to 18.8 kg in 2005). In Hong Kong, per capita consumption remains higher than in mainland China, at about a fairly constant 26.5 kg to 27 kg per capita. Meanwhile, in South Korea, per capita sugar consumption is also increasing, up from 19.8 kg per capita in 1991 to 26 kg per capita in 2005.

What these comparisons show is that China's per capita sugar consumption is likely to continue to grow, not having reached the same levels as its neighbouring countries, i.e., the countries with the closest cultural and cuisine traditions to those of China. But China could see trends that are seen in more-developed countries, compared with which, China's per capita consumption rate is still relatively very low. For instance, in the US per capita consumption has stuck at about 31–32 kg per capita for some time, whereas in Canada, this figure is about 44 kg per capita and in Australia closer to 50 kg per capita.

In India, a country often compared with China for its similarly rapid economic growth in recent decades and large, increasingly urbanized population, sugar consumption rose from about 13.8 kg per capita in 1991 to 19.6 kg per capita in 2005, showing a similar rate of growth as seen in China, but at a more advanced stage. Indians drink a lot of sugary tea, which the Chinese do not, as yet, which probably accounts for India's higher consumption levels compared to those in China. However, it is worth noting that China is a patchwork of

Table 12: **Per Capita Sugar Retail Sales and Consumption Volume & Value, 2001–2007**

	2001	2002	2003	2004	2005	2006	2007	% Annual Growth 2001–2007
Retail								
KG/capita	0.64	0.71	0.75	0.82	0.93	0.99	1.02	57.85
RMB/capita	2.64	2.89	3.18	3.81	4.49	4.96	5.71	116.25
Consumption								
KG/capita	7.41	9.09	8.05	7.65	7.39	9.21	10.04	35.54
RMB/capita	17.53	27.21	23.31	19.31	21.56	24.73	39.28	124.01
Population (m)	1,261.3	1,274.5	1,287.9	1,301.2	1,314.6	1,328.0	1,341.3	6.35

Source: International Sugar Organization/Indian Sugar Association/China Sugar Association/FAOStat/Access Asia.

cuisines and some use far more sugar and are aimed at sweeter teeth and tastes than others. For instance, eastern China's cuisines are particularly high in sugar and chefs seemingly quicker to throw more sugar into their dishes.

The growing consumption of sugar, both at home and in restaurants, in fizzy soda drinks and sugar-based confectionery as well as a growing ingredient in any numbers of convenience foods or ready meals, is also having a side effect that impacts China's healthcare system. When the China Youth Development Foundation (CYDF) conducted a survey of Beijing's schools and pupils' health in 2005, the NGO found that after myopia (nearsightedness), decayed teeth was the biggest problem affecting kids (obesity was sixth after inflammation of the mucous lining covering the inside of the eyelid and the surface of the eyeball (trachoma), low red blood cell count (anemia) and infestation of the intestine with roundworms (ascariasis)). It seems that despite the claims of many fizzy-drink manufacturers and confectionery companies, China's growing sweet tooth was doing the nation's dentistry no favours.

Salt – Goitres Down, Blood Pressure Up

Of itself, salt doesn't make you fat, but its inclusion in processed foods is symptomatic of the problems associated with the shift in diet towards more of those processed foods, and can create some ancillary health problems of its own, which, combined with obesity, adds to the detriment of the average consumers' health, and increases the strain on health services to deal with the outcome of increased salt, sugar and fat consumption. It is therefore useful to include here a summary of the changes in salt consumption in the Chinese diet.

In 2006 China surpassed the US to become the world's largest salt-producing nation, with an output of 48 million tonnes, compared with the US total of 46 million, and a world total in that year of 240 million. Chinese salt production increased by 56 per cent in the decade up to 2006, and now represents one-fifth of global production, according to The Salt Institute, the industry's trade association. China is therefore not short of salt. This might lead you to believe that the problems associated with salt consumption in China are a simple case of too much. However, this would be a simplification of the situation.

As with most things in China, regional variations in salt consumption are significant. Overconsumption of salt is a problem in many areas of the country. In fact, raised blood pressure (defined as a systolic blood pressure of 140 mmHg or over) is one of the leading causes of death and disability among Chinese, and much of this is related to a high salt intake. However, rates of the health problems related to high salt intake, such as hypertension, stroke and cancer of the stomach, seem to be much higher in northern China, where they are at almost pandemic levels. It is in these parts of China that the per capita consumption of salt appears to be highest, and where the reduction of salt intake seems to meet with the highest resistance.

But there is another health extreme related to salt consumption in China. It seems that in western China (Xinjiang, Qinghai, Sichuan, Gansu, Chongqing and Tibet) one of the key health problems related to diet is a lack of iodine intake. Iodine deficiency is most typically associated with remote inland areas. Most salt prepared for human consumption has iodine added to it, in order to supplement iodine intake into the average diet. This habitual addition of iodine has pretty much wiped out iodine deficiency in most developed countries. Iodine deficiency is a major cause of goitres (swelling in the neck due to an enlarged thyroid gland) as well as cretinism.

Yet, as an article in the *China Daily* pointed out, according to a Ministry of Health survey at the time, that iodine deficiency was widespread in the above provinces and that the incidence of iodine deficiency disorders (IDDs) had increased in areas where, according to a survey in 2000, the problem had been practically eliminated. According to Li Sumei, Director of the National Reference Laboratory for Iodine Deficiency Disorders under the Ministry of Health, '…there were 700 million people living in iodine-deficient areas, and a significant number of them suffer from varying degrees of IDDs.'[6]

According to Li, the problem seems to stem from the lack of iodization in edible salt. For example, 39 per cent of table salt in Tibet was not iodized, while in Hainan (a relatively well-developed island province in southern China) the level was 22 per cent. Even in Beijing, it was found that 16 per cent of salt was not iodized, mainly because there is a booming trade in uniodized, fake-branded salt. China has made significant inroads in adding iodine and therefore in reducing health problems associated with uniodized salt, but much remains to be done and it is necessary to remain vigilant to the problem.

Thus it is that Chinese consumers are increasing their intake of salt, and in an increasing numbers of areas of the country, escalating to dangerously high levels, but without getting any of the possible benefits from added iodine. Bao Shanfen, a researcher at Beijing's People's Liberation Army (PLA) General Hospital found that many families in six surveyed districts in Beijing used too much cooking oil and salt, with some taking in as much as 13 to 15 grams of salt a day.[7] By way of contrast, the UK's Food Standards Agency recommends that children 1–3 years of age consume no more than 2 grams of salt per day rising to 3 grams for those aged 4–6, while children 7–10 should consume no more than 5 grams a day. Another survey, this time conducted in Taiwan by the Consumers' Foundation, Chinese Taipei (CFCT), where the national diet is comparable to mainland China, warned about excessive levels of salt in packaged food products including popular items such as dried plums and instant noodles.[8]

It is also clear from several consumer surveys conducted by several agencies that Chinese consumers are blithely unaware of how much salt they consume in prepared foods, both from catering establishments and from packaged processed foods bought from retail outlets, in the same way that most are not aware of the amounts of added sugar and fat. It is important to note that it is not just the sometimes staggeringly high levels of sodium in processed and pre-prepared foods as well as fast foods that are a problem, but the amount of salt being added to traditional Chinese cuisines as well. Merely staying out of the junk-food joints is only half the solution when it comes to controlling salt intake in China.

Oils and Fats – The 'Hidden Ingredients'

By 2006 the Chinese, both urban and rural, were eating approximately 42.2 per cent more edible oils per capita than they were ten years previously. For instance, Shanghai citizens' daily intake of edible oil had grown from 28 g to 50 g. However, retail sales volume (per capita) only grew by 13.9 per cent over the same period, while non-retail consumption (catering and food processing) grew by 54.1 per cent. This is interesting for a variety of reasons.

Firstly, retail sales of vegetables per capita pretty much stayed the same in terms of volume over the 1997–2006 period, based on the official data. If this is the case, then people didn't need to buy 13.9 per cent more oil in order to cook more vegetables. No, what they have been cooking more of in oils is meat.

Secondly, if per capita retail sales volumes of edible oils is growing less than other areas of consumption, this means it comes from catering and food processing, unless the Chinese have all taken to fuelling their cars with rapeseed oil. This is important, because, when you cook your own food, you can control how much oil/fat you use. But you cannot control this with food cooked for you, either by restaurants or food-processing companies making your ready meals. Even if manufacturers state the nutritional information (not widely available at Chinese restaurants, and only recently forced onto the food processing industry) on menus or packaging, it is hard to compare fat contents in percentages or grams with the proportions you might use when cooking at home – a tablespoon or a dash, etc. – it's an imprecise and confusing science.

You can see why processed food manufacturers think it's a good idea to put more fat into the food they make. Basically, oil is a cheap ingredient. The average price of cooking oils has generally declined most years, with price increases really only in 2003, 2004 and 2007. Over the period, oil prices have barely grown at all. It has therefore comprised a very cheap ingredient. Using oils as a basis for sauces, manufacturers have increased the amount of sauce over other more expensive ingredients, such as meat, and bulked up with rice (or other carbohydrates) and vegetables. This also makes for richer-tasting food that makes the consumer feel like they are getting something really special and tasty. The same logic applies in catering. It means that food manufacturers and caterers are using more of the cheaper ingredients, and less of the dearer ones, and thus generating better profit margins per serving. In competitive markets, such as catering and food processing, this is good for margins, if not crucial to business survival.

The danger is that consumers don't necessarily know how much oil they are consuming when eating pre-prepared ready meals or when eating out at a restaurant or fast-food joint, in the same way that they do not know how much added sugar and salt – the so-called 'hidden' ingredients – they are consuming. In this, China is no different from most other countries. The problem in China is the pace of dietary change, and the role that hidden cooking oil increasingly plays in the new diet.

Domestic prices for cooking oil started to rise in late 2007 and 2008, sparking some concern among consumers and, of course, the social-harmony-obsessed government. Eventually, in June 2008 the government scrapped tax rebates on exports of 36 varieties of cooking oil products, including vegetable, soy, peanut and sunflower oils, in an attempt to drive down domestic prices. The move was designed to encourage exporters to shift to domestic sales and therefore help increase domestic supply. Cooking oil appeared to be a touchstone of consumer concern over rising food prices; in late 2007 a stampede occurred among a crowd waiting to buy discounted cooking oil at a branch of French supermarket chain Carrefour in the city of Chongqing. Tragically, three people were crushed to death. Smaller cooking oil-related riots occurred elsewhere around the same time, including at a branch of the UK supermarket chain Tesco in Shanghai.

Alcoholic Drinks – China's Beer Belly

Within the realm of food and beverages, perhaps nothing symbolizes the massive change within Chinese society in as much as the consumption of alcoholic drinks. Overall alcoholic drinks consumption has changed hugely over recent years. Much of the bulk of both volume and value sales in China used to come from grain spirits, which included everything from expensive bottles of Maotai ('liquid razor blades' as American news anchor Tom Brokaw once called it) to the mass of locally distilled rotgut in an old pop bottle. But times have changed. Spirits are increasingly seen as what Grandpa drank before he died of the ravages of hard labour and poor healthcare (not to mention the smoking and hard liquor), despite attempts by the drinks giants such as Pernod Ricard to relaunch and rebrand traditional spirits. They still sell significant amounts but the age demographic is high and most is consumed at restaurants rather than the expanding number of bars across China.

The hype around spirits consumption in China is massive, but the reality is that apart from expensive imported 'badge drinks', spirits in overall terms are in massive decline. Not only are they not popular with younger generations, the government has actively sought to discourage their consumption, due to most of what was being consumed being pretty toxic stuff, and cause of much haemorrhaging of healthcare funds and labour days lost due to sickness (not to mention recent crackdowns on drunk driving in many cities). The Western spirits brands are trying to revive the market (advertising firms have made fortunes from saturation advertising campaigns) and some brands have achieved success, but it seems the heyday of spirits was the late 1980s and early 1990s when badges of affluence were worn more openly among China's new rich. This may not be good news for Scottish whisky distillers hoping for 1.3 billion malt aficionados, but may be beneficial for China's collective liver.

In place of spirits, the government insisted that if the Chinese are going to drink, it should be beer. And so they have – with a vengeance. The Chinese ditched spirits (retail volume consumption declined by nearly 28 per cent between 1999 and 2007) and took up drinking beer (retail volume increased nearly 680 per cent between 1999 and 2007). For those few in China who can afford a wine habit, their consumption of wine has grown by nearly 185 per cent

Table 13: **Growth in the Total Market Value and Volume for Alcoholic Drinks by Sector, 2003–2009**

RMB m, Current Prices	% Growth, 2003–2009
Beer	125.02
Wine	136.96
Spirits	221.38
TOTAL	19.48
Litres mn	
Beer	66.8
Wine	141.00
Spirits	102.34
TOTAL	38.68

Source: Access Asia from various Chinese official sources, trade associations, manufacturer information.

between 1999 and 2007. However, the spirits industry has deftly switched its production towards a higher end and this has paid off, with spirits sales rallying between 2003 and 2009 to register volume growth of over 100 per cent, faster than beer at 67 per cent over the same period, but still behind wine at 141 per cent.

This means that the mass of Chinese who drink have switched from spirits (and mostly traditional Chinese spirits) to beer. This has meant switching from low volume/high alcohol, to high volume/low alcohol. The switch to higher volume has meant that as well as all that water to process it, the Chinese are consuming much greater quantities of the carbohydrates (read sugars) that are a key component of beer. While the rates of occurrence of sclerosis of the liver may have declined due to less spirits being consumed, there are considerably more Chinese now proudly sporting a beer belly.

And it is not just the amount of beer that is being consumed, it is the way that it is being consumed, too. Many more young Chinese urban white-collar workers, most of who have a fairly sedentary lifestyles and work in offices, are going out to bars and nightclubs, drinking beer until late at night. This is different from the typical Chinese beer drinker of a couple of decades ago, who would more typically be a middle-aged factory worker or labourer who had a bottle of beer with their dinner before heading off to bed so as to get enough sleep before another early start and another day's hard work.

Beer consumption looks likely to continue to rise rapidly over the coming years, if the Chinese beer makers have their way. Although China overtook the US as the world's largest volume beer market in 2006, per capita consumption in China is about a quarter of the level seen in European markets such as the UK and Germany, and about half the level seen in comparable neighbouring East Asian markets, such as Japan and South Korea. The brewers see in these statistics the potential to continue to greatly expand their market.

China's leading brewers are currently frantically buying or building production capacity in the new growth regions of China, in order to tap into the new market potential in relatively low per capita beer consuming regions. Driving up the market is the easy option for the brewers, who would otherwise have to compete much more directly with each other, which means becoming more cost efficient – much harder to achieve. The huge amounts of advertising expenditure being pumped into selling more beer are matched only by the investment in developing the logistics to increase market penetration of beer into more of the market.

Even in developed regions of China, where beer consumption is already relatively high, the increasingly leisure-oriented consumption patterns of Chinese consumers is leading them into an increased variety of social situations where they are more likely to drink more beer. They are eating out more, as we have already discussed, but they are also going to more bars, nightclubs and karaoke parlours, staying more frequently at more holiday resorts, going out to leisure complexes, such as cinemas and bowling alleys, where beer is on sale.

Beer consumption can only be expected to keep on growing. Add to this the new growth in wines, and overall alcohol consumption is growing even faster. What this will mean for the future health of the Chinese is no mystery; the effects on health and healthcare spending caused by increased alcohol consumption are well documented in countries that have been through rapid growth in the alcoholic drinks market. Yet again, though, the problem that China faces that cannot be predicted accurately by the circumstances in other countries, is that its alcohol consumption rate growth is so much more rapid than has been the case in most other countries. China's beer belly is set to expand.

Soft Drinks – Fizzy China

You'd think that healthcare experts would be pleased that the Chinese consume so much fruit juice, and that consumption is growing faster than carbonated ('fizzy') soft drinks (CSDs), the two sectors having grown in volume by 203.9 per cent and 105.5 per cent, respectively, between 2001 and 2007. It's true that dentists might be bemoaning the high acid and fruit sugar content, but think of all the 'vitamins and goodness'! 'Vitamins and goodness' are the unique

Table 14: Growth in the Total Volume Market for Soft Drinks by Sector, 2001–2007

	% Annual Growth, 2001–2007
Carbonated soft drinks	105.49
Concentrates/dilutables	36.49
Fruit juices	203.86
Sports drinks	85.74
Mineral water	148.94
Soya drinks	46.42
Dairy drinks	32.15
RTD tea	87.21
RTD coffee	80.61
TOTAL	109.29

Source: Access Asia from trade sources and manufacturer information.
Note: RTD = Ready to Drink.

selling points (USPs) that soft drinks marketers use to promote their fruit-juice-based soft drinks, but much of what is consumed is not as pure and innocent as it might seem.

Much of the fruit juice sold in China is not pure juice. In fact, finding pure, untampered fruit juice is not that easy in Chinese supermarkets, and most that is available is made artisanally at juice bars and the like. The bulk of what is called fruit juice is reconstituted concentrate, usually with added sugar, and often with added colours and preservatives to revive the moribund lustre of the original fruit. Not that this has stopped a rash of products being labelled as '100 per cent juice' just as there are myriad products from chewing gum to fizzy drinks that erroneously label themselves as 'sugar free'. Of course, as consumers began to want no-added-sugar products, so the manufacturers switched to nerve-jangling alternatives, chiefly the artificial, nonsaccharine sweetener aspartame (known better in the West under brand names such as NutraSweet and Canderel, etc. and itself the subject of a public controversy due to possible health risks).

The approximately 150 per cent growth in mineral water consumption might also lead you towards optimism, but this simply reflects again the power of advertising, coupled with the rather sorry state of China's tap water supplies.

The Chinese population has only grown by about 1 per cent a year since the turn of the century, though per capita consumption of CSDs and fruit 'juices' increased by 101 per cent and 185 per cent respectively. This adds a lot of fizz, aspartame and sugar to the average diet that was not being consumed less than a decade ago. Also, as with all total per capita figures, these total national figures hide much slower growth in poorer rural regions of China, and much, much faster growth in richer urban areas.

So it is that the healthcare workers of China are not that pleased about the sharp rise in soft drink consumption among the population. They are also very nervous about the fact that the fast-food, marketing-led consumer culture that has caught on among China's younger generations is creating an environment where these younger Chinese are likely to consume even more sugar-filled soft drinks than before, further adding to the already numerous causes of rising childhood obesity (and to the poor dentistry among school children noted by the authorities) among urban Chinese, and that this environment is spreading to more of the country as other cities and regions rise up the income ladder.

The Hidden Dangers – MSG, Trans Fats and Interesterified Fats

No discussion of China's diet and its evolution can ignore the issue of monosodium glutamate (MSG), a sodium salt of glutamic acid, a nonessential amino acid, widely used as a food additive and commonly marketed as a 'flavour enhancer'. The Chinese consume large amounts of MSG, as do many other Asian societies and the patrons of Chinese restaurants around the world. MSG is found in all manner of components of the modern Chinese diet, from pre-prepared stocks and stock cubes (which are enjoying rising sales), condiments, frozen dinners, snack foods such as flavoured potato chips, virtually all fast food and the omnipresent Chinese quick-eat of instant noodles.

However, the Chinese do not consume as many other foods that may counteract MSG (taurine-containing raw fish, and meat) as the Japanese do. MSG is basically a flavour enhancer, used to intensify food taste, and virtually all the MSG produced goes into food for human consumption, with a small part used in animal feeds.

According to a report on global MSG production and consumption, published in January 2007 by SRI Consulting, China leads the world in terms of both production of MSG and its consumption.[9] The report notes that total world consumption of MSG was almost two million tonnes in 2006, valued at US$2.3 billion, and that consumption has increased very rapidly in recent years, in large part thanks to the Chinese market. China is the world's largest consumer and producer of MSG, and in 2006 represented 52 per cent of global consumption, and 57 per cent of global production. The 5 per cent difference represents the growing volume of Chinese exports, as MSG becomes a major new trading item for Chinese businesses. China is now the world's largest exporter of the chemical.

Scientific opinion on whether there are any particular ill effects from the consumption (at 'normal' levels) of MSG remains split. However, there seems to be mounting evidence that there is a possible link between MSG consumption and human susceptibility to obesity. In a German study entitled 'Obesity, voracity, and short stature: the impact of glutamate on the regulation of appetite' which included data sampling on over two million German subjects over two years, the researchers came to the following conclusion:

> The present study for the first time demonstrates, that a widely used nutritional monosubstance – the flavouring agent MSG – at concentrations that only slightly surpass those found in everyday human food, exhibits significant potential for damaging the hypothalamic regulation of appetite, and thereby determines the propensity of world-wide obesity. We suggest to reconsider the recommended daily allowances of amino acids and nutritional protein, and to abstain from the popular protein-rich diets, and particularly from adding the flavouring agents MSG.[10]

Closer to home, the INTERMAP Co-operative Research Group conducted a study of 752 healthy Chinese (48.7 per cent of whom were women) between 40 and 59 years of age, randomly sampled from three rural villages in north and south China, and determined that MSG intake was positively related to BMI.[11]

In a country where MSG consumption levels are already high, the consequences of this kind of research result could be very significant. Clearly, more investigation needs to take place in China, but it would seem that, although cutting MSG consumption would not be a cure-all for the obesity problem in China, significant reduction of MSG consumption might prove to be a significant factor in aiding overall obesity level reduction. However, this would require further scientific research and for it to gain any credibility in China, would most likely need to be conducted there. Also, when MSG is such a significant export and domestic market commodity, business interests within China will not be keen to see any critical scrutiny of such an easily produced and valuable commodity.

Of course, the easiest way to cut MSG consumption would be for more people to be aware of the problem. This has started in China with a growing number of restaurants following a trend, seen in the Asian catering industry in Europe and North America, of restaurants advertising themselves as 'MSG-Free'. This trend accelerated following the popularizing of the notion of Chinese restaurant syndrome (CRS), also called monosodium glutamate symptom complex (and first suggested in the US in the 1960s by Dr. Ho Man Kwok in the *New England Journal of Medicine*[12]), which remains scientifically unproven but posits that MSG consumption can lead to flushing, sweating and a sensation of pressure in the mouth or face. Dr. Ho Man Kwok wrote:

> I have experienced a strange syndrome whenever I have eaten out in a Chinese restaurant, especially one that served northern Chinese food. The syndrome, which usually begins 15 to 20 minutes after I have eaten the first dish, lasts for about two hours, without hangover effect. The most prominent symptoms are numbness at the back of the neck, gradually radiating to both arms and the back, general weakness and palpitations.

True or not – and Britain's *Observer* newspaper covered the controversy by noting, 'If MSG is so bad for you, why doesn't everyone in Asia have a headache?'[13] – many consumers believe it in what has been termed 'MSG-phobia'. Increasingly so, it seems, in China, too – in Beijing and Shanghai some restaurants have started to do this – though typically at the more expensive end of the market. In general however, scientific opinion remains divided and general public awareness in China remains low.

A problem with MSG is that diners don't actually see it. Similarly with trans fats and interesterified fats. They're increasingly banned in states across the US, with major corporations being forced to remove or replace trans fats included in their products in the developed world (McDonald's fast food, Oreo cookies, etc.), but little or nothing seems to be happening about trans fats in China. The trans fat ban caravan is currently working its way around the US and now across the EU.

Why are trans fats bad? Without going into details of chemistry that we do not really understand, trans fats are built differently from other unsaturated or saturated fats. Basically, their linear structure means that their molecules can lay tightly bundled together, forming a hard fat that doesn't melt at low temperatures, and has a lot longer shelf life. This is great for companies making baked foods or restaurants that need fats to fry food in, that they last as long as possible. All good for those fragile profit margins.

However, their hard structure makes trans fats rather difficult for us to dissolve. This means that when we consume them, these fats tend to stay untouched in the bloodstream longer, and can therefore build up into fatty layers of gloop that can clog up arteries. Think heart attacks! Then, if that wasn't bad enough, they also seem to be a rather effective insulin suppressant, which is not good news if you are planning on becoming diabetic. Trans fats both cause and compound obesity related problems.

The problem for China is that trans fats legislation and control remains negligible. It is therefore almost certain, given the financial pressures put on food manufacturers and caterers in China, that trans fat use in these industries is widespread. Both Starbucks and McDonald's have made public statements that they no longer use trans fats in China, and other chains are working towards phasing out their use, but there continues to be a significant proportion of the food manufacturing industry in China that will not cease to use trans fats until their use is formally legislated against. This seems rather a long way off at present. Indeed, most Asian governments (the exceptions being South Korea and Taiwan) seem to feel that banning trans fats is unnecessary. Even Singapore (a country which has become a byword for banning anything and everything) has so far refused to bring in a ban despite repeated and vocal public calls to do so.

Given China's scarcity of trained dieticians, lack of legislative control, poor regulatory control over the food industry across the country and a general lack of consumer awareness about the issues surrounding trans fats, the health problems caused by them are not likely to diminish very quickly. Meanwhile, the health problems caused by their widespread use in food preparation will continue to accumulate.

What is worse is that in the search for ways to replace trans fats, food scientists have come up with something new called interesterified (pronounced 'interest-terrified') fat. This is an oil that has been totally hydrogenated (i.e., hydrogen has been added), making it fully saturated. Being too hard to use for food, this is then mixed with liquid oils to form a margarine-like product. In early January 2007, a scientific report presented by a joint UK/Malaysian research team suggested that these new interesterified fats are potentially even more harmful than trans fats, being even more effective in suppressing high-density lipoprotein (HDL) levels (in healthy individuals, about 30 per cent of blood cholesterol is carried by HDL), raising blood glucose levels and suppressing insulin levels.

When product labelling, even in highly regulated markets, is not strong enough to require disclosure of all types of fats, and public understanding of the ill effects of these trans and interesterified fats (or even of their existence) is low, it is difficult to see how consumers are supposed to protect themselves and cause market forces to drive these products off the shelves. The Singaporean government seems to feel that market forces will drive trans fats out of the market, but given the mounting scientific evidence that these fats are potentially lethal, it is very odd that a government that likes to legislate out of existence anything that it deems mildly deviant or detrimental should baulk at banning trans fats. And, of course, the market rejecting them depends in large part on the wider public having heard of them, something the food industry is keen not to happen.

As for China, if its government is aware of the trans fat issue, it is keeping very quiet about it, and observers have yet to see any significant research coming out of China about levels of trans fats consumption, or any correlations between their consumption and health detriments. Since most of the edible-oils trade in China remains state-controlled, it seems logical that any ban instituted by the Chinese government would quickly be executed on the ground, and that would be the end of trans fats in China. But, if you consider how the government has struggled to get tobacco advertising banned, when the tobacco market in China is even more of a state-run monopoly, perhaps the politics and vested interests involved are significant hindrances not just towards controlling trans fats, but even producing legislation against them.

Food Poisoning: Bad Practice

It is not just the rising fat and additives content of Chinese consumers' diets that are making headlines in China. Food safety is now one of the key consumer rights issues in China, and is set to become an international trade issue. It is also inadvertently driving sales of pre-packaged and prepared ready meals as consumers come to identify them, rightly or wrongly, with safety.

After a spate of food poisoning that resulted in 138 deaths and more than 7,000 cases of serious illness during 2002, the central government set up a new China Food and Drug Administration (CFDA) to replace the State Drug Administration. The CFDA includes food, herbal products and cosmetics in its remit, as well as coordination of the food-related supervisory functions of China's health, agriculture, quality inspection, and industry and commerce agencies. One of the body's first tasks was to set up an effective monitoring mechanism for the processing and sale of food products, including premarket checks on food.

The CFDA is focusing particular effort on follow-up action, with more nurses to interview patients and their families. Apart from routine surveillance, the department will do research into the activities of mosquitoes and rats to assess their risk to the public. The department also plans to conduct studies on the possible risk caused by dioxins and the safety of genetically modified (GM) foods.

All such moves indicate a rising awareness of the need for tighter controls on food hygiene, something the government thinks chimes well with its broader national agenda of fostering the party's desired Harmonious Society. In the past, mass poisonings, particularly at school and college canteens, have led to large protests. News reports of food crises such as bovine spongiform encephalopathy (BSE) in the UK have become well known amongst a highly news-literate Chinese populace, and so food hygiene has become a major concern of Chinese consumers especially when faced with avian flu, Blue Ear disease and outbreaks of foot and mouth disease in China itself. In addition to this, press reports of tragedies involving fake foods, such as the swollen head syndrome affecting infants that was linked to fake formula milk in 2004, have alarmed consumers and led to central government intervention. That scandal broke in Anhui province in April 2004 when 13 babies from Anhui's Fuyang city died after unknowing parents bought fake milk powder from rural markets. Approximately 200 infants suffered malnourishment, leading to a medical complication called 'big head' or 'swollen head' disease by local residents. Investigators uncovered more than 100 factories making fake formula powder consisting mostly of starch and water, and ultimately prosecuted manufacturers, retailers and complicit government officials.

At the beginning of 2007, US pet food suppliers needed to recall over 100 brands of cat and dog food that had been tainted with melamine and caused a rash of pet deaths. This highlights the issue of food production standards in China, as much of the pet food sold in the US, including that tainted with melamine, comes from China. Sourcing food from China is an increasingly risky business, and the tainting of pet food in the US was no freak accident.

This was proved tragically correct with the Sanlu milk disaster of 2008 when milk and infant formula tainted with melamine from one of China's largest dairies, Sanlu, found its way into the retail channel. By November 2008 China had reported an estimated 300,000 victims and six children dead from kidney stones and other kidney damage, while a further 860 babies were hospitalized. The melamine appeared to have been added to the milk in order to cause it to appear to have a higher protein content. Though Sanlu became the main target, government inspections later revealed that the problem also existed to a lesser degree in products from 21 other Chinese dairy companies, including leading brand names such as Mengniu, Yili and Yashili. The Sanlu scandal was a repeat of other food scares in that it involved corporate malfeasance combined with corrupt local government officials and an ineffective food safety regime. Public faith in Chinese-made food and beverage products understandably sank to an all-time low, one it is still to recover from.

Consequently, Chinese consumers are increasingly afraid of their food. A recent survey by China's Food and Drug Administration found that 65 per cent of Chinese consumers are concerned about their food supply, and it is easy to see why. Within the month of April 2007, there were four separate incidents of mass poisonings at a school, a hospital and two workplace canteens. In Hong Kong, new food safety laws have been introduced following a series of food scares after imported fish and eggs from China turned out to be contaminated with potentially cancer-causing substances. The eggs had been injected with the carcinogenic substance 'malachite green', used to make the yolks of rather inferior eggs look 'more yellow'. In 2005 Yum! Brands' KFC restaurant chain received plenty of bad press after one of its products was found to contain the banned Sudan-1 dye, a carcinogenic food colouring. It was detected after public and official concern led to China launching a national food safety inspection when Sudan-1 was detected in a pepper sauce brand, Meiweiyuan, produced by the Guangzhou-based Heinz-Meiweiyuan Food Co., Ltd. The tainted KFC products had been produced for the company by a supplier. Incidents like the Sudan-1 scare show several things:

(1) That China's food economy is increasingly linked into the global food economy in terms of ingredients used as well as imports and exports of foodstuffs;
(2) That suppliers and supply chains needed close monitoring as well as manufacturing facilities, restaurants and retail outlets;
(3) That the press was now able to report these problems relatively openly and that the public would react to them.

China's president, Hu Jintao, has been prompted by all this to urge his country's farmers and food processors to improve food safety. There is also more legislation on its way; national guidelines for food and drug safety, already State Council-approved, but yet to be 'promulgated', i.e., the rather cumbersome Chinese bureaucracy's way of saying formally made public. However, whatever the central government says and does, it is the local authorities, and often the regulators, too, who show little or no desire to deal with, or even admit to this widespread problem, a problem that spreads ever wider as China's food products enter more of the global market.

Much of the problem is due to ignorance and carelessness, while some is pure malice. Putting carcinogenic colours into egg yolk to make them look more 'yellow' exemplifies ignorance; mistakenly putting rat poison into a hospital breakfast, carelessness and the Sanlu scandal, sheer malice. Because the legislation is not yet in place, nobody is informing, training or policing the food-processing industry. And even once legislation is in place, it is hard to see how this will really make practices change, or how the government will police an industry that spans thousands of companies.

To enforce such legislation would require new 'food inspectors' across most of China who would need training, monitoring and safeguards to prevent collusion with malicious manufacturers and corrupt officials. But, there is no telling how well qualified these food inspectors would be, nor the qualification of the people training them and if not paid well, they will inevitably be liable to pressure from those willing to offer them bribes to look the other way. It is also unclear what kind of executive authority they would have. For instance, it might be that inspectors could fine people for transgression on the spot, which would simply create a new niche sector in the bribery market and has already led to outrage when similar street inspections have been deemed to be unfairly fining people. Many see the myriad layers of inspectors that already roam the streets of China's cities as tantamount to licensed extortion. Also, it will be interesting to see whether the new legislation stipulates when and how frequently food products need to be checked and certified along the supply chain, and indeed, whether those failing to ensure the safety and regulation of their supply chain will be punished or simply allowed to disavow the problem, claiming it was all the suppliers fault, as has often been the case to date.

Companies could spend more time policing their own suppliers. However, consider the case of Mercedes-Benz, a very rich company with a high-profile brand to protect. But even Mercedes-Benz has been taken to court several times in recent years because some of the cars and vans they sold have been faulty (sometimes dangerously so) because their parts suppliers have been selling them substandard parts. After the first time this happened, Mercedes-Benz doubtless tightened the measures they use to scrutinize their suppliers. But, it occasionally still happens. It would be much harder to track supplies of ingredients from thousands of suppliers, especially if the crop supply shifts location by season, as has been seen even in a company as wealthy, well staffed and international as KFC, which was seemingly unable to track its suppliers efficiently. With profit margins in the Chinese food-processing industry being wafer thin already, there will be little economic incentive for many companies to invest in improving practices in order to comply with legislation that is poorly policed.

Going Green...Maybe

In Europe and North America, 'ethical' consumption is all the rage at supermarkets. From Fairtrade to organic food retailers, such as the UK's Planet Organic and America's Whole Foods, sales are up. In the UK alone, Fairtrade says sales are up 62 per cent over the last four years, while it is estimated that the UK's ethical food market will top US$4 billion by decade's end (though by way of contrast, Britain's total grocery market is worth in excess of US$230 billion), according to *Ethical Corporation* magazine. In the West, the drive towards ethical, organic and green foods seems to be driven by rising incomes and the adoption of more ethical lifestyles by the middle classes. The major supermarket chains are getting in on the act in a big way; most have launched organic food lines, tried to reduce unnecessary packaging and offer environmentally friendly shopping bags (in China, too, plastic bags are now not given out freely but charged for to discourage their use, following government legislation). The greenness and 'organic-ness' of some of their products are questionable, but the move is in the right direction.

Driven by fears of tainted foods, an increasing number of Chinese consumers – those that can afford it – are opting to buy organic where possible. Companies have begun to cash in on the trend, with a sharp increase in 'green' products appearing on supermarket shelves.

In the mid-1990s Wuyuan, a tea-growing county of 330,000 people high in the hills of northeastern Jiangxi province, was perfectly suited to benefit from this change in consumer buying habits. The county, at the head of six different rivers and surrounded by forest, banned all factories. In 1997, the county's best-known product, green tea, passed the EU's stringent organic food tests and was certified for sale there. The same year, the county's monopoly green-tea producer, Wuyuan Green Tea, was renamed Wuyuan Organic Foods. Since then, the company has secured EU certification for organic mushrooms, edible fungus and ingredients for Chinese medicine. It is now seeking certification for chickens and sesame paste.

The rise of Wuyuan Organic comes against not just the backdrop of surging Western demand for organic foods, but also of a nascent – but quickly developing – domestic market in China itself, driven by fears of unsafe foods. Sales of organic foods by China's 800 government-certified organic producers reached US$4 billion in 2001, some US$140 million of which comprised exports. Both figures represented 20 per cent growth over the previous year. Specialized supermarkets in China's big cities now stock a wide range of organic produce, according to the China Organic Foods Research Centre (COFRC) and many leading chains such as Shanghai's listed supermarket chain Lianhua now have organic shelves in selected stores. This sort of move by the dominant city-based chain operators into organics and green food follows the trend for specialists to open in the big cities. Lianhua's new green shelves followed hard on the announcement that Anhui-based green retailer Guoqi Green Supermarket was to expand into the Shanghai market, while a number of smaller independent organics specialists are already open for business across the city.

Though gaining awareness, it is currently the case that a small number of Chinese consumers are shopping for green and/or organic foods primarily because of an environmental conscience. The main driver is more likely to be worries over poor hygiene, the rash of recent food contamination scares and tainted produce. Either way, generally good news, and if consumers are increasingly willing to pay a little more for green or organic foods, then hopefully this can both raise incomes somewhat in the countryside, and also improve farming techniques and practices. Nothing has improved rural production techniques and standards more than the little payments or incentives for produce offered by the man from the rigid and centralized Chinese state food ministry being replaced by the Japanese supermarket chain buyers offering high margins for high-quality produce. Still, there's a long way to go. Companies selling refrigeration and farm-to-fork logistics equipment and technology still report that sales are hard to find, and funding for upgrading production in the rural areas is scarce.

With domestic demand for organic produce hopefully set to surge as consumers turn their backs on pollution-laced crops, provinces across the country are scrambling to find remaining patches of pristine countryside to be used for organic farming. While toxins and other pollutants have blighted much of China's most fertile countryside, several regions – notably mountainous areas in central provinces such as Jiangxi – remain comparatively unscathed. But these areas are few and far between.

This brings us to the thorny issue of green and organic standards in China – or rather the confusion over these standards. At the moment, 'green' certificates are being issued by a range of government and quasi-government institutions, including the China Green Food Development Centre (CGFDC) in Beijing and the Organic Tea Research and Development Centre (OTRDC), as well as a growing number of foreign certifiers setting up shop in China, such as ECOCERT International and Bio Control Systems (BCS) from Germany, the Institute for Marketecology of Switzerland, the Soil Association of the UK and the Organic Crop Improvement Association (OCIA) from the US. If the consumer is not to become bewildered by this mass of certification, some order will be required.

Originally established by the Ministry of Agriculture in 1992, the COFRC is now under the China National Seed Group Corporation, a state-owned food company. The Centre has set up its own certification scheme that closely mirrors EU and US schemes to monitor food products. This involves close checks not only of the soil, air and water quality to ensure the absence of toxins which might enter food, but also production methods to ensure they are natural and not harmful to humans or the environment. So far, Japan recognizes the COFRC's standards, with Germany and France expected to follow.

Not a week passes without a startling revelation in the Chinese media about the toxicity of the country's staple foods. A study of fruit and vegetables sold in Beijing in 2002 revealed that 20 per cent contained illegally high pesticide residues and alerted the media to the problem. The COFRC asserts that despite bans, the widespread sale of illegal pesticides continues. Such revelations have consumers (at least those with sufficient income) scurrying for organic labels.

GM Foods – Frankenstein's Kitchen?

In April 2002, experts estimated that the Chinese had consumed more than 20 million tonnes of genetically modified (GM) foods to date. Most GM food products currently sold on the local market are not labelled as such, so people are unaware that the food they are eating is biologically engineered. China itself produces little GM food such as grain or oil plants, though it does grow bioengineered non-food products such as pest-resistant cotton.

The first GM plant was born in the US in 1983. However, mass production and commercialization of bioengineered crops did not begin until 1996, when China started to import such products. China's imports of GM crops, including soybeans, had reached 80,000 tonnes by 1996, 2.8 million tonnes by 1999 and 7.5 million tonnes by 2000. Imports topped 10 million tonnes in 2001, meaning that the country's imports of bioengineered products had increased more than 100 times over this six-year period.

China's three most popular bioengineered crop imports are soybeans, corn and rapeseed respectively. In 2001, the country imported 15 million tonnes of soybeans, roughly equivalent to its own production of naturally grown soybeans. China uses imported soybeans as raw materials for soybean oil, tofu (bean curd) and soya milk. More than 80 per cent of soybean salad oil, a high-grade oil product, is made from bioengineered soybeans.

In March 2002, China implemented new safety certification and labelling rules for GM products. US soybean exporters were worried that the new rules might affect the US$1 billion annual trade in soybeans between the US and China, some 70 per cent of which is genetically engineered. However, negotiations with US trade representatives resulted in a compromise whereby China issued preliminary safety approvals for such products and granted a transition period of nine months until December 2002, when the new rules took effect. Once again, the consumer is all too often and invariably unaware of when their food is GM and when it is not.

And So in Today's HFSS World...

In China's increasingly modern and sophisticated cities we now see the same pressures and attitudes as in other global advanced urban centres; mothers complaining of having no time to shop, prepare food or cook and a feeling that cooking is hard work, while eating out or ordering in is both easier and more convenient. At the same time, the supermarkets and convenience stores have stocked their shelves with an abundance of processed products that don't require forward planning and little if any preparation time.

HFSS (high in fat, salt and sugar) foods then increasingly become the norm for the more rushed breakfast period, as families dash to school and work with packed lunches and ready meal dinners. Again, as elsewhere in the world, the food industry has increasingly developed products (many of which are HFSS) targeting these consumers, and has subsequently marketed them heavily to mothers and children. Outside the home, demand for take-away meals and affordable eating options has increased, home delivery is at the end of the phone line (courtesy of myriad independent restaurants as well as the likes of McDonald's, KFC and Pizza Hut), and again the catering industry has responded with the expansion of fast-food outlets, many of which base their entire menu ranges around HFSS products. All of these factors combine to mean that ultimately, parents, even if they are aware of the problems associated with HFSS foods, have reduced control over what their children eat, what forms the basis of their diet and they find it increasingly impossible to monitor their family's HFSS intake.

On top of this, there is what has been referred to as a 'knock-on effect' whereby consumers eating more fast food, convenience and pre-prepared meals are also less likely to eat fresh fruit and vegetables, while children especially develop a grazing and snacking culture, further increasing their intake of HFSS food products. In Western society, less authoritarian parent/child relationships and children's own growing spending power have meant that children increasingly control their own eating patterns, and this invariably raises their intake of HFSS foods. In China, the situation has been different, as discussed later in this book, with single children being increasingly spoiled and parents and family members finding it hard to deny their offspring what they demand, which is often high in fats, sugar and salt.

Identifying the 'Evil'

In the West there has been a tendency equate the 'obesity epidemic' with a single identifiable 'evil' in the diet – a prime suspect if you like – trans fats and interesterified fats are the latest 'evil' within the scientific community and much of the health community, but there have been others before (remember the media concerns over high-fructose corn syrup?), while the general public may just talk more generally of crisps, sweets, McDonald's, junk food and/or fizzy drinks. But it is the cumulative change across the national diet that has made the difference – food, beverages, oils and ingredients as well as trans fats and interesterified fats. No one addition or single change would have caused this problem. The fact is that, particularly for China's urban middle class, their diet has changed radically and seemingly definitely in terms of both volume and variety.

But where are the Chinese buying all these HFSS foods?

Chapter 5

SHELVES OF FAT – FOOD RETAILING IN CHINA

Where Has All the Fresh Food Gone?

One of the major contributors to China's change in diet has been the development of the country's food retailing industry. Increasingly busy urban Chinese seem to have less and less time to shop, with so many other demands being made on their time. In this sense, urban middle-class Chinese have become as 'cash rich and time poor' as anyone else, meaning that they increasingly buy their food where it is convenient for them to do so.

In the previous chapter, we dissected the statistics on the growth in food sales, and the increased availability of food, much of which has remained relatively very cheap. A crucial shift, noticeable from the statistics for fresh produce, is the growing prevalence of meat in the diet. However, there has also, concurrently, been a massive growth in consumption of processed and packaged (pre-prepared) food, the growth of which has been significantly faster than that of fresh food consumption. Partly this is attributable to the development of new food manufacturing sectors, in response to rising incomes and more discretionary purchasing, which of course started from a very low base. Also, as we touched upon in the last chapter, there is the increase in the promotion of these new manufactured food products. Large food retailers in China have given over increasing floor space to ready meals. Indeed, when the British retail giant Tesco entered China they announced as a key plank of their entry strategy that they would launch up to 500 own-label 'value' products in China, many of these being the ready meals the chain is so well known for in the UK. However, perhaps even more significant to the change in how urban Chinese consume food is the way that they buy food now, compared to the recent past.

Twenty years ago, people in China's major cities would cycle to wet markets most days to buy the fresh fruit, vegetables, meat, fish and poultry to cook for their main evening meal. This would be supplemented by a weekly visit to stores to buy tinned and dried foods. But, in the last 20 years, these wet markets have gradually disappeared from the streets of China's city centres and from many of their suburbs, pushed out by a combination of spiralling downtown land prices, massive urban redevelopment and hygiene concerns.

Now, a weekly drive (or taxi ride) to the local hypermarket is more the norm in China's cities, combined with repeated visits to smaller supermarkets or convenience stores to top up their weekly shop. Consider that in China's eight largest cities, between 1996 and 2005, wet market traffic declined by between 50 per cent and 54 per cent, while hypermarket and supermarket traffic went up by as much, if not more. The wet markets are increasingly gone and in their place stand convenience stores (c-stores), supermarkets and hypermarkets. For a growing number of urban Chinese consumers the nearest and most convenient source of fresh food is now a supermarket rather than a wet market. Interestingly, after 2005, government statistical publications stopped detailing the development, or decline, of China's wet markets, such is their decline in the grand scheme of things in the new China.

Meanwhile, the newly developed inner-city areas have created space for increasing numbers of hypermarkets, supermarkets and c-stores. For example, in Shanghai, the number of convenience stores grew by nearly 250 per cent between 2000 and 2005, including the large chains operated by Japan's Lawson as well as local competitors, while in Beijing, Guangzhou and, more recently Shanghai, the 7-Eleven chain competes with local c-stores. These new retail formats, being driven by the need to generate profit from low margins by selling more lucrative products, sell proportionally small amounts of fresh produce, compared to packaged, processed foods. C-stores sell little, if any, fresh produce at all.

People can and will only buy food that is readily available, and with fresh produce becoming much less so, consumption of processed packaged foods has risen dramatically (see Table 14 below). Total volume sales of the processed foods and beverages with high quantities of HFSS (and MSG) have generally grown at twice the rate of fresh fruit and vegetables, meaning that consumer intake of these foods are twice as significant in the diet than fruit and vegetables, as was the case at the turn of the century. And this only accounts for retail sales, and does not include intake from food bought at catering outlets.

Now consider the growth in per capita spending on these products. What must be considered when looking at these figures is that these are per capita statistics for the whole country. Much of the sales of products such as chilled ready meals and savoury snacks are made pretty much entirely in urban areas, and many older Chinese consumers have not developed a taste for some of these products, so basing per capita consumption on the total population does not give a true indication of the per capita intake for people who do eat these foods, and it is clear that those who do eat them, primarily the new urban middle classes, eat much more than is shown here. A rough but perhaps more helpful calculation would be to take China's urban population and factor out

Table 15: **Per Capita Volume and Growth of Retail Sales of Selected Snack Food Products in China, 2003–2009**

	2003	2009	Volume Growth
	KG/Capita	KG/Capita	2003–2009
Ice cream	0.59	1.27	115.64
Cakes	0.02	0.05	108.88
Sweet biscuits	0.07	0.15	108.95
Chocolate	0.04	0.09	117.70
Candy	0.05	0.10	93.55
Chilled ready meals	0.09	0.20	114.96
Savoury snacks	0.15	0.30	97.99
Sodas	4.28	7.20	68.18
Alcoholic drinks	7.61	17.87	134.90
And, by way of contrast:			
Fresh fruit	5.85	12.48	113.16
Fresh vegetables	50.01	80.64	61.26

Source: Access Asia.

the largely subsistence-surviving rural population, or just take China's 150–300 million middle-class consumers and see their per capita consumption.

What is most significant about these figures is not the actual per capita volumes, but the rate of growth in per capita consumption. Again, remember that these are only retail sales figures, and the alcoholic drinks data does not include consumption at hotels, restaurants or catering (HoReCa) establishments, the addition of which would greatly increase these volumes. While average purchased volumes of vegetables grew by about 61 per cent, all of the processed foods, high in sugar, as well as fat and salt (in many cases) grew by at least twice that rate.

The relative decline in consumption of vegetables (or China's increasing waistlines) is not necessarily the direct fault of retail industry development. Nor can it be blamed directly on the loss of inner-city wet markets. These factors certainly have contributed to making it more difficult to buy fresh fruit and vegetables, but other influences are more significant.

Busier Lifestyles – Changing the Way People Act

With the massive changes that have occurred in urban Chinese society in the last three decades, it is hardly surprising that Chinese consumers' lifestyles have changed considerably. Many of China's cities have been practically rebuilt and some, the most famous example being the aforementioned Shenzhen, have been built virtually from scratch. People no longer live in the neighbourhoods they were brought up in or even the same city or province. Mobility of labour, whether the peasants leaving their inland farms for the factories of China's eastern and southern coast or the fresh Hubei province graduates heading for desk jobs in Shanghai, is increasingly common. Whole industries have been replaced with new ones, so employment has changed radically, both the types of jobs and the conditions of employment.

The prospect of home ownership has also appeared. This not only means that more people are saving to buy a home and looking at locations to live in, but also that they are working harder to achieve home ownership, and once in their home, have to continue working hard to keep up with the mortgage payments and maintain their generally high savings rate – all at a time of rising living costs virtually across the board from subway fares to medical fees. No wonder people have little time to spend on food shopping and cooking – even in their brand new kitchens. Indeed, increasingly, Chinese people are simply working more to buy a kitchen, but cooking less in it.

Products once common have vanished, to be replaced by totally new ones. Cars and motorbikes have replaced bicycles. Bicycles have become not just redundant (replaced by e-bikes and scooters) or unfashionable, but on today's busy roads in Chinese cities, downright dangerous (and in some cities actively discouraged). Similarly, not only are fresh vegetables not readily available in many convenience stores, but even those that are available are often not in great condition, and have probably been farmed using pesticides, chemical fertilizers and other 'ingredients' that consumers are increasingly becoming alarmed about – for good reason as we've already seen.

All this change, within a generation, has created a huge social shift, and people have had to adapt fast. Open to new ideas and ways of living, as well as aspiring to new, previously unattainable lifestyles, Chinese consumers have adapted quickly to accept new food products and ways of eating. Working long hours in new office jobs, people increasingly rely on convenience foods from convenience stores located (conveniently) on their commuting routes. Since 2004 the Beijing Municipal Government (worried about hygiene and the fact that the city didn't look 'modern' enough) has been phasing out street food stalls to replace them with c-stores – Beijing's stated aim in 2004 alone was to see 500 new chain supermarkets and c-stores open in the capital. They achieved this and the number is still rising. It is also more common for people to order in a delivery of fast food from an outlet close to their office, rather than go out to eat, or to prepare their own lunch at the start of the day. Eating out in the evening, sampling the richer dishes available cheaply at the many restaurants, is often more convenient than going home to cook a meal. Eating out is also the Chinese equivalent of going to a pub or bar in other cultures; it is where people socialize, and food is the integral backdrop to most social encounters in China. Who pays for the meal in a restaurant in China is as eagerly contested with much mock restraining and reaching for wallets as buying the next round is in an English pub.

Retailers (and the catering trade) are not so much shaping this change, as responding to the demand created by it. That demand is for convenience, and for those few additional moments that people don't have to work, study or commute, it is a demand for the time to socialize, usually around food. Likewise, if there are pre-made baby foods in jars, readily available from nearby stores, which save time feeding the children, then great. This makes life easier, and people thank the retailers and manufacturers for this in rapidly growing sales. Until very recently, few people in China have really had much spare time to sit back and consider questions about the nutritional values of such products, what the additives used in foods are, the effects on their health or the effects on their environment in terms of packaging waste, manufacturing energy consumption or the carbon footprint of the chill chain. That may change now that the five-day workweek is almost universal in white-collar jobs, and after a period of acquisition and consumerism, perhaps the new middle class can relax a bit and consider how it utilizes its leisure time, but at the moment the larger trend remains aspiration. And so China has gone to the shops.

Shopping: China's National Sport

When studying Chinese back in the 1980s, one of the facts and figures that the then government liked to get included into the prescribed language courses, was that *taijiquan* (tai chi) was the national physical pastime, and thanks to this being China with over a billion people, was perhaps the most popular 'sport' in the world. Now, by far the most popular participation 'sport' in China is shopping. Shopping and consumption includes everything the urban Chinese could want. The excitement of being on the cusp of obtaining the marvellously new, the social whirl of people met and conversations held, the chance to sample foods never tried before, or even the comfort of foods well-known, the colours, the smells, the air conditioning, the buzz of the city.... Of course, China's High Streets are slowly homogenizing with the same brands and logos and looking increasingly alike – what the Parisians, proud of their independent *boulangeries* (bakery shops) and *charcuteries* (delicatessens), dismissively (but correctly) refer to as 'Londonization'. In China it's less of a problem, as rather than seeing this process as eroding national traditions and culture, it's all viewed as 'international', 'cosmopolitan' and the most beloved word of party officials, 'modern' – adjectives the Chinese government loves to see attached to its cities.

Shopping has always been an important facet in Chinese society, ever since market towns sprang up to sell the produce of their surrounding rural fields and orchards. The markets were where local grassroots politics was shaped, where businesses were built and fortunes made. They were the meeting places for all of Chinese society, where news and gossip – as well as Imperial edicts – got their airing in a time before mass media; multiplexes have replaced street opera now. During Imperial times, the merchant classes were ranked even below labourers, but now the shopkeeper (or more probably the retail developer) is the king of a growing commercial empire in the huge megacities of China, lodged in marble-clad palaces of consumption.

What has also been remarkable has been the sharp rise of organized retailing in China, which has meant a squeezed position for the mom n' pop stores and independent fresh-food stores and wet markets. Other developing retail environments have typically not seen this sort of rapid organization by chain retailers. In India, for instance, where legislation has limited local chains from growing, and effectively kept out foreign chains, organized retail had only a 3.2 per cent share of total retail sales in 2005.

Sales are shifting to the organized sector; a 2005 survey of mom n' pop stores in China, conducted by the investment bank CLSA Emerging Markets, found that 76 per cent of their sample in Beijing, Guangzhou, Hangzhou, Shanghai and Wuhan had seen a drop in sales over five years, an average of 12 per cent – while their net profits decline was steeper at 33 per cent, indicating margin squeeze as the mom n' pop stores sought to compete with the new competition of c-stores and supermarkets.[1] Interestingly, the steepest declines

Table 16: **The Growth of Organized Retailing in China, 2000–2015**

US$ Billions					
Year	2000	2005	2010	2015	2000–2015 CAGR*
Total retail sales	205.38	437.21	1,181.63	2,081.61	16.70
– Organised retail sales	29.28	106.19	312.12	595.81	22.25
– Organised retail share (%)	14.26	24.29	26.41	28.62	+14.36 % points

Source: Access Asia from various sources.
*CAGR = Compound Annual Growth Rate.

came in those cities in the survey (Wuhan and Hangzhou) where organized retailing was most recent and consequently less developed and also where consumers were less wealthy. How can a mom n' pop store compete when, at best, they typically stock just 200 to 300 different products (stockkeeping units, or SKUs in retail trade parlance), less than a typical 1920s-era American corner grocery and incomparable to a modern hypermarket with perhaps in excess of 30,000 SKUs? This situation has exacerbated since 2005.

Individuals, couples and whole families will spend their weekends cruising the malls and major shopping streets of the main cities in China. Many have been spectacularly successful, others have failed to draw the crowds for various reasons; either way, over 400 giant shopping centres had been opened throughout the country by 2005, with developers showing no signs of slowing down. There, shoppers can soak up the images of what they aspire to have, advertised by celebrities who already have it all. Supermarkets can help create a middle class – low-priced items freeing up money for families to spend on cars, homes, education and other amenities of life and generally stimulating expenditure in the economy (a theory the Chinese government most definitely subscribes to in its ongoing desire to drive consumption rates upwards). Shopping areas have become the theme parks of China, while the real theme parks have largely gone bankrupt, unable to compete in providing a good day out. It is commonplace to have street promotions that resemble pop concerts or fashion shows on during key shopping days, making the shopping experience more like going to a funfair than going out to buy your weekly groceries. 'Shopping festivals' are now all the rage among local business promotion associations, even though nothing new or special is on offer. The message is clear – get out there and shop – it's almost elevated to a patriotic duty by some party officials.

For much of the working week, people are busy making the money they need to feed their consumer lifestyles, getting by with only buying the bare essentials in expectation of releasing their pent-up spending power at the weekend. This shift in emphasis has led to the continued demise of the fresh produce wet markets in inner cities. The emphasis has changed to the weekly one-stop-shop. A symptom of this is that having to buy everything all at once, rather than gradually, over the week (as used to be the case), means that a logistical problem has created itself for these shoppers. How do you get all this stuff home?

For most, the taxi is the solution. However, for those with the cash to afford a car, private transport is now available to more and more people. Retailers have developed outlets catering to the rising number of families with a private car, and are turning destination shopping into a family outing experience, centred on the car. In the West, we are all familiar with this effect, and how it has come to change the High Street or Main Street of the average European or American city or town. This effect is now beginning to take hold in China, too.

As more Chinese shoppers use cars to shop, so they begin to see the potential to use the car to solve other logistical issues: getting the kids to school, taking the kids to cram school, taking the kids to McDonald's for their school friend's birthday party (or through the new McDonald's Drive-Thrus for instant fat and starch without even opening the car door) – and so it goes. Soon, kids get used to sitting down all the time, and balk at the idea of actually walking anywhere. Again, remember that these social changes have all happened *within one generation*. Today's Chinese parents haven't been able to see this situation coming, as their counterparts in the West have. The same changes in the US began at the end of the Second World War – over 60 years ago. In China, similar amounts of change have taken less than half that time. Therefore, everything is new. In fact, the only thing that is not new is constant change. It is therefore no real surprise that Chinese consumers do not see the resulting effects of such rapid lifestyle shifts until they have become acute.

The changes that have come to China's cities have been dramatic and likewise, the retail landscape has changed beyond recognition in the country's cities over the past few decades. New suburbs and housing complexes have arrived with new retail areas, to serve the shopping requirements of the increasingly concentrated urban population. Shanghai alone has planned and is well on the way to completing a projected ten satellite cities (really large suburbs) each with a population of approximately one million people. People, by the hundreds of thousands, are either being relocated to these suburban satellite cities or opting to live there, exercising what the Scottish economist Adam Smith identified in the eighteenth century, in his *Wealth of Nations*, as the trade-off between time, convenience and money – live in town and pay more rent, but have more time (as you are closer to shops) or choose to live in the suburbs and pay less but, 'pay the difference out of this convenience'.

In Shanghai, between 2006 and 2009 the number of people per square kilometre living in the city rose by 3.3 per cent, reaching 2,375 people per square kilometre (Km^2). Such concentrations of population produced an environment that could sustain larger retail complexes, including ever-larger malls, hypermarkets and big-box home improvement and furniture retail outlets on the fringes. Many of these new developments have been created through foreign investment in new retailing joint ventures and more recently, (as the retailing laws have allowed) as Wholly Owned Foreign Enterprises (WOFEs) lured by the persuasive (yet misleading) call of statistics quoting over a billion potential shoppers. Chinese retailers have learnt, copied and adapted (occasionally improving upon) the formats the foreigners have introduced.

The malls and hypermarkets also needed to keep people interested in shopping, and used the fast-food outlets to supply quick, cheap food to keep the masses marching down the shopping aisles and into the food courts. Hungry for outlet space, the fast-food chains have been quick to fill any vacancy. There's been a fast-food land grab and the prime-location malls and hypermarkets are where they find the greatest levels of potential consumer footfall.

Remember, Chinese cities have changed from the austere days of post-Cultural Revolution survival to the glittering consumer cities they are now, within just one generation. This new generation now knows nothing other than what exists today, with scary winter tales of yesteryear hardship having become the folklore of the elderly. Young Chinese now understand the concept of 'hanging out at the mall': a concept that would obviously have been alien to their grandparents' generation. Their entire habitat is decorated with branded signs and consumer enticements. Little wonder, then, that their behaviour and perceptions of lifestyle are utterly different from the previous generation. This sharp contrast with the past makes it even harder for their parents' and grandparents' generations to relate to these youngsters, or to advise them about it. Indeed, the older generations are even more bamboozled by the rate of change seen in their cities than their offspring.

So from every angle, Chinese consumers' shopping habits are being manipulated by the wider forces of social change. But in the end, the Chinese love to shop, so what do they care?

Supermarket Sweep

Just over 20 years ago, in 1988, you could count the number of supermarkets in China on your own fingers, and even those were only supermarkets by dint of some very generous elasticity in the definition of what a 'supermarket' is. Ten years later there were already 14,000 or so supermarket outlets across China. However, most of these were really only individual grocery stores that were over a rather vague definitional threshold, and were not really proper supermarkets. The appearance of proper supermarket chains is more recent. Of those counted as supermarkets in 1998, probably only half were what would today count as coming under the definition of 'supermarket'.

By 2000, supermarket outlets, which are part of chain groups, and where the individual store size is over 1,000 m², reached a total of over 4,139, a total which grew to about 28,800 by the end of 2008. With the exception of Tibet, there are supermarket chains now established across all of China's provinces.

The sector now generates about RMB710 billion (US$104 billion) in annual sales; that's 12.2 per cent of total retail sales, or 34 per cent of total retail food sales. The rapid growth of the supermarket sector is making the leading supermarket retailers into some of the biggest retail groups in China.

Not only are there new homegrown Chinese supermarket giants emerging, but international colossus such as Walmart, Tesco and Carrefour are there, too. They have, for the most part, entered the Chinese market only in the past decade or so. French company Carrefour was the first to really commit to the China market, entering through some nifty footwork around foreign retail restrictions outside of the key cities open to development at the time, and paying requisite fines in order to keep politicians out of their hair, Carrefour has taken a strong lead among foreign grocery retailers in China. It was the first truly national grocery chain across China, opening up in such far-flung places as Urumqi in the far west of China. Carrefour also set a quick pace in the race to cover as much of the growing domestic consumer market in China as quickly as possible. Others entered the market later, most notably Walmart, which began catching up with Carrefour by

Table 17: **China's Leading Supermarket Retailers, 2009**

Rank	Company	2009 Turnover	2009 Stores
1	Lianhua Supermarket	67,170	5,599
2	RT-Mart	40,432	121
3	Carrefour	36,600	156
4	CR Vanguard	34,764	1,074
5	Walmart	34,000	175
6	Suguo Supermarket	33,236	1,852
7	Nong Gong Shang Supermarket	26,738	3,331
8	Wumart Holdings	26,100	537
9	A-Best Supermarket	17,236	109
10	Trust-Mart	16,500	104
11	Wenfeng Dashijie	15,665	978
12	Tesco	13,300	79
13	Lotus Supercentre	13,000	77
14	Metro Jinjiang	12,023	42
15	Wuhan Zhongbai Chain Warehouse	10,506	139
16	Yonghui Supermarkets	10,218	268
17	Shandong Jiajiayue	10,120	489
18	Beijing Jingkelong	10,064	247
19	Renrenle Chain Commerce	10,038	90
20	Xinxing Group	9,878	532

Source: China Chain Store & Franchise Association (CCFA), NBS, Access Asia.

buying up existing local competitor chains in order to gain a sniff of the leadership position. More recently, the big newcomer expanding fast is Britain's Tesco.

The frantic pace of the race for a presence across China is with good reason. China is only now seeing the development of a real domestic consumer economy worth tapping into. Prior to that, it was important really only as an export manufacturing base, as local consumers just didn't earn enough to make them that interesting, unless they were exceptionally well off, so low-cost, fast-moving consumer goods (FMCG) retailers just weren't going to make much money out of selling day-to-day stuff to Chinese consumers. But the export economy has driven up the value of the wider economy, and with it the average income of Chinese consumers, permitting ever more of them to buy life's little luxuries while they do their grocery shopping. And, as we've seen, it's the little luxuries that make the retailers money, not the bags of potatoes and fresh fish.

Supermarket retailing in China is, like everywhere else, now all about margins. Expensive boxes of chocolates, elaborate chilled ready meals, rich, tangy sauces – these are the products that have higher margins. These are the branded products, the ones that have an image attached to them, a lifestyle aspiration, something you can use to appeal to the hopes, fears and vanities of your target consumers. The more of these expensive things you can sell, the more likely you are to make a profit in China. The problem is still that profit margins in supermarket retailing in China are quite small. Typically about 3 percent, but with rising rental, heating, lighting and staff costs, there's a lot of squeeze. The solution to this problem is to (a) sell more of the expensive stuff (which is often high-fat, high-sugar, high-everything else) and (b) to just sell more – period.

To sell more in volume, you need more floor space, and more shelves selling to more people. This means getting as many stores located in as many up-and-coming, tier-two and -three cities across China as you can, as quickly as you can. You also need to develop an efficient supply chain in order to get products as cheaply and efficiently as you can into your stores, so that you can keep more of the eventual retail price. It comes down to economies of scale. However, then you have the annoyance of competitors, all trying to do the same. The race has therefore been to get to the regional markets, as they open up to real levels of consumerism, faster than the competitors. The aim is to establish market share ahead of anyone else. Once you have that share, your ability to develop volume sales and economies of scale in the longer term are much improved, even if that means taking a bit of a hit in the short to medium terms.

So, all of these grocery retailers, who, combined, are beginning to hold a tight grip on an increasing share of the total retail market – and certainly the

Table 18: Comparison of China's 10 Leading Foreign-Invested Grocery Chains, 2004–2009

China Turnover (RMB mn)	2004	2005	2006	2007	2008	2009	% Rise
Carrefour China	16,239	17,436	24,800	29,600	33,819	36,600	125.4
RT-Mart	11,630	15,700	19,587	25,675	33,567	40,432	247.6
Walmart	7,635	9,934	15,032	21,315	27,822	34,000	345.3
Trust-Mart	12,000	13,200	14,000	14,000	16,400	16,500	37.5
Tesco	7,010	7,920	9,300	12,500	13,500	13,300	89.7
Lotus	7,394	10,060	13,500	11,797	13,000	13,000	75.8
Metro Jinjiang	6,364	7,546	9,367	11,079	12,646	12,023	88.9
Auchan	3,521	5,000*	6,200	5,731	8,152	9,860	180.0
PARKnSHOP	3,243	3,795	4,708	5,078	3,960	3,582	10.5
E-Mart	–	–	–	–	3,200	3,500	–
China outlets (no.)							
Carrefour China	62	78	95	112	134	156	151.6
RT-Mart	47	60	68	85	101	121	157.4
Walmart	43	56	71	102	123	175	307.0
Trust-Mart	88	96	101	101	104	104	18.2
Tesco	31	39	47	55	61	79	154.8

Lotus	41	61	75	70	76	77	87.8
Metro Jinjiang	23	27	33	37	38	42	82.6
Auchan	11	13	16	20	31	35	218.2
PARKnSHOP	31	37	44	45	43	39	25.8
E-Mart	–	–	–	–	18	20	–
China average turnover per outlet (RMB mn)							
Carrefour China	261.92	223.54	261.05	264.29	252.38	234.62	–10.4
RT-Mart	247.45	261.67	288.04	302.06	332.35	334.15	35.0
Walmart	177.56	177.39	211.72	208.97	226.2	194.29	9.4
Trust-Mart	136.36	137.5	138.61	138.61	157.69	158.65	16.3
Tesco	226.13	203.08	197.87	227.27	221.31	168.35	–25.5
Lotus	180.34	164.92	180	168.53	171.05	168.83	–6.4
Metro Jinjiang	276.7	279.48	283.85	299.43	332.79	286.26	3.5
Auchan	320.09	384.62	387.5	286.55	262.97	281.71	–12.0
PARKnSHOP	104.61	102.57	107	112.84	92.09	91.85	–12.2
E-Mart	–	–	–	–	177.78	175.00	–

Source: China Chain Store & Franchise Association (CCFA), NBS, Access Asia.

food market – are scrambling madly to beat each other to the market. The bigger companies are able to take more of a hit on profits for a longer period. Sheer size does matter. But, eventually, even the likes of Carrefour and Walmart will need to make a decent profit. These companies have shareholders, and what shareholders want is dividends. Their shareholders want payback from the money taken from the company and invested into China. If China doesn't begin to pay, then it begins to be just an ongoing drain on potential dividend earnings for shareholders, and their patience is not eternal. In October 2009 there was a story in the news of how some Carrefour investors were suggesting the company pull out of its non-European business in order to improve their earnings. Obviously, the executives in charge will have to placate such short-termism on the part of its investors, but it is doubtful that it will pull out of such a rapidly growing and potentially lucrative future market as China.

The pressure is therefore on the retailers to turn a profit as quickly as they can in China. But, with margins so slight, how can they do this? After all, there is only so much efficiency you can achieve, even if you are as skilled a stuff-shunter as Walmart. This brings us neatly back to food. Food will typically make up about 90 per cent of supermarket shelf space in China, the rest being toothpaste, toilet roll, nappies, underwear, etc. Fresh produce, as we have already stated, makes next to no profit – it's a loss leader. The imperative is therefore to sell more manufactured food. The stuff that is minced, boiled, pasteurized, pulverized and then injected full of sugar, salt, acidity regulators, colourings, flavourings and preservatives that have become the stuff of daily existence in the 'developed' world.

The problem is convincing consumers that they really need this stuff, rather than the cheap fresh produce they have quite happily been buying for generations. This is where the marketing deals with food manufacturers come in. Special promotions are a big thing in Asian supermarkets, and China is no exception to this. You can hardly move round many Chinese supermarkets without uniformed marketing girls, wearing heavy makeup to mask their acne under the unflattering glare of fluorescent supermarket lighting, trying to get shoppers to sample the latest Nescafé coffee drink, some branded, processed, herb-flavoured cheese, or any number of day-glow gloopy sauces or salad 'dressings' and the like.

The major food groups (the corporations, not the nutritional elements) are all there, glad to push at a new group of recently moneyed consumers who haven't yet developed the cynicism that such marketing usually founders upon.

Selling-Up the Farm

Meanwhile, down on the farm, three pieces of government policy have had a hugely significant effect in altering rural lifestyles. Eager to promote the rural economy of China in order to close the income disparity between urban Eastern China and the rural hinterland, the Communist Party has pulled several command levers within the domestic economy to get more rural people earning, spending more money and consuming more.

One of the most important levers has been a scheme to encourage chain store retailers to enter the rural market, converting rural village stores into bannered franchises of the leading urban chain stores in each region. The chain operators help local store managers to improve management, inventory control, marketing and the use of IT and, in return, they get quick access to rural consumers. With significantly lower rates of income, the rural retail market is very much a volume game, with economies of scale very important to making the venture viable. The more stores shifting more goods, the better. Distribution efficiency also becomes imperative, and many chains not only supply goods to rural stores, but also use those stores as depots to collect fresh agricultural produce to be transported back to the main depots, so that that produce can then be distributed onwards to chain-owned urban outlets, making the truck's return journey pay for itself with a backload.

This scheme is important because without it, no matter how much more rural consumers might be earning, if there are no stores to spend their money in, that cash will just end up in savings. For mass-market goods manufacturers, the rural market has now become that much more viable, and the expansion of organized retail into rural areas is helping many domestic and foreign manufacturing companies keep the growth chart pointing upwards. Rural markets can now become consumer markets, with goods to consume, bought from organized retail outlets, whereas before, there was only subsistence purchasing of absolute necessities from agricultural depots and basic necessity supply stores.

It's not just that the infrastructure has changed, but the rural mindset has, too. Rural dwellers can now buy things that they otherwise would not have. They are now comparing products based on price and brand, based upon what they have read about products in adverts. All of a sudden, rural Chinese are worth advertising to. Now, branded display units are appearing in many rural stores. Even chilled and frozen food cabinets are appearing in some rural stores, thanks to the fact that rural households are now buying appliances.

Hence, important policy number two, the rural appliance rebate scheme. The rural appliance rebate scheme, which gives rural residents a 13 per cent rebate on selected white goods and consumer electronics, has provided a sense of hope to manufacturers as they face falling demand due to the global financial crisis, which has severely impacted their export market and left them with high inventory levels. To an extent, the programme has released the pent up demand for affordable household appliances and consumer electronics in the rural market, where the ownership of key white goods and consumer electronics remains relatively low, especially when it comes to refrigerators, air conditioners and washing machines. The ownership of refrigerators was only 26.1 per 100 rural households in 2007, compared to 95 in urban households, which can be partly explained by the fact that farming communities traditionally have less need to store their foods, as they can buy fresh produce from the markets or get it from their own farms. Owning a refrigerator can be costly, too, as it increases electricity bills.

The programme was initially launched in the provinces of Henan, Shandong (including Qingdao city) and Sichuan, in December 2007. Following the success of the initial scheme, the programme was later expanded to nine more provinces in late 2008, followed by a nationwide rollout in early 2009. The number of items eligible for the rebate has increased from three to ten, which earlier comprised refrigerators (including freezers), mobile phones and colour TVs. The additional seven items were washing machines, air conditioners, computers, water heaters (electric, gas and solar), microwave ovens, induction cookers and motorcycles.

From a food-lifestyle point of view, clearly the type of foods that rural Chinese consumers can now buy has altered because they now have the equipment to store and cook foods that they did not have before, and the ownership of this equipment means they can buy new types of food products, such as chilled and frozen foods, and microwaveable TV dinners. Clearly, having to pay for the electricity to run these appliances also means that rural households need to have consistent cash incomes throughout the year, and that means more rural workers are tied to regular salaried jobs, as well as tending their own seasonal crops and herds. But for many rural households, where most able-bodied family members have gone to the cities to find work, keeping the farm going is becoming more a chore than a benefit.

That is why important policy number three is the change in agricultural land lease regulations. Without getting technical, previously, rural farmers could not sell-on the lease for the land distributed to them by the government in order to grow their own crops. So, even if they had no use for the land, they could not legally rent it out to someone else to use. That has all changed, and they can now legitimately sell the lease, usually to large farming cooperatives, which are now busily buying up leases to adjacent land parcels in order to form large plots of land for intensive, industrialized farms.

This has two hugely significant influences for the future. Firstly, rural households have a new source of income (from their land lease) while they are freed to go off and find better-salaried jobs in towns and cities, or to set up their own manufacturing or service industries. The net result for the future will be more wealth generated in and for the rural communities that until very recently remained largely subsistence consuming communities.

At the same time, large-scale mechanized and organized farming is at last taking over from private dirt farmers in the production of China's food. This will mean better quality control, higher crop yields, higher volume output and a wider variety of crops, including more exotics and cash crops. These organized farm cooperatives are now working very closely with the major supermarket and hypermarket retail chains, as well as the large catering operations, to secure supply deals. Out of this, large-scale agricultural groups will emerge, and China's agriculture will, after centuries of barely any change, become a modernized industrial concern – agribusiness. The change in consumer lifestyles in rural China is likely to be even more dramatic than has already been seen in urban China, and is really only just beginning.

Finally, the last component of ensuring the widespread distribution of food across the country is the distribution and logistics system and this is also undergoing radical change.

Problems of Distribution – Changing the Way Food is Supplied

The physical shape of China provides many challenges to manufacturers in getting their product to the consumer. Not only is China big, but it is mountainous, crossed by numerous large rivers (many prone to flooding) and despite the massive infrastructure projects of the last 20 years, still has poor road infrastructure in many regions. This makes just getting products to shops difficult, never mind in good order and with minimum waste and spoilage. The lack of even a basic chill-chain outside the major cities makes moving fresh produce around difficult, and adds to costs, typically distribution and logistics can account for up to 18–20 per cent of a product's cost in China compared to approximately 10–12 per cent in the EU and as low as 8 per cent in North America.[2]

The cost of distribution eats into the profit margins of manufacturers, who have to add this to the price to retailers, and so the retailers are only interested in products that have a higher profit margin. Fresh fruit and vegetables are simply not profitable (unless exported to Japan or another arable-challenged market). If anything, for supermarkets, they are an unintentional loss leader. They know that people go to supermarkets to buy fruit and vegetables, but that they will only make money from selling other more profitable products. These are the packaged, processed ready meals, ice creams and ready-made sauces, etc. All of these products also have the added advantage of being packaged and preserved, with long shelf lives and low spoilage rates in transit.

Take, for example, a typical c-store in the centre of Shanghai as an illustration of the motive behind stocking particular food products. A sample survey, conducted by one of the official statistical agencies in China, found that the typical 90 m² store in downtown Shanghai had a sales revenue of about RMB26,500 (US$3,817) per month in 2005, of which RMB1,000 (US$144) came not from sales, but from fees paid by food product manufacturers to have their products placed on a prominent shelf (known as 'slotting fees'). However, total expenses for such a store each month was RMB26,350 (US$3,795). This means that a typical c-store in Shanghai makes only RMB150 (US$22) in profit each month, including the fees paid by manufacturers! This makes these stores very vulnerable to any adverse factor in the market, such as bad weather keeping shoppers away, producer product price inflation eating into what margins there are (as we've seen, they are negligible), new competitors in close proximity (an ongoing problem in Shanghai) – the list is endless. Many such outlets are in a precarious position and with retail rental agreements often as short as six months in Shanghai, it is little wonder that the c-store that opened the other week is suddenly empty and closed or seems strangely denuded of stock all of a sudden (they can't afford to buy any more). Chances are it failed to hit even the US$22 a month average profit.

The decision for such retailers is therefore clear. In order to survive, store managers must stock the products that have the highest profit margin, with the longest shelf life, the lowest possibility of being damaged in-store and the highest possible income from manufacturer slotting fees. This is a consideration that not only affects c-stores, but all food retailers, including supermarkets and hypermarkets.

Additionally, the inflationary food prices of 2008 didn't help margins. Yet, in many cases, prices should have risen more, but to remain competitive (and after urging from the government in the name of social harmony) many manufacturers were forced to restrain price rises by taking a margin hit. This means that manufacturers are making less profit on their products, so need to sell more volume, also giving them a major incentive to concentrate on products with the attributes described above. Bear in mind that in most FMCG categories there are multiple manufacturers offering a range of brands all with an ever more bewildering range of sub-brands and flavours; this creates overcapacity and brand crunch (as well as rising slotting fees due to the growing number of competitors), engendering intense competition through pricing which mitigates inflationary rises in the price of packaged foods somewhat. This constant new product introduction is confusing for the consumer and also benefits nobody as much as the retailer selling shelf space and earning slotting fees. It also leads to some hasty launches of products that would perhaps best have been culled in the development stage, such as Nestlé's infamous watermelon-flavoured Kit-Kat or Shanghai Guangming (Bright) Dairy's chocolate-flavoured cheese slices, which rather failed to excite the consumer and left many browsing shoppers simply bemused.

And the products with these higher margins are what, exactly? They are certainly not fresh fruit and vegetables, that's for sure. Indeed, they tend to be packaged or frozen foods, processed snacks, confectionery, soft drinks and the like. All having lower manufacturing costs, longer shelf life (thanks to the packaging and preservatives), tend to have more cheap ingredients (such as potato starch, salt, sugar, etc.) and little nutritional value. The commercial imperative to survive in the tough retail market in China is forcing the industry, from manufacturers to wholesalers to retailers, to supply more of these food products.

Can Retailers Change the Chinese Diet for the Better?

Perhaps all is not lost for the Chinese diet, or for a healthier relationship between retailers, caterers and consumers. A healthy cynicism may develop leading people to think more about what they are buying and their diet, and stores and restaurants can respond to this. What is more, many retailers are now beginning to understand that consumers want more from life than a prescription Western diet. In fact, many Chinese consumers are looking back into their own cultural traditions for some kind of sense within the morass of so much change in such little time. Retro-Chinese style is becoming a palpable movement, both in art and the media, but also in product packaging and even in the design of new shopping streets made to look like *Ye Olde Cathay*.

And this is perhaps the key point. Although the rapid change in China's society created the opening for the foreign food manufacturers and retailers to get into the market and start redesigning the lifestyles of Chinese people, that self-same frantic pace of change is now creating another new demand. Many Chinese consumers are no longer aspiring to simply ape their Western counterparts' lifestyles, but are aspiring to achieve a lifestyle that is Chinese, but new. There is an ongoing exploration, among Chinese people at the moment, to identify what it means to be Chinese now. China's role in the world has changed. It is more important, both economically and politically, and the Chinese realize this. All of a sudden, being Chinese is something to be especially proud of, and being Western is just something that Westerners do.

It is not mere luck that the Chinese government speaks about its core 'Harmonious Society' policy gambit. Harmony has been a key theme within

Chinese philosophy since the year dot (which, in China, was a long time ago), and the concept of harmony – including inner-peace, cohabitation with nature, social stability, etc. – has strong cultural resonance with Chinese people. The recent revival of interest in Buddhism and practicing tai chi all are symptoms of this. Harmony is also increasingly being sought in simple daily life, including demanding clean food and products with low environmental impact. Those seeking such foods may be a small minority at the moment, but the trend should grow as incomes allow.

The problem that China still faces, though, is that much of the damage created by the rapid change of the past is already done. The retail structure of China's cities is now set in concrete (and marble), and only more brutal change can alter that. Rather than this, the Chinese retail market is being forced to redecorate its image to suit a more Chinese perspective. Local foods are back on the menu again, even though steak consumption still continues to rise. The variety of food available in China now is vast, reflecting the varied needs and wants of a varied people. Retailers now have to respond to these changes in consumer demand as much as they shape it.

Certainly, the organic food lobby has changed the way retailers source their foods. Furthermore, increased vegetarianism is also being reflected in there being more 'health' foods available on the shelves. And as the awareness of the obesity issue spreads from the newspaper and TV coverage to the evidence staring them in the face, some Chinese consumers and retailers are realizing that there needs to be a change. The problem is, as with most things in China these days, that it is a minority within the wealthy urban elite that shows these progressive traits. The rest of China is still playing catch-up, still aspiring to eat hamburgers, pizzas, fatty steaks, sugary doughnuts and salty fried snacks. Also, even having the best will to attain a healthier lifestyle often does not translate into real action. Ingrained habits are hard to shift, especially if it means going to a gym and working up a sweat. Harmony is fine, but only if it is convenient and quick.

Yet, there is still a role for retailers to play in changing things, and they are becoming open to more positive social responsibility. Many c-stores are located adjacent to schools, specifically in particularly densely concentrated cities such as Shanghai. These stores have, after government intervention, started to display signs about sales of cigarettes to minors, but are still emporiums of high-fat and high-sugar foods.

Also, take as an example the fact that a few supermarkets in a few cities had begun encouraging shoppers to reuse plastic bags. Admittedly, this was because local governments, unhappy with their cities lying under a snowy carpet of 'white waste', were beginning to find ways to curb the consumption of plastic bags. The important thing was that there was a positive response from retailers. This shows that they can be responsive to such social issues as environmental damage and human health, if cajoled and prodded in the right way, at the right time, by the right people. As it turns out, cajole turned into coerce, as the government introduced a complete ban on most plastic shopping bags at the beginning of 2008, and enforced it from June 2008. Despite the predictions of some, the public has by and large accepted and embraced the plastic bag ban.

However, progress is often a case of two steps forward, one step back. A case of the back step is vending machines. Vending machines are increasingly common in China. They first appeared in the country around the busy Sanlitun area in Beijing, but have since been popping up everywhere across the country; Qingdao sea front is lined with vending machines selling biscuits, fizzy drinks and confectionery as are the platforms of Shanghai's subway, to name but two high-traffic locations. The machines sell almost exclusively snacks, fizzy drinks and confectionery.

What is clear is that any attempts to improve the dietary health of Chinese consumers will need the cooperation of the Chinese retail industry. But the retail industry will need an incentive. Retail margins, as demonstrated above, are too narrow for them to make any grand philanthropic gestures devoid of any monetary gain. They will need to see that there are enough customers who are demanding healthier food before they will commit valuable shelf space to such products, even if they do come with a higher price tag, and a higher potential margin. In that sense, Shanghai is not so different from Sheffield or Sacramento.

The retail industry in China is under increasing pressure from new government edicts, regulations and laws, all aimed at improving the way companies – and that includes retailers – conduct their business. Most plastic carrier bags, as of June 2008, were banned, as already mentioned. But on top of this, other new laws on packaging recycling mean that manufacturers and retailers will become responsible for the cost of reclaiming and recycling used packaging. New government agencies will have the right to police and fine food manufacturers using illegal ingredients, or substandard manufacturing processes. Now the incentive to provide better products and services is coming from a combination of consumer demand and government edict. The pressure is certainly mounting.

Chapter 6

FAST FAT – THE IMPACT OF FAST-FOOD IN CHINA

The Fast Food Nation

Hand in hand with the changes that the development of retailing in China has brought upon what and how Chinese people eat has been the change in the catering industry. Most big supermarkets have a fast-food outlet right outside. Even stand-alone supermarkets and hypermarkets have 'lobbies' (basically mini-malls) usually stuffed with eateries of various forms, all designed to provide fast and convenient food to fuel shoppers on their way round the supermarket aisles – shopping malls all have the requisite 'food court'. Food shopping can therefore be a reason to eat out, or an excuse to do so.

The issue of obesity in China is one created by a combination of factors. Changes in retailing are a contributor, but not solely to blame. The rise in the fast-food market is another contributor, but again, not all fast food is bad, and it's not simply a question of the Western chains, but also of Chinese cuisine often being as bad, if not worse, despite the widespread perception of many consumers that it is all intrinsically healthier than Western food. However, the combination of the effects of these two factors has a much greater compound effect than each individually, and adds to a total sum of more food being consumed.

It's not just China's economic growth that's fast, but its food is pretty damn quick too. If you believe a survey by ACNielsen, conducted in late 2004 and published in January 2005, some 97 per cent of Chinese people were already eating out at fast-food restaurants, ranking China in the top five of a total of 28 markets surveyed. The 28 countries were spread across Asia-Pacific, Europe and the United States, and included over 14,100 consumer interviews. The survey found that in China 30 per cent of respondents ate at fast-food restaurants two to three times a month, and 26 per cent once a month or less. Three per cent said they ate fast food more than once a day, and 6 per cent of them ate it every day. Twenty-one per cent of respondents ate fast food once or twice a week and 11 per cent three to six times a week. The survey also found that lunch was the most popular fast food time for 91 per cent of Chinese consumers. Fifty-six per cent of those surveyed also chose to eat take-away breakfast.

So, what would such figures convert to in total population terms, assuming that the survey gives a fairly accurate guide to the proportion of consumers? Well, firstly, as the survey was done mostly online, we have to assume that the figures only really relate to urban consumers – there being few rural fast-food outlets, anyway. Given that by the end of 2007 the urban population of China is estimated to have reached 521.2 million people, then some 156.4 million ate fast food two to three times a month, and another 135.5 million would eat fast food once a month or less. That's 291.9 million people.

However, of these there are some 109.5 million eating fast food one to two times a week, and 57 million eating fast food more than two times a week. You also have the 31.3 million who eat fast food once every day, and 15.6 million who eat fast food more than once every day! That's a market of 208.6 million Chinese people eating fast food at an average of once a week or more.

So, out of the total urban population in China of 508.6 million people, about 292 million are eating fast food once a month. That's 56 per cent of the urban Chinese population, assuming the survey is close to representative of the facts. To check if these assumptions are based on a realistic market size, we can look at the market value figures.

In 2006, based on estimates by Access Asia, the total value of the catering market in China was somewhere in the region of RMB1,035 billion (about US$132 billion). Of this, the value of the fast food market is estimated to represent about 43 per cent of the total value of the catering market, or RMB442 billion (US$65 billion). There were an estimated 33 billion fast food transactions in 2006, with an average value of RMB13.32 (US$1.70) per transaction. This figure for total transactions, based on industry data, makes sense if you add up the likely number of transactions based on the ACNielsen survey. Therefore, the 15.6 million urban Chinese who are eating fast food at least once a day, sometimes more, are probably spending US$620 or more per annum on fast food, out of a total average annual urban wage of US$2,300 (that's 27 per cent!).

What is more significant is the growth in both the value and volume of fast-food sales. Between 1997 and 2006 the total value of the fast-food market grew by about 900 per cent, with the total number of transactions increasing by 517 per cent, meaning that the average value per transaction had increased by about 62 per cent over that period. So, not only were the Chinese visiting fast food outlets more frequently (average transactions per outlet were up by nearly 120 per cent since 1997), but they were spending more money while they were in such outlets. The number of outlets increased by over 180 per cent over this period, which also means that the fast-food market had penetrated into more regions of China, and the neighbourhoods of more Chinese consumers.

Table 19: **China's Fast Take-Up of Fast Food, 1997–2006**

Fast Food's 10-year China Growth	1997	2006	% Growth
Total annual transactions (million)	5,380	33,187	516.9
Daily transactions (million)	14.74	90.92	516.9
Total market value (US$ million)	5,656	56,518	899.3
Total number of outlets	206,153	582,800	182.7
Average value of transactions (US$)	1.05	1.70	62.0
Average annual transactions per outlet ('000)	26.09	56.94	118.2

Source: Access Asia.

If you consider that the ACNielsen survey was conducted at the end of 2004, and that the total number of annual transactions between then and the end of 2006 grew by 29 per cent, then either the numbers of urban Chinese eating fast food has gone up by 29 per cent over that period, from 291.9 million people to 376.5 million people in 2006 (or from 56 per cent of the urban population of China to 72 per cent), or the existing 56 per cent of urban Chinese who ate fast food at the end of 2004 are now eating 29 per cent more fast food than they did then! Most likely, the number of people eating fast food, and the volume they individually eat each year, have both gone up.

The Chinese (at least urban Chinese) have therefore weaned themselves onto a diet of fast food with amazing speed. As we noted, fast food is not the sole cause, or necessarily even the primary cause, of China's obesity rise, but it is a factor and it is a market that has grown stunningly fast. So why have such convenience foods and eating habits done so well? Perhaps, we first need to look at how China has in some ways always had a tradition of fast food.

Like Most Things, the Chinese Invented Fast Food!

Apart from the kind of cooking done at home to feed the family and the high cuisine practised in the imperial palaces, or the food produced by the restaurants and teahouses, there has always been another facet to Chinese cuisine – the market food stall vendor. The traditional market has been around in China for aeons, time enough for such vendors to work out how to create tasty snacks at low cost (in terms of ingredients and cooking fuel) so they could be cooked very quickly and be charged at a low price to suit the pockets of the other traders at the market. Be they bags of roasted peanuts, steamed buns, stuffed dumplings, kebabs, fried noodles, battered, deep-fried 'whatever', the market food vendors of ancient China knew how to make tasty fast food. These traditions live on in the many 'food streets' and snack stalls around China (despite the government's slow eradication of street food due to hygiene concerns and the overwhelming desire to appear 'modern'), while many traditional fast foods have also appeared reinvented in pre-packaged, frozen and chilled varieties on supermarket shelves.

Part of Chinese food's appeal in the Western market, especially when initially introduced, was its relative simplicity to cook and its speed of production. Part of the simplicity was the fact that the carbohydrate in every meal, as with Indian food, is largely a white blanket background of rice, although Chinese food also has noodles. The rest of the meal is what you think about – the meat, the fish, the vegetables and the sauce.

One of the problems with basing your diet around rice is that although you get a high level of carbohydrates (sugars to give you energy), rice has very little in the way of micronutrients. Also, most of the carbohydrates in rice do not last long and generally run out faster, leaving you hungry again sooner. This leads to more frequent meals and snacking to fill in the gaps in energy between meals. The traditional Chinese diet is designed around light meals and between-meal snacks, rather than the large meals with slow-release carbohydrates (such as starch) in the West. Much of this has been determined by the role of rice in the Chinese diet. In China, rather than ask if someone is well, you ask them, 'have they eaten rice today?'

So, not only do the Chinese tend to eat light meals, with frequent snacking in between, they also tend to get much of their nutrition from the non-staple part of their diets, both at meals and in snacks. Fruit, nuts and seeds have traditionally played a key role in the snacking part of the Chinese diet, and this continues to be the case. Likewise, products such as dried fish and seafood, preserved fruits and pickles, are all snack foods, but with a deliberately nutritious aspect. These snacks are not an indulgence, so to speak, but are rather an essential supplement in the Chinese diet.

This works when you have a traditional eating pattern, linked to a traditional working day (often labour intensive for at least part of the day) and traditional foods, often highly nutritious. Even though much of traditional Chinese food is fried, there is low fat content, as the process of stir-frying relies on small amounts of oil, most of which only penetrates the very surface of the food due to the speed of the cooking. Also, meat content (and therefore saturated fat content) tended to be smaller in more traditional diets, and most of the meat eaten tended to be leaner. The problem with the traditional eating patterns came about when first the main meals changed, then the snacks, but the habit of snacking between meals did not change.

Imagine you begin your day with a deep-fried stick of batter from a street vendor. Sounds horrible, but they are popular as a breakfast food in China and very tasty. What they provide is the carbohydrate overdrive needed to kick-start the body in the morning and keep you going well on the way to lunch, when you normally have some rice and vegetables. But what if you have a hamburger for lunch instead? The rate of daily fat consumption suddenly gets an unexpected midday supplement that the body is not used to, nor needs. Likewise, if you still eat fried peanuts as a snack, this further adds to the additional fat intake.

It is not that fast food is particularly bad *per se*, although it was never the healthiest option, but the key problem, especially in China, is how it fits in with established diet and eating habits. It adds to the fat, without adding much nutrition. People do not easily adapt to replacing something old with something new, and so when fast food arrived in China, it really just added a lot of fat and sugar to a Chinese diet that really didn't need it; it needed more iron, calcium and iodine instead.

So, into China came the Western fast-food concept of measured portions, apportioned processes and foods designed to fit the necessities of the process rather than the nutritional needs of the consumer. It began not very long ago, and WOW, how the market has grown!

The Colonel and the Clown: KFC and McDonald's Compete for China

The year 1987 was significant for many reasons. From the perspective of this book, it was the year that KFC (then still known as Kentucky Fried Chicken) opened its first outlet in China – the first Western fast-food outlet in the PRC. And what a place to open – right on the corner of the iconic Tiananmen Square, almost next door to the Great Hall of the People, and right under the very-preserved nose of Mao Zedong himself. It took archrivals McDonald's until April 1992 (five years later) to open their first outlet, and they've been playing catch-up ever since.

From 1997 to 2007, the number of KFC outlets in China increased nearly ten fold, from 216 to 2,000. KFC is a division of Yum! Brands, who also own Pizza Hut (more on them later), Taco Bell (which entered briefly and then exited the China market) and Long John Silver's. The Greater China division of the company also includes Taiwan and (strangely) Thailand, with most of the outlets located in the PRC. This division produced US$200 million in profits in 2005, up from US$20 million in 1998. This means that the average profit for each outlet in the 'China' division is US$83,000. Based on the figures released by the Chinese government for Yum! Brands outlets in China, which are mostly KFC, total revenues were in the region of US$1,440 million, which would mean profit margins in the region of 14 per cent. This is way ahead of anyone else in the Chinese catering market, let alone the fast-food market.

Compare this with McDonald's. In 2004 McD's had only 600 outlets, compared to KFC's 1,400. McDonald's sales were RMB3.55 billion (US$429 million), compared to RMB11.87 billion (US$1.43 billion) for KFC, while McDonald's average sales per outlet were therefore RMB5.9 million (US$713,000) per outlet, compared to RMB8.48 million (US$1.02 million) per outlet for KFC. By 2005, Yum! had 34,000 (mostly franchised) restaurants around the world, 2,000 more than McDonald's.

However, between these two companies, we have seen China's fast-food industry rise from nothing in 1987 to at least 2,800 outlets (for KFC and McDonald's alone) 20 years later. This means that there have been at least 100 new KFC or McDonald's stores opening every single year in China. The average turnover per store across the two companies is about RMB7.71 million (US$931,000). If the average fast-food transaction is about RMB9.65 (US$1.41), this means that the average number of transactions in each store, each year, is about 800,000, or 2,200 per day, or 91 per hour (if all are 24-hour stores), or one-and-a-half transactions per minute. In other words, the stores are busy.

This represents about 1.6 billion transactions each year for these two companies alone. But even these large numbers are nothing when you consider that there were some 33.2 billion fast-food transactions in 2006. Yes, there are the Pizza Huts and Burger Kings and other Western fast-food brands, but most of the rest of the market is smaller local companies. But both KFC and McDonald's continue to strive for growth across China, seeing the existence of all these other transactions not as a healthy competitive landscape, but as a challenge to their domineering pride. Gradually, city by city and town by town, the Colonel's face and the Golden Arches are appearing right across China. In the case of KFC, this amounted to one new outlet each day in 2005.

What is interesting is that China has forced these global behemoths to adapt to the Chinese market, rather than for Chinese consumers to adapt to their prescriptive menus. For KFC, with its core ingredient being the already Chinese staple meat of chicken, this has been a relatively quick process. KFC had more than just a first-mover advantage on McDonald's, given that beef burger consumption was quite alien to the traditional Chinese diet.

McDonald's – Beefing Up

The fast food chains are major advertisers (as shown below, in the competitive Shanghai market KFC, Pizza Hut and McDonald's are among the five largest advertisers the city), although it is noticeable that the larger regional Chinese/ Asian restaurants chains are also major advertisers at a local level. However, when it comes down to sheer weight and spread of advertising spend within the catering industry, the clear leaders are McDonald's and KFC.

McDonald's is a major TV advertiser. In one of its earlier TV campaigns (2001), the company aired adverts aimed at children, promoting a free bubble-blowing machine and showing children flying over houses (notably new, modern estates and not the old Beijing *hutongs*) and landing at a freestanding drive-thru McDonald's outlet – then a new concept in China. In the same year, the company targeted adults with a campaign that used comedy with an advert promoting the company's free spicy chicken wings. In the advert, a man was shown putting a wedding ring in a box of spicy wings and giving the box to his girlfriend with the intention of proposing. In the event, she turns out only to be interested in knowing where the wings are, and is not interested in the ring.

What McDonald's was trying to do then was to get more Chinese through their doors, as they were losing trade to other fast-food outlets, particularly KFC. McDonald's was trying to appeal to all age groups, but particularly to families. It was also trying to compete with KFC on its home turf – chicken. However, this has now all changed.

After taking over as President of Marketing and Sales of McDonald's China in late 2007, Gary Rosen began experimenting with changing what McDonald's is in China. His new emphasis was a change of image for McDonald's from a family-friendly, magical place to a more alluring place for China's urban adults. It started with the appearance of McCafés in urban centres, with plush sofas and coffee tables – a not altogether successful experiment. The emphasis also shifted in terms of the McDonald's menu in China. Rather than trying to

Table 20: **TV and Print Ad Spend by Brand for Shanghai 2008 (RMB Million)**

Source: China Media Monitor.

pander to local specialities and fight the 'chicken wars' with the likes of KFC, McDonald's, in true reactionary fashion, focused on its core product – beef burgers, as well as trying to exploit the market for cheap coffee and ice cream (notably more successful, though low margin).

A recent key advertising drive was an insert advert in newspapers and magazines. This in itself is nothing special, except that the insert was a large McDonald's napkin, which would fall out onto the lap of the reader when they opened the publication. Inside, there was an advert, which challenged the reader to 'imagine what you could do with this enormous napkin? Think for a moment how you could use it to wipe away sauce from your mouth… so much sauce, it will cover your entire mouth….' The idea was to work on the appetite of hungry commuters, and on their imaginations, making them feel a desire to eat beef. Campaigns targeting young modern mothers have been another approach, with kiddie gyms in outlets; the new urban mum could use McDonald's as a place to take five, rest in hygienic surroundings, while the children ate burgers and played.

In addition to the sensory assault of the napkin insert, McDonald's has been spreading its broader message through the Chinese market by developing a long-term 'beef education' campaign. Using the slogan 'Do you have enough beef?' McDonald's has 'challenged' young Chinese people through various media channels. The company invites customers to register within stores as a 'beef person', join the 'beef club' online, share in the 'beef experiences' of celebrities, and has engaged the opinions of nutritionists willing to stake their name to the nutritious qualities of beef. The aim is to make Chinese consumers believe that beef is good for them.

McDonald's believes that Chinese consumers are ready, willing and able to eat more beef. However, despite the good signs now, there is a potential spanner in the workings of this idea over the longer term. Firstly, there are mounting concerns about obesity levels, child and adult. Many nutritionists and health experts have been quoted in the Chinese press as being concerned about the rapid increase in people's red meat (read beef) intake as consumer incomes have grown, and intimate direct links between the rise in beef eating and the expansion of China's waistlines.

Another potential problem for beef is food prices. Since 2006 food prices have been rising. Basically, food prices are catching up with reality and the rest of the economy. Also, as grain and other crop prices rise, this adds to an increasing cost for meat production. In a country where arable land is severely limited, and where crop imports are a rising part of the economy (raising alarm bells with the Chinese government over food security), the justification of using such limited land resources to raise beef, when so many other food crops could be produced on the same area of land, is creating a market environment where beef prices will increasingly be pushed upwards. Also, much of this beef is raised on soya beans, the bulk of which are imported – the beans go into the cows, the cows go into the burgers – why not just put the beans into the people? Furthermore, bulk import costs have risen fast lately due to there not being enough bulk cargo vessels (everyone's been building container ships instead of bulk ships), and the laws of supply and demand are strict – fewer ships, higher shipping cost. This could make eating beef an increasingly expensive luxury again, as it was in the past – which is not a good situation for a mass-market, fast-food operator whose business relies on beef as its core product.

However, McDonald's has seen sense in regard to competing with KFC in the 'chicken wars'. According to some analysts, KFC's profit margin is almost twice as large as McDonald's, 19 per cent versus 10–11 per cent in 2005, while KFC also has twice the number of outlets that McDonald's has and is growing faster (see Table 22), though both are now engaged in home and office delivery wars. Thus, McDonald's has backed off from its direct fight with KFC, a fight it was obviously going to lose, and has retrenched into its beef heritage. This approach could work in China, so long as prices do not escalate beyond the market's means. But even if local production and import prices do remain viable, China is not the US of the 1950s, despite the many parallels drawn by mistaken commentators. The cultural differences alone are too large. For instance, despite the push on beef, over 50 per cent of McDonald's sales in China are still chicken-based, with beef products only representing 35 per cent.

What McDonald's seems to be pushing towards is presenting itself as having the choice of the best fast-food beef, chicken and fish dishes, and thus mark itself out as different from its competitors.

In September 2006, McDonald's changed its China menu, but adhered to its own convention in keeping the number of items on the menu the same in order to help its customers 'more effectively make choices'. When the new menu came out, its Asian-flavoured beef, chicken and sticky-rice wedges had disappeared from McDonald's China menu. However, Gary Rosen states that this is not a departure from the localizing of its menu, declaring that 'We would absolutely not 100 per cent 'localize' our menu in China, since McDonald's is a Western brand, but we are also hard at work in the flavour laboratories we have in mainland China and Hong Kong, coming up with menu items that meld with the lifestyle of Chinese people, and that suit the taste buds of Chinese consumers.' The fact that McDonald's has 'flavour laboratories' in mainland China and Hong Kong seems to add kudos to consumer fears of Frankenstein food supplied by big business, rather than abate them. Despite this, there have been few obviously healthy choices added to the McDonald's menu board in China, with the possible exception of the Corn in a Pot product launched February 2006, compared with numerous sweet, sugary pies, cold coffees, ice cream variations, etc.

However, the company has done its own research to prove that Chinese consumers don't want McDonald's to give them a facsimile of their own local dishes, but rather Asian-adapted Western products. This is leading not just the thinking in terms of menu development, but is also leading to several 'strategic adjustments' including the redesign and feel of stores, setting up strategically located new stores, establishing drive-thru stores and overhauling such things as purchasing, supply-chain building and management. The company hoped to spread its new message through 850 stores in China by 2008 (rising to a projected 1,350 by 2011), and will be pushing its new thinking through its considerable advertising expertise and budget.

Just how far that budget stretches became clear when McDonald's developed a reality TV show for children in China. Combining the Olympics and a competition-based reality TV show, the company found an ingenious way to advertise to children. McDonald's worked with the International Olympic Committee and CCTV to provide a reality TV-type competition show, allowing the winning 300 children an opportunity to participate in many different types of programmes at the Beijing Olympics. With less than a year to go to the opening of the Beijing Olympics, the appearance of the show 'Olympic Cheering Little Champions', which began airing in October 2007 was an attempt by McDonald's to circumvent any laws against advertising to children that exist in China (very few), while also trying to ride the wave of Olympic fever.

The linking of healthy lifestyles in childhood and beef-based fast food also raised a few eyebrows. During the programme, the child contestants first took part in a test and then an artistic and essay contest. The contestants had to show their understanding of the meaning of the Beijing Olympics 'One World, One Dream' slogan in order to win a chance to continue. After this, the children then participated in intelligence and athletic competitions with children from other countries, in order to find the final winners.

It is not just in the West that commentators are expressing some concerns that a fast-food company, the International Olympic Committee and the central TV mouthpiece of a communist government should be working together to promote cram-school-style education principles alongside consumption of high-fat-content food among children. Indeed, there were a rash of comments on blogs and websites where Chinese people expressed concerns over this 'arrangement'.

KFC – Chickening Out

While McDonald's is re-finding its belief in beef as its core product, despite the mounting concerns over links between increased beef consumption and rising obesity levels, KFC is continuing to harry its key competitor by promoting chicken as a lean and healthy product, confronting the obesity and food hygiene issue rather than shying away from it. KFC's 'New Fast Food' positioning is clearly a defensive move to head off any bad press. The new positioning by the company is summed up in several key phrases, used by the company in its own advertising and marketing:

- Tasty & safe
- Balanced nutrition
- Based in China
- Embodies high quality
- Healthy living
- Unlimited creation[1]

While the worldwide obesity crisis has emerged over the last decade or so, leading to many people pointing fingers of accusation directly at the fast-food industry, parts of the industry have been busy trying to change their ways – and their menus – in order to deflect such accusations away from themselves, and, presumably, onto somebody else – anybody else. In KFC's case, this has meant developing healthier food and beverages by establishing a 'food health inquiry committee', experimenting with new menu selections, changing the flavour of its foods to better match the tastes of Chinese consumers and improving its dissemination of information about nutrition. KFC has also gone to great pains to be seen as encouraging young people to participate in physical exercise, while promoting its healthy food policy.

The result of all this is KFC's so-called 'New Fast Food' movement, which it is trying to turn into a future guiding principle for the development of the Chinese foodservice market. So, we have a huge corporate organization with a predominantly red logo design, an elderly benevolent paternal father figure as its godhead and a catch-phrased political movement! Perhaps it is no surprise or coincidence that the first KFC outlet in China was opened right next to the Great Hall of the People in Beijing.

The 'New Fast Food' campaign is based around retreating from the old way of doing things, and replacing them with methods that consumers should respond positively to, especially given the growing consumer frustration with fast-food companies and their own expanding torsos. KFC is therefore ditching much of its traditional Western fast-food positioning; it is increasing the range of choices on its menus to include more Chinese-Western fusion dishes, rather than reducing them; it is now trying to move away from so much deep-fried food and use more cooking styles; it is trying to include more vegetables in its dishes to suit Chinese tastes; it is attempting to continually change its menus on a seasonal basis, discourage overeating, and, move more towards a Chinese model of food hygiene and safety.

In this sense, KFC is increasing its operational costs, while at the same time encouraging people to eat less! That it is not doing this outside China calls into question its credentials as a benevolent organization. However, what appears to have changed may not be all that different in practice. The menu may have changed, but still includes fried chicken and potato chips, which no doubt rank still as the lead items in sales volume terms. So despite the rhetoric, it is most likely that this is more tinkering than fundamental policy change. What IS significant is that consumers do seem to be believing this tactic by KFC, and that, as far as KFC is concerned, is what matters.

Most significant to the market is that KFC is way ahead of its competitors, and is simply maintaining its lead. The others, including McDonald's, are all frantically playing catch-up. This means that KFC will continue to tinker with its menu and market this tinkering at its leisure, while the other competitors will be ploughing much more time, money and effort into coming up with new advertising angles to win consumer interest. And KFC is a massive advertiser in China, indeed, the second largest brand after Olay beauty products.

One last area where KFC seems to be doing better than McDonald's is in the coupon deals it gives out. This is very important to most Chinese consumers, as

Table 21: **TV and Print Ad Spend by Brand in China, 2008 (RMB Billion)**

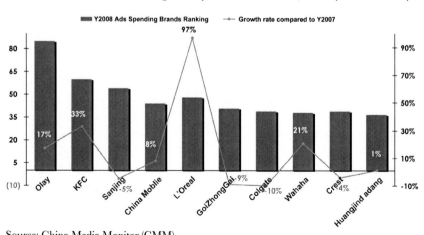

Source: China Media Monitor (CMM).

about half of Chinese customers at either chain use coupons. However, KFC tends to reward coupon users with better deals than McDonald's. For instance, KFC often gives coupons for money off its core chicken meals. However, McDonald's rarely provides coupons for money off its beef meals, perhaps because the beef is so much more expensive. Whatever the reason, the consumer population notices such things, and it is in such minor matters as these that the fast-food giants are either winning or losing the battle for hearts and minds in China.

The plan has been for both companies to rapidly move into as many regions of China as possible, while also increasing their penetration level in each of the major cities. They employ the young – mostly undergraduate students, – and they aim mostly at the young – predominantly school children. They do this through targeted advertising, by marketing (both apparent and more under-the-counter means), by setting up shop as close to schools as local laws allow – local laws for such things often being the stuff of myth. The target market is children, and only appeals to young adults as a secondary market, perhaps because they have control of, well, young children.

The cheapness of such fast-food meals is a key to their success, and an indicator as to why so many Chinese choose to eat fast food from such outlets. This cheapness has created not only increased demand, it has increased the fast-food proportion of Chinese food consumption, and this is where the contribution to the problem of obesity comes in.

Coffee and Pizza: Exotic Imports for an Eclectic New Consumer Class

Less obvious a hit in China than KFC or McDonalds, but still expanding rapidly across the country, are the number of pizza places. Pizza Hut, the leading pizza chain in China, had 201 stores by mid-2005 and 430 by 2009, which, compared to the chains of outlets created by KFC and McDonalds, might seem small, but they are there, nonetheless, doing good business, too. And it's not just Pizza Hut; others are there, too. The details and statistics are not as important as the fact that these pizza places have introduced a new item to the Chinese diet – cheese.

Cheese might not seem that important, and it is certainly still very much a minority food in the Chinese diet, but it is significant. Significant in that the existence of pizza chains in China, their continued existence and flourishing business, indicates that Chinese consumers are trying very hard to like cheese – to get what pizza is all about. In a country where dairy consumption was virtually unheard of only a few decades ago, and where lactose intolerance remains high, it shows that many Chinese will try very hard to adopt imported eating trends in order to appear more urbane and sophisticated. Were this salad (apart from the risks associated with that in China due to chemical residues), this might make sense, but pizza? Cheese? Cheese is a product totally alien to the Chinese diet. Indeed, when the authors were first in China, the Chinese would complain that Europeans smelt of cheese!

But pizza chains do exist. Sure, they have had to develop local versions of their most popular dishes, dishes with 'Chinese characteristics'. The aim is obviously to attract additional local customers. Most successful at this has been Pizza Hut, who developed the *Xinyi* (Goodwill) Pizza for Chinese New Year. They have managed to draw customers into their restaurants using decorations of large red Double Happiness signs, firecrackers, traditional poetic couplets and the Chinese character *Fu* (fortune) hung upside down according to tradition, along with displays of traditional Chinese handicrafts, calligraphy and paintings. Pizza Hut even altered its trademark red roof of the 'Hut' from its original trapezoidal shape into a design outlined with a Chinese calligraphy brush, and then filled in with red. They have come up with pizzas including ingredients such as eels – a local speciality.

It is not hard to see other examples of how exotic foreign foods are being pushed into the Chinese mainstream by appealing to the youth/young adult market. One such innovative example of this is the showing of a full-length feature film, which is, in fact, an advert for Starbucks on the Shanghai subway system. Again, coffee, in the country that is the source of the whole tea-drinking habit, might seem anathema, but coffee shops such as Starbucks are now everywhere in China's tier-one and tier-two cities.

Entitled *A Sunny Day*, the soap-opera-style, boy-meets-girl film was played, from early November 2007, exclusively on thousands of flat-screen monitors on Shanghai's subway cars and station platforms for the 2.2 million commuters who use the Shanghai subway system every day. It played for over 40 weekdays in instalments, while Internet relays allowed those who missed an instalment to catch up with events online. The Starbucks logo, its outlets and its drinks featured as integral parts of the story, and the lead male character in the film was Huang Xiao Ming, a 29-year-old pop star – an established star – sometimes described as 'China's Justin Timberlake' (meant as a compliment, apparently).

The advertising industry promotes this invasion into places where people are in transit, and where they are not actively engaged in work or other tasks, as helping to eliminate boredom. Certainly, many commuters like having something to look at, and enjoy the distraction of the entertainment provided. This has probably helped a lot of the brands advertised to increase consumer awareness and raise sales. However, the media saturation does possibly have some long-term problems for advertisers if consumers begin to feel that they cannot escape from constantly being barraged by advertising messages.

As well as Starbucks, there are other chains that have opened up, many direct copycats and competitors elsewhere in the world, such as Costa Coffee and The Coffee Bean & Tea Leaf. Likewise, there have been less successful entrants, such as the continental European (in its broadest sense) themed Délifrance. Whether successful or not, what these concepts have planted into China are the habits among certain consumers for eating cakes and drinking coffee with cream and sugar. We could produce endless statistics on the growth of cake and coffee consumption, but that would miss the point. The key significant factor is the existence of these products, and a continued growing market for them among a population already getting more than enough carbohydrate and fat. Cheese might not be a big sector in the food market, in relative terms, but sales are high enough for importers to increasingly bring new products into China and for local dairy companies to start launching cheese ranges.

Ergo, it is not as simple as pointing a finger at imported foreign fast-food concepts and laying the blame for China's obesity problem at the door of these foreign corporations; the Chinese are just as culpable for delivering added fat to the Chinese diet. It could, of course, be argued that all the local manufacturers are doing is creating pseudo-foreign foods in order to win consumer interest and without the foreign influence, they would not go down this route. Despite several good reasons why that argument does not stand up, one overarching reason is that if you look at the Chinese-cuisine fast-food industry, which is based on traditional Chinese dishes and cooking methods, and look at the fat and sugar content of the sauces they use, you find that they are just as bad as the foreign imports – and perhaps worse.

Wonton 'U' Like – The Rise of Domestic Fast Food Chains

Whether you visit a Zhending Chicken outlet or a Mala Noodle, go for a Little Sheep hotpot, a Fumao fish chain or some duck soup fast-food outlet, there are many things that strike you as common between them. First off, they all look like facsimiles of some Western fast-food chain or another. Next, they maintain the same hygiene levels, the same garish staff uniforms, the same limited-menu concept, all the familiar trappings of the Western fast-food experience. They also all tend to use thick, sticky sauces full of sugar and salt, and seem to fry everything. You could ask for something you would expect to be fairly healthy, but would often find that the dish you get is just as weighed down with gloopy sauce as if you'd asked for sweet and sour pork.

The issue is not to do with Western food, but the way fast-food culture and marketing creates expectations in consumers for that massive oral senses assault. The amount of sugar and salt in many of these dishes is enough to put you on a serious high for some hours. And this is perhaps why fast food gets the massive amounts of repeat business that it does, both in China and elsewhere – it gives you a high, a buzz. It is almost addictive, whether it be a burger or fried ribs. And this is perhaps why fast food seems to have created such a problem.

Imagine you're a local fried-chicken chain in China, trying to eke out a living pursuing market share from KFC, and times have been tough. There are examples of this for sure, and we would look at chains such as Rong Hua Chicken in Beijing, which opened its first outlet there in 1994. It took two years for the chain to achieve RMB1.5 million (US$187,000) in monthly sales per store. Six years later, however, Rong Hua Chicken closed its last store. Some blamed a lack of standardization for the chain's demise and its failure to set strict rules on raw materials and food-processing methods. It also failed to standardize services or unify the layout and design of its chain stores. This led to uneven levels of quality within the individual stores, and consumers quickly lost interest.

How, then, do you avoid being another Rong Hua? Well, as described above, you go for the garish uniforms, the Western-style outlets, the simple menus, etc. But you also have to have a hook to your food. Most foodstuffs have fairly subtle flavours, so the way you stand out is by adding an extra flavour hit. You see it in the West, too, with spicy wings, BBQ sauce, etc. Well, the same has been happening in China, with sweet and sour sauces getting both sweeter and sourer, black bean sauces getting sweeter, saltier and gloopier by turn – the examples are numerous.

So, just a problem of the Chinese fast-food industry, you think? Well, the problem is, the more people eat of these strong sauces, the more they get used to them. Manufacturers of off-the-shelf sauces sold through supermarkets and other stores and increasingly promoted vigorously on cookery programmes, have to keep up with the hit-hungry taste buds of their consumers, and bottled sauces are getting sweeter and saltier.

And so it goes on until you reach the situation where China is now, where many of the foods in many restaurants are highly flavoured, very sweet, salty and probably contain all kinds of flavour and colour enhancers. Of course, you then get the foreign fast-food chains starting to see the potential of this burgeoning Chinese-style fast food.

Enter KFC and its new Chinese fast-food chain. In 2004 Yum! Brands, owners of KFC, launched its East Dawning chain. As with other Yum! restaurants, the efficient and brightly branded chain is expected to win strong appeal with Chinese consumers, but this time with a decor and menu that is Chinese. The chain offers standard versions of traditional Chinese dishes such as noodles, rice, soy milk and other favourites, including fried dough and plum juice. Simplified Chinese food. Keep it simple so you can sell it cheaply, restrict consumer decision-making, rely upon cheap untrained staff and keep all the costs to an absolute minimum. Do this, and you can make a profit. Add a lot of cheaply made sauce for that instant oral sense attack and the subsequent sugar rush/salt palpitations, and you're on to a winner. It is clear that a lot of the fast food being sold to Chinese consumers is not good for them, especially if eaten in significant quantities, which is increasingly the case. However, can the current obesity problem in China, or elsewhere for that matter, really be laid directly on the doormat of the fast food companies?

A Plethora of Fast-Food Choices

KFC's China journey has become legendary; books have been written about it (we're only adding to an already crowded shelf of KFC China-related books), business schools provide case studies on the chain's success and the business press has lapped it up, both in China and internationally. But is it sustainable? Not that KFC is about to go out of business in China anytime soon, but will they become increasingly yesterday's fast food, as consumers find themselves lured by ever more fast-food giants in China's major cities?

KFC China's same-store sales dropped 4 per cent in the second quarter of 2009, the first time they had ever fallen. This was bad news. In press interviews, Yum! blamed cautious consumer spending, thanks to the 'global recession.' But was this the only reason? The Chinese were still eating out with gusto; total catering revenue nationwide jumped nearly 20 per cent in the first half on the same period in 2008. Yet, KFC announced that they expected same-store sales to be flat for 2009 – had China fallen out of love with the Colonel? Traditionally, fast-food chains such as KFC do well in any consumer spending downturn; cautious consumers look for cheaper meal deals and the ability to budget their spending in advance. This was the case during the 1998/1999 Asian Financial Crisis when KFC's same-store sales in China grew robustly and KFC used the decline in retail rents to expand aggressively.

There were other factors at play, though, in urban China in 2009. The major pressure on KFC's same-store sales comes from increasing competition in China's tier-one and tier-two markets. Rather than one major competitor eating its lunch, KFC faces a host of new and improving competitors nibbling away at the margins of its established outlets. As we have noted before, the same phenomenon of falling same-store sales among market leaders – despite rising overall consumption numbers – was also visible in supermarkets and department stores.

The range of new and/or aggressively expanding competitors in the fast-food sector is astonishing. In mid-2009 McDonald's was planning another 500 stores over the next three years while Burger King (12 outlets at the time) was aiming for 300 outlets by 2011, targeting younger consumers. Other players at around the same price point include Japan-based Yoshinoya, which aimed to increase its then 211 outlets to 1,000 within five years; US sandwich brand SUBWAY, which is fast expanding through a franchising model; and the popular Taiwanese coffee and bakery chain 85 Degrees, which planned to open 90–100 stores by the end of 2009.[2] The food offerings from Starbucks, The Coffee Bean and Tea Leaf, and Costa Coffee were also increasingly varied and available at reasonable prices.

For consumers with a sweet tooth, Dunkin' Donuts was planning to do battle with the ice cream chains Häagen-Dazs, Coldstone Creamery and Dairy Queen as well as the donut chains Mister Donut and Krispy Kreme. Dunkin' Donuts announced plans to open 100 franchise locations in Shanghai, Jiangsu and Zhejiang over the next few years. Most of these expansion plans should be taken with a hefty pinch of salt, but the trend to fiercer competition is clear. Domestic fast-food chains are also expanding quickly. The best example is the Kung Fu (*Zheng Gongfu*) chain, which features a Bruce Lee logo above its 270 locations nationwide (in 2009). And let's not forget Yum!'s own new

Table 22: **Selected Fast Food Brands in China, 2009**

Brand	Established (in PRC)	No. of Outlets (August 2009)	Expansion Plans
KFC	1987	2,600	370 new outlets in 2009
McDonald's	1990	850	500 more outlets by 2011
Dairy Queen	1992	170	100 more outlets in 2009
Yoshinoya	1992	211	1,000 outlets by 2013
85 Degrees	2007	42	91 more outlets by 2010
Dunkin' Donuts	2008	6	100 outlets by 2011
Subway	1995	128	actively seeking franchisees
Pizza Hut	1990	430	10–15 outlets per year plus additional home delivery stations
Papa John's Pizza	2003	118	250 outlets by 2011
Burger King	2005	12	300 more outlets by 2011
Kung Fu	2002	270	Planning to IPO
East Dawning	2005	18	N/A
Little Sheep	1999	376	60 new outlets by end of 2009

Source: Access Asia from company information.

concept East Dawning (with 18 stores), plus Little Sheep, a popular chain of hotpot restaurants with 375 outlets, in which Yum! had acquired a 20 per cent stake. With fierce competition from dozens of expanding foreign fast-food chains, quickly improving local players and independent operations, it is hardly surprising that KFC was suffering in its core market.

Supersized in China

In this respect, China has been no different to other nations – when people start to eat out more, they tend to eat and drink more in total. China has embraced the 'eat all you can' deal, the buffet and the set lunch as quickly as anywhere. When eating out, people eat more than in the home; leaving food on a plate is like leaving money on a table. But leaving food really means not leaving it, but taking it home to be reheated or rehashed up the next day – *liang fei, liang shi* (a Chinese variation on waste not, want not).

In China, the idea of supersizing hasn't really become what it is in the US or Europe. Rather than taking on massive portions of food, it is more a case of increased portions more frequently. Used to the habit of snacking during the day, and eating lighter meals, the snacks in between meals are becoming meals in themselves, in terms of their size. From a 'little and often', we are getting to people eating the same amount they would normally eat during a meal, in between the meals.

Two key environmental factors are coming into play to create this situation. The first is time. Free time is a scarce commodity in China's busy cities and towns. Getting hungry means stopping for meals, which means taking time to go out and eat. If you get hungry mid-morning, you can order in a 'snack' to tide you over until lunch. To make it worth being in the snack-delivery business, you need to charge enough per delivery, which means you need to supply enough to justify the cost, so you increase the portion size. The assumption is that if you have a hearty mid-morning snack, you won't need to go out for lunch. But then your colleagues invite you out to have lunch with them, so you go, and you eat another meal. It is the 'meal between meals' that the fast-food industry best serves, and where the danger of snacking lies. It is not that portions are necessarily too big; it is the number of meals, and the fact that the additional meals are of the processed/manufactured kind that lend themselves to the fast-food market. Then, after work, you meet up with friends for a 'bite to eat' and end up having another meal. One of your friends then invites you out for a few drinks at a bar, as it's Friday. The session lasts a while, and before heading home, you all order in some bar 'snacks'. It is easy to understand how this cumulative, unconscious effect can add more food intake to the normal diet.

The second major issue is, as already touched upon, portion size. As we've already said, it's not so much that portions are much bigger. What tends to be the issue is that Chinese people can afford to go out to eat more than they did before. Eating out is a major part of a typical Chinese social life. So, groups of people meet up at restaurants, perhaps trying out a new place they haven't been to before – the turnover of restaurants is pretty rapid in many cities. Because there is a group of people, they each want to order the dishes they individually fancy the taste of. Ordering invariably takes place while other conversations are ongoing, and before you know it, rather a lot of dishes have been ordered. All of these dishes individually are probably a meal in themselves, but they are meant to be shared. The problem is that the group tends to order so many of these dishes, it is easy to end up with a table heaving with food and a group of diners struggling to wolf down food so as not to waste it.

Chinese consumers are getting through main meals, often to group-induced proportions that exceed what an individual would normally eat if they were eating out alone, and interspersed with fast-food mini-meals in between. This is not comfort eating so much as social environment creating a situation where people are eating more frequently and with more volume on each occasion.

How Much of the Obesity Problem is Related Directly to Fast-Food?

Is there a proven link between fast-food and obesity? Legally, no. But do not be surprised if the attorneys-general of several US states begin proceedings against fast-food companies at some point in the future, just as they did against the tobacco companies, in order to compensate themselves against the increased costs of healthcare created by obesity. They will attempt to prove, in law, that fast-food creates obesity. However, until then, there is only circumstantial evidence (and gut instinct!), that suggests that fast-food is a major contributor to the obesity problem.

And such legal actions would have a lot of public support. This is not necessarily because of any proven link, but certainly the media, many physicians and many vocal consumer groups all point the finger at fast-food as a major cause of obesity in the US, and the Chinese are beginning to come to the same conclusion. In Asia, it is not just the Chinese. Malaysia is also seeing a similar process beginning to happen. Likewise in Hong Kong, Taiwan and Japan. Even in South Korea, where body consciousness is very high, people are getting fatter, and they are seeing fast-food as the reason.

It is also the case that, as with pre-packed and ready meals bought through supermarkets, it is hard for consumers to gauge their intake. For instance, the

UK pressure group Consensus Action on Salt and Health (CASH) has worked out that many fast-food meals contain at least twice the recommended levels of daily salt intake for children – they calculate that a family of four sharing a Pizza Hut 'meal deal' would each consume 12.3 grams of salt, nearly two-and-a-half times the recommended daily maximum for 7–10 year olds.[3]

But can you really simply blame fast-food? After all, people are also leading more sedentary lives, whilst many people still smoke and are drinking much more alcohol than they used to. They are also eating more unhealthy food bought from retail outlets, as opposed to caterers. It could be argued that the consumer is to blame for getting fat and that their pointing the finger at the fast-food industry is shunning responsibility for their own bad habits. You cannot ignore that there is probably a strong case for saying that a significant portion of the problem can be blamed on the individuals.

However, this argument really only stands up if you are talking about a few individual, freak cases. But the obesity problem in the US and China, as elsewhere across a wide variety of cultures, has reached epidemic proportions. The only thing that really acts as a common link between the problems across so many countries is the existence of fast-food, and a lot of it.

Let us consider the situation in the US, to put the situation in perspective. The number of Americans characterized as overweight grew from 47 per cent in the late 1970s to over 65 per cent by 2002, including 31 per cent clinically obese, according to the US Center for Disease Control. The US government has calculated that the medical costs attributable to obesity reached US$75 billion in 2003, about half of which was paid for by taxpayers through public healthcare schemes. In 2005, the *Journal of the American Medical Association* attributed about 112,000 premature deaths in 2000 to obesity.[4]

The US problem is severe, and it perhaps gives a foretaste of what is to come in China. It is clear that people are getting fatter, that it is costing the country a huge amount of money to care for this overweight population, and that the problem is killing people. But nobody has yet proven a link, legally, between the obesity problem and fast-food. However, since the beginning of the 1970s, the US fast-food market grew from sales of US$6 billion to about US$134 billion in 2005, according to *The Economist*.[5] So, at the same time that the American population has become significantly fatter, the fast-food industry has grown significantly larger in terms of its sales. Fast-food has also spread into nearly every community in the US, as has obesity. Europe is not far behind.

The other factor that has been crucial in the fattening of America, and could be the key to the problem in China, is that fast-food is very cheap, relative to other foods in the same market. This cheapness is very much due to the way that fast-food is made and delivered. There are good reasons why the price can be kept relatively so cheap. Mass buying of food ingredients from factory farms, mass production techniques leading to mass distribution, and the relevant economies of scale that can be employed in such large operations, all add to the cost savings. It is also no coincidence that most fast-food outlets employ teenagers – they are cheap labour. A limited menu of easy-to-make meals also helps to limit the costs of equipping and running the kitchen. Also, the fast-food restaurants tend to be wipe-clean, from the kitchens to the eating area. You can do the whole lot with a bottle of disinfectant spray.

Economies of scale and functionality add to the ability to sell at a low price. And it is low price, coupled with convenience and speed of delivery and the ubiquitous branding and marketing machines found everywhere that sells fast-food to people. Obesity from eating too many hamburgers is not exclusively a disease of the urban poor in the US – this has nothing to do with not being able to afford to eat better. Indeed, food in the US is relatively very cheap.

Of course, China is still cheaper, as shown repeatedly by *The Economist*'s famous Big Mac Index, where world currencies are measured against the cost of a single Big Mac in each country. *The Economist* works out purchasing power parity (PPP) using a base currency to measure the price of a product in different countries. Under this system, in 2008 a Big Mac costs US$3.57 in the United States and US$5.34 in the euro area, US$4.57 in Britain, but just US$1.83 in China.

It is not an issue of people not knowing that fast-food isn't really good for them. Most people do tend to know that fast-food is high in fat. However, it is unlikely that they understand just how high in calories fast-food is. In his Academy Award-nominated film, *Super Size Me*, Morgan Spurlock stated that between 1971 and 2000 the average American woman's daily intake of calories rose from 1,542 to 1,877, and that the average American man's calorie intake grew from 2,450 to 2,618. The US government recommends a daily calorie intake of 1,600–2,000, for women and 2,200–2,400 for men, with lifestyles including at least some 'light physical activity' But, what many people just do not realize, is that one fast-food meal can represent as much as their whole daily calorific intake!

A KFC meal can have as much as 1,600 calories, which is a lot for a meal that weighs less than half a kilogramme, plus a large fizzy drink. And this is by no way the most calorific of fast-food meals. Little wonder then that many people do not realize that if they eat a fast-food meal every day, plus continue to eat other meals and snacks, then they are adding a significant amount of fat to their diet. It is also very unlikely that many people will realize how much extra exercise they would need to burn off that additional fat, each day.

Although nobody has successfully brought a case against any fast-food company for making them fat, the fast-food companies are already responding to a perceived change in their public relations. Much is made of this trend in the West and how consumer pressure against the fast-food giants is forcing them to change their menu items to include more healthy foods, such as salads. But China is not being left out of this. Some consumers are beginning to point the finger at the fast-food companies for their children's weight problems, and the notorious Chinese bloggers (who have been instrumental in naming, shaming and forcing contrition and compensation from other foreign companies who have failed to serve the consumer well) are beginning to criticize the fast-food companies and their means of making money.

A further similarity between China and America is that in both countries, when the little man feels aggrieved against a huge corporation or a government department, they do not take this to their elected representative; they take it to their lawyer. China is becoming highly litigious, and it has been those companies whose products have been faulty, poisonous, explosive, abrasive, etc., that have been the main targets of many high-profile cases.

No wonder, then, that fast-food companies are looking again at their menus and working out ways to make them healthier. In China, where fast-food companies have invariably had to alter their menus, anyway, in order to appeal more to the tastes of local consumers, they have perhaps far more room to make such manoeuvres, both in order to keep their food popular, and to make it healthier. Perhaps there is some sense that there needs to be some self-regulation by fast-food companies to help reduce the risk of future prosecution by either overweight individuals or disgruntled governments that have seen their budgets inflated by rising healthcare costs.

There is perhaps no way to prove fast-food's complicity in the obesity problem of a nation, although for an individual, such a case might be made. However, what is apparently clear is that fast-food does not help the problem. The coupling of a rise in fast-food consumption, and more fatty, sugary convenience foods in the retail stores, – driven by a newly convenience-oriented lifestyle – and a lack of exercise, are creating a lethal combination.

Despite more and more consumers being aware of the risks, they are still buying what is bad for them. Why? Well, perhaps as well as acknowledging lifestyle changes and lack of time, we need to look more closely, not at what is sold to consumers (and how they are living their lives), but more at how they are persuaded to buy it.

Chapter 7

SELLING FAT – PROMOTING FAT
IN CHINA

Who Persuaded the Chinese that They Like Coffee?

We've already touched upon how diets have changed in China, and how the retail industry has come to shape the direction that these changes have taken. We have also touched upon how the catering and retail industries have moulded each other, and in turn created a new retail environment in China's cities. But if Chinese people are eating more and new types of food at home or outside, then partly they've been sold those foods through advertising and marketing, often with a helping hand from the government. Whatever the claims of the industry to a nobler calling, advertising agencies and marketers simply attempt to sell stuff to people, convince them they want it, and so are a key part of a changing diet and lifestyle. At the same time, the government is keen to expand consumption in all fields to better the balance the economy and unlock people's savings, and are just as keen for consumers to eat more, thus promoting changing lifestyles through their propaganda.

Take dairy products, a good example of where brands, advertisers and the government have all combined to push up consumption. In the 1980s dairy products in China consisted of plain yoghurt (which people drank from recyclable ceramic bottles), some ice cream and condensed milk used in cooking. You could get cheese, but it was expensive and available only in stores aimed at foreign expats. Cream was available in Nestlé one-serve portions for those same expats who drank the awful coffee stuff. That was about it. Most Chinese people, having never really consumed dairy products (apart from yoghurt, which contains a live culture of bacteria which helps digest the dairy fats), were lactose intolerant. Give them a pint of milk to drink, and they would be very ill. So how did the dairy industry in China get so big and successful?

Partly because there was lobbying by interested parties outside China – those interested in creating a market for dairy products in the then newly opening consumer market. And partly, there was a belief by some sectors of the Chinese government that Chinese people needed more dairy in their diet, with a lack of calcium in the average diet being a key issue. Whatever the motive, various government-promoted and dairy industry-sponsored campaigns to increase dairy consumption, especially among children, came about. Such initiatives included supplying milk powder to the parents of newborn children and then providing them with discount vouchers to keep on buying the brand. Not surprisingly, a certain Swiss dairy products manufacturer was a vanguard in this 'social welfare' campaign. There have also been campaigns to promote the supply of subsidized milk to children at primary schools in many provinces and cities, aided by various foreign and local dairy companies as well as governmental agencies. These campaigns, which began in earnest in the late 1990s and early years of the twenty-first century, have had some success. A series of campaigns helped boost the number of Chinese who claimed to drink milk daily from 33 per cent in 2001 to 45 per cent in 2002 (though nearly 30 per cent of Chinese still claim never to drink milk), while yoghurt consumption rose by several per cent over the same year. A government- and dairy-sponsored schools campaign to introduce milk to children's diets claimed to have reduced lactose intolerance by 16 per cent among the kids – that's a significant number of potential new dairy consumers.

But where did all this dairy come from? To begin with, there was not a great deal of supply within China, so imports were needed. But it soon became apparent that this was too expensive, and that a domestic dairy industry needed to be established. Funding for the development of this industry came from leading dairy manufacturers, in the form of joint venture partnerships, as well as foreign government investments – such as from the EU.

At the same time, fast-food companies were bringing alien foods such as cheese into the Chinese market along with beef burgers and pizzas. Meanwhile, coffee companies were trying to get the Chinese to like coffee – with the hope that they might begin to buy it. It wasn't always an easy sell. With coffee, especially if you dislike the bitter taste of it, came the inevitable creamer. The concept of cream thus entered the market. Likewise, the concept of cake entered mainstream Chinese consumerism. Although less heavy than Western cakes, Chinese cakes, along with lots of sliced fresh fruit and chocolate whorls, are often smothered in whipped cream (often synthetic) and tend to be very sweet. Yoghurt was less of a hard sell, especially if you improved on the local product by adding fruit, sugar, preservatives and emulsifiers to the pot!

When it came to dairy products, Chinese consumers, whether they really liked it or not, had to give it a try. Eventually, many consumers did get used to dairy products, and even developed a tolerance to lactose. Now, the food aisles of Chinese supermarkets have as much UHT milk (Ultra High Temperature processed milk) as you would expect in a supermarket in Germany. Not happy with simply importing product ideas, the Chinese dairy industry has begun to innovate too with new 'localized' flavours and products that may not always taste good, but make it up in fat and sugar content.

So who did persuade the Chinese that, despite its bitter taste, they should really be drinking coffee? It would be easy to blame the likes of Starbucks, but they really only followed in the footsteps of others and weren't pioneers. Prior to the Starbucks phenomenon hitting China, powdered coffee brands like Maxwell House and Nescafé were already well established. Admittedly, sales were slow at first until the brands realized that Chinese households typically did not contain several essentials for the coffee drinker – cups and saucers, teaspoons and milk – but they got around that by selling gift packs including a jar of coffee, a jar of powdered milk, two cups, two saucers (neither ever used because people preferred drinking from the jars the coffee came in!) and a teaspoon, and then successfully launching powdered premix coffee sachets that included the powdered milk and sugar (wine sellers had a similar problem, having to give away corkscrews in the early days). Fast-food outlets helped people to spread the good news, and soon the market was ripe for the Starbucks, The Coffee Bean and Tea Leaf and Costa Coffee's of this world to spread across China at the rate of a caffeine-pumped express train. Before anyone knew what was going on, instead of drinking tea, people were trying to drink coffee, steeped in milk and sugar to temper the flavour, which to most Chinese, not used to bitter flavours, was hard work.

Thus, from drinking tea, which has virtually no fat or sugar, the Chinese began drinking coffee drenched in full-fat milk and sugar, even though they didn't really like it. Which begs the question 'Why?' The answer is a simple one – marketing. Coffee culture was sold as the sophisticated, Western/cosmopolitan thing to do for all those urban middle-class strivers with an outward-looking view on the world, a sense of style and taste and a penchant for the finer things in life. Coffee was sold as part of a 'lifestyle' package – one of the more enduring buzzwords of modern China. If you wanted to be more cosmopolitan, and get a job in a foreign company (as most people did, and many still do) then you had to know how to drink your coffee.

Of course, there has been a backlash, helped along by the marketers and advertisers with some consumers now going back to drinking tea with a vengeance. And not drinking just any old tea, but the finest Chinese teas – at a price – and bought from or consumed in some of the trendiest, retro-Chinese-chic teahouses that have appeared in and around the major cities.

Meanwhile, children themselves have become more demanding and know their brands – thanks to marketing – but not their contents (again thanks to the smoke and mirrors of advertising and lax legislation). Survey after survey in China has revealed that the typical diet of obese children is characterized by particularly high consumption of convenience foods, carbonated drinks, dairy products and low intake of homemade foods, fresh fruit and vegetables.

The Chinese may not have taken to grazing and snacking in quite the same way as has occurred in the West, but the sheer number of new products and the range of retail outlets where they are available (all backed by widespread advertising) means that consumption has increased. This is a problem, since we tend to associate greater variety with greater freedom of choice, both personally and within a society. This means that we tend to associate choice with liberty, the bogus democracy of shopping. However, it still leads to obesity levels increasing, and fat intakes up all around.

It is a political conundrum. In a political democracy it is often said that the country gets the idiot it deserves, certainly the one it votes for (usually). Yet, in a consumer democracy (such as China's food market essentially is) what do we get? In this case, the power of advertising to exploit and manipulate the weaknesses emerging in social relationships (among peers, between parents and children, etc.) in order to increase product sales, which is something that such advertising can manipulate in a way that develops a self-sustaining momentum, where those relationships reinforce the pressures to rely on the advertised products; this leads to control of the freedom of choice by the advertisers. In this case, we do not choose the idiot we deserve; we are told which idiot to choose. This process is helped along by the severe constraints on press freedom in China that, as well as censoring sensitive news, means that fashion, lifestyle and travel journalism (to name just three sectors) are rarely independent and usually marketing- or PR-company-driven advertorially (though rarely highlighted as such to the unwary consumer).

Chinese consumers are not naïve, but they are not as cynical and circumspect about the motives behind big business as consumers in the West can be – yet. The fact that their economy is developing so rapidly has changed their whole country and society so quickly and profoundly means that Chinese consumers are perhaps particularly vulnerable to the influence of those who have the monetary resources and lengthy experience in the dark arts of consumer manipulation. The fact that dairy and coffee consumption have risen so rapidly in a country where dairy and coffee consumption were previously anathema, because people really didn't like them and couldn't digest them, indicates that this manipulation of consumer habits is much more directly successful than we would perhaps like to admit. Meanwhile, advertising and marketing 'professionals' feel rightly proud of themselves for being able to shape trends.

The advertisers have also latched onto certain key themes from Chinese culture to aide their campaigns, whilst ignoring those that might limit their success. For example, the image and idea of the plump child as being a totem for the idea of health, vitality and future prosperity has been husbanded by many companies selling to the Chinese in recent years. Yet nobody is promoting the local traditions set in place to act as a counter to consumption, such as the Buddhist tradition of fasting at regular intervals, which usually meant simple abstinence from meat, but often meant a general reduction in food intake. The monthly fast, however, has seen a resurgence alongside the resurgence in Buddhism itself, and the growth in the number of vegetarian restaurants in China's cities provides evidence that this is a concrete trend, counter to the all-consuming culture promoted by the advertisers, and that Chinese consumers are increasingly aware of their diet, their health and the fact that big business does not always have their best interests at heart, despite what feel-good media messages might proclaim.

Advertising and Obesity

The relationship between advertising and obesity is a long and well-documented one internationally, though to date, the discussion of the link between the advertising of fat-inducing foods and drinks and obesity, particularly among the young, has been muted in China. This lack of a discussion has not been due to any particular government clampdown or censorship, but instead, due to the general climate of rapid growth in advertising and fast-changing lifestyles that have meant that no time has yet been found for such discussions. Yet they will have to happen soon.

In countries where the combined phenomena of rising incomes, longer working hours, more working mothers, time-poor/cash-rich parents, etc., have taken place earlier and over a longer period of time, of course the discussion has occurred and solutions been sought. This has often led to scandals; the Coca-Cola company wrote to Coke's advertising agency in a memo designed

Table 23: **Ad Spend on Food, Health Food and Alcoholic Drinks, 2007–2008**

Category	Spend 2008 (RMB bn)	Y-o-Y Growth (%)
Food Products	14.8	4.6
Health Foods	8.7	22.6
Alcoholic Drinks	6.1	16.9
Total Ad Spend (all categories)	190.0	9.1

Source: China Media Monitor (CMM) from China State Administration of Industry and Commerce (SAIC).

to be sent to magazines that they 'require all insertions placed adjacent to editorial that is consistent with each brand's marketing strategy…We consider the following subjects to be inappropriate: hard news, sex, diet, political issues, environmental issues…'[1]

In the UK, a survey by Ofcom (the independent regulator and competition authority for UK communications industries) encompassing 'Children's food choices, parents' understanding and influence, and the role of food promotions', stated: 'Academic research confirms that hours spent in television viewing correlate with measures of poor diet, poor health and obesity among both children and adults. Three explanations for this have been offered (1) television viewing is a sedentary activity that reduces metabolic rates and displaces physical exercise; (2) television viewing is associated with frequent snacking, pre-prepared meals and/or fast food consumption; (3) television viewing includes exposure to advertisements for HFSS food products.' As well as television, the report noted peer pressure ('My friends like it'), 'pester power' where children continually request certain foods (the 'nag factor') and, perhaps most importantly, promotions (e.g., special offer/in-store promotions) of HFSS products, as influences on children's food choices.[2]

Most academics agree that before four or five years old, children regard advertising as simply entertainment, while between four and seven, they begin to be able to distinguish advertising from programming. The majority have generally grasped the intention to persuade by the age of eight, while after eleven or twelve they can articulate a critical understanding of advertising. Thus, globally, advertisers try to appeal to younger children through the use of bright colours, lively music and the use of cartoon characters or celebrities, while teenagers are presented with an argument or a proposition regarding the product; simplistically put, the product is cool, new, tasty, trendy, etc. Again, at this age celebrity endorsement is popular and the stars are influential. Interestingly, the Ofcom report noted earlier also specifically mentioned that 'TV advertising may have a more powerful influence on obese children, engaging them in a more emotional/physical way than it does children of normal weight.'

Advertising has become a ubiquitous part of Chinese urban life – hoardings, TV, radio, elevators, the back seats of taxicabs, the Internet. There's no escaping it – below or above the line. In the last two decades Chinese consumers have been inundated with advertising from every angle. This is not just because the advertising market was an early beneficiary of the economic reforms and went rapidly from very little to an incredible amount, but also because a bewildering range of new products from

SUVs to shoes, web sites to pop concerts are now vying for people's attention and money. In a market where a regular visitor to a supermarket is still being confronted by a couple of dozen new products and brands they've never seen before every time they wheel a trolley round the aisles, the need to promote brands has been intense. Crucially, with all these new products, brands and services piling into the market vying for consumer's attention, building customer loyalty has been problematic. The Chinese have been on a massive two-decade-long 'taste test', trying the whole gamut of new products – rejecting some as too expensive or just too horrible, and accepting others. This has meant that brands have had to keep up the advertising pressure, and consequently the spend, to stay in the game. For many sector-leading brands even a small dip in ad spend can lead to an almost instant loss of market share as a competing brand moves in and takes the available ad space and occupies the consumer's attention. This has meant that ad spend-to-sales ratios have been even higher on average in China than in Europe or North America.

With vast lifestyles changes and the resultant openness to new ideas, Chinese people have evolved into eager consumers of advertising and other media messages. Household TV ownership is almost universal in urban areas, with advertising slots becoming ever more frequent. Even the programmes on TV are selling something. Consider that many cookery programmes on Chinese TV, which are very popular with older women, tend to be sponsored by a food product, such as a cook-in sauce, with the product often being used in the programme. This incursion of advertising is also found in magazines and newspapers and in all forms of transport, and most major sporting events are sponsored by at least one food or beverage brand – the 'advertorial' is widespread and not always clearly defined from the regular editorial. The messages being promoted are hard to escape, and do have an influence on how consumer behaviour develops.

Above-the-line advertising is often reinforced in the supermarkets and c-stores, where in-store point-of-sale (PoS) advertising, as well as salespeople promoting certain products by serving free samples, is very common. The retailers are glad to get the additional income (marketing and promotional fees) from the marketing companies and manufacturers who want to promote their products this way, too. Profit margins in the Chinese retail sector are very slim, so any additional income that can be derived from direct marketing campaigns in-store is welcomed by the retailers.

Similarly, the so-called 'slotting fees' paid by manufacturers and brands to have their products displayed on the most visible store shelves are another significant boost to income for retailers, and have even become a major slice of leading retail company profits. And the manufacturers that pay the biggest fees tend to be those selling the products with highest percentages of fat, sugar and salt. The reality of these kinds of economic considerations are foremost in the minds of retailers and push the provision of fresh produce (which is of less financial benefit to the retailers) further down their list of priorities. When Chinese supermarket retailers first started using the 'loss leader' technique so familiar in Western stores, they chose to loss lead Coca-Cola rather than carrots.

The role of packaging in advertising a product, bringing it to consumer's attention and persuading them to buy it is also crucial. Products aimed at children tend to emphasize fun packaging and again, as with TV advertising aimed at the young, use bright colours and cartoon characters. For older kids and teenagers, brands can impart a 'cool' status through packaging. For young upwardly mobile white collars, convenience and trendiness, as well as internationalism, are the major points emphasized in China.

Brands are able to attract both children and parents through packaging and advertising by persuading parents that children will like and eat this or that product, and then there is the fact that brands are generally seen as indicators of quality, intrinsically better than unbranded goods – yet they are differentially skewed towards the promotion of HFSS foods. While this is a global trend reflecting the advertising spending power of the major brands it is also true that in China the brands are better associated with other factors that are at present ranked as more important by many parents, such as better hygiene, quality and food safety. With the Asian Development Bank estimating that 300 million Chinese people annually are affected directly in some way by tainted food, this is no small concern and recent major food scares such as that over fake formula milk that led to the tragedy of swelled head syndrome and other mass poisonings at schools, canteens and restaurants, have parents rightly concerned. Large and well-known domestic and international brands offer some degree of surety to parents, and this is often reinforced through advertising and packaging in China.

Moves on Advertising

To date, few serious restrictions have been placed on food advertisers in China regarding advertising HFSS products or advertising directly at children and the young. However, the Chinese press has reported initiatives such as the 2006 International Congress on Obesity in Sydney, where the International Association for the Study of Obesity called for a global statutory ban on the advertising of non-nutritious and junk food to children in order to tackle the global epidemic of obesity.

As calls for limits on advertising HFSS products to children grow internationally, from the American Academy of Paediatrics to the EU and many others, so China's statutory bodies are expected to respond, too. Chinese academics and healthcare professionals have also noted that a host of countries including Sweden, Norway, Denmark, Belgium, the UK and Greece, now limit ads directed at children. In some Western countries this has already led to some purveyors of HFSS foods, such as McDonald's and Kraft, to announce that they will promote more healthy foods and curb advertising to young children for snack foods. Though as we have seen in China, such moves by the likes of McDonald's have come at the same time as setting up drive-thru restaurants and young mothers clubs.

Despite a slow start compared to many Western countries, product placement and embedded marketing in Chinese TV has been around for a while and is now common in movies, too. There have been a number of reasons for this, including a slight lag behind Western marketing techniques and the fact that the majority of Chinese films, until recently, have been ancient historical dramas, films around the revolutionary exploits of good communists or kung fu epics – not the best places to place cans of Coke or luxury watches. Now, Mainland movie directors are coming out and inviting product endorsements to help them offset the rising costs of their movies.

Through greater access to foreign films, either legally at cinemas or on TV, or through widespread access to pirated DVDs, Chinese audiences have grown increasingly used to product placement. Pierce Brosnan advertising watches as James Bond was a successful campaign in China, while Western films that have been released in the PRC have been able to leverage their corporate endorsements; for instance, the promotion of Sony products including mobile phones and HDTVs with the Chinese release of *Spider-Man 2*. The level of product placement and movie tie-ins that Chinese audiences have been exposed to in Western films has already been parodied in China with popular Chinese comic actor and movie director Ge You's successful and critically acclaimed *Big Shot's Funeral* (2001).

There was for some time a certain artistic reluctance on the part of some Chinese filmmakers to accept product placement in their movies. However, the highly successful director/actor Stephen Chow, whose film *Kung Fu Hustle* (2004) was a major success across Asia and also somewhat of a success in the West, announced that for his future films (which are now quite big budget by Chinese standards), he will willingly accept star endorsements, co-branded merchandise, events and wireless and Internet tie-ins.

You Sold Us the Fat, Now Sell Us the Cure

Advertising agencies, marketing outfits and PR firms are just hired guns; they will work for anyone who walks through the door with a chequebook in their hand. Over the last 20 years, advertising agencies in China have made good money from food manufacturers, beer companies, fizzy drink brands, food retailers and, especially, fast-food giants. They will continue to do so. But now they will also start to make money from those offering cures for obesity – Weight Watchers, fat farms, slimming pills, diet plans, cosmetic surgery, 'magic bullet' pharmaceuticals. They persuaded many Chinese to get fat; now they'll convince them they know how to slim them back down again. Growing concern over an obesity epidemic in China will be good news for the advertising people whether the response eventually turns out to be measured and sensible or dumb panic. They personally have little interest which. They know that they can sell the idea that their client can 'cure' fat, and also know that this is highly unlikely – if they could, then they would have made a fortune and retired to watch all the skinny 'cured' people walk by.

Given the experience of the West, we can expect the advertising community to present fat as universally bad and to encourage overweight and obese people to actively dislike their physical shape (though that is not our intention, simply to highlight the point at which being overweight becomes hazardous to health).

Of course, fat can equal profits for a number of businesses, the magazine sector included. Following the trend in the West, a rash of magazines on men's health, women's beauty and fashion all discuss issues of weight, obesity, dieting and body image at great length. And magazines discussing body image find themselves tapping into a major issue of interest among Chinese at the moment. Advertising, it seems, can have it both ways. However, where advertising is running into a few problems with the public is with advertising to children– and it is with children that concerns about rising obesity levels are most concentrated and concerned.

Chapter 8

LITTLE FAT EMPERORS – OBESITY AMONG CHINA'S CHILDREN

One Family, One Child

If the rise of obesity has become a subject of concern and heightened awareness in China, then it is the specific issue of child obesity that has come to the forefront in both the media and the public mind. Again, China is in a sense no different from other nations in this regard. Obesity concerns became heightened in any number of countries when studies showing that child obesity rates were rising became wider public knowledge. The US, the UK, Singapore and other nations have all gone through prolonged handwringing over the issue of child obesity in recent years. As Sander Gilman has noted, 'Fat children signify a basic change in society for the worse.'[1] And this is as true in China as elsewhere. Chen Chunming, head of International Life Sciences Institute Focal Point in China has said that 'Problems of obesity will not only influence children's physical and psychological development, but also become a 'time bomb' for the country's future economic development and public health system.'[2] However, parental awareness is often still low. As one Beijing mother, interviewed on her purchasing decisions, commented to the authors in 2009, 'No sacrifice is too great to give my child all the things I didn't have in order to insure her happiness.'

What is specific about China and important to note in the wider debate on obesity and its causes, is the country's unique and long-standing One-Child Policy. China is gradually rescinding the One-Child Policy. However, for those children now adding to the growing rates of obesity in the urban middle class, they may later in life ask themselves how far the responsibility for their weight and health problems are linked to the policy under which they were born.

Launched in 1979 after the population topped one billion, the One-Child Policy remains the most ambitious of the Communist Party's many attempts at social engineering. But implementation has always been patchy. Today, only a surprisingly low 20 per cent of children under 14 are from single-child families, according to the State Family Planning Commission (SFPC). However, the policy has been most effective in cities and consequently, the number of one-child families is far higher. In urban China, residents have faced heavy fines and can lose their jobs if they have a second child. Many couples prefer fewer children and cannot afford or have room for any more. But in the countryside, where parents depend on children to help them, especially sons, resistance has been widespread and continual.

In 1995 Beijing approved a pilot project in six rural counties where family planning workers would try to limit births by expanding health services for women, providing more information about contraception and allowing couples to make their own decisions. Then in 1998 the UN population agency encouraged China to take the experiment a step further, providing funding and training to 32 rural counties that agreed to eliminate the birth permits, targets and quotas, and stop promoting abortion as part of family planning. According to Chen Shengli, a senior SFPC official, health workers across the country have been impressed by the results of the UN project, with many also choosing to abandon birth permits and quotas. Xie Zhenming, a senior official at the government-affiliated China Population Information and Research Centre who campaigned for the changes, estimates that cities and counties accounting for nearly a quarter of China's 1.3 billion people have eliminated birth permits and quotas over the last five years. And about half the population now lives in jurisdictions that allow women to choose which type of contraception to use. This, at least, is the idea, though not necessarily the reality.

When the One-Child Policy was introduced, it was meant to last for only one generation, long enough to control the nation's population explosion, but short enough to avoid distorting the age structure beyond all repair. In 2004 the National Strategic Research Project Group on Population Development was formed to advise on the next course of action. When its report was published in January 2007, the recommendation was simple: do nothing. The main conclusion of the report was that, for the population peak to be controlled at around 1.5 billion, the national gross birth rate over the next 30 years must be 'stabilized'. According to the latest government statistics, 36 per cent of the population is still required to follow a strict one-child policy in the richer coastal provinces, while 53 per cent may have a second child if their firstborn is a girl, in 19 of the poorer provinces. Those families that belong to 'national minorities' follow looser regulations, while there is no family planning policy at all in Tibet.

Unsurprisingly, the policy has not always been popular, and the recent nationwide population census led to an influx of babies abandoned at orphanages, as people feared the penalties – which can include fines in urban areas, or your house being bulldozed in rural areas – for breaking the rules. Rural families in China have been targeted with inventive campaigns to

Table 24: **Percentage Breakdown of China's Population by Age Group, 2003–2009**

% of Population	2003	2004	2005	2006	2007	2008	2009
0 to 4 years %	6.57	6.52	6.46	6.40	6.34	6.28	6.22
5 to 9 years %	9.66	9.58	9.50	9.41	9.32	9.23	9.14
10 to 14 years %	7.90	7.84	7.77	7.70	7.63	7.55	7.48
15 to 19 years %	7.57	7.58	7.59	7.61	7.62	7.63	7.65
20 to 29 years %	19.46	19.49	19.52	19.56	19.59	19.63	19.66
30 to 39 years %	16.23	16.26	16.28	16.31	16.34	16.37	16.40
40 to 49 years %	13.33	13.36	13.38	13.40	13.42	13.45	13.47
50 to 59 years %	8.25	8.26	8.28	8.29	8.31	8.32	8.33
60 to 64 years %	3.57	3.57	3.58	3.58	3.59	3.60	3.60
65 years + %	7.45	7.55	7.64	7.74	7.84	7.95	8.05
TOTAL	100.00	100.00	100.00	100.00	100.00	100.00	100.00

Source: Access Asia from the National Bureau of Statistics.

encourage family planning, including being paid not to have more children, or campaigns in the countryside attempting to appeal to entrepreneurs. One sign that appeared in villages read, 'If you want to get rich, have fewer kids and raise more pigs.'

As far as this book is concerned, the major result of the One-Child Policy is that expectations for the one child are now exceptionally high. There are no 'second chance' parents, so the pressure not to fail in raising their child is intense. This pressure leads to the heavy investment in babies and young children in order to get a good return from them in their adult years. Many parents were raised in a China that was materially deprived and still in political turmoil. In the new China, with a social reward system characterized by a heavy dependence on academic performance, many parents wish to compensate for their own loss by providing everything for their children right from the baby stage. Many of these parents are what are known as 'lag-behind' consumers as they missed out on the consumer boom of the 1990s and are now spending heavily on their children to compensate for this.

The generations of one-child children in China have come in for their fair share of criticism – spoiled, pampered little brats unable to look after themselves, given everything they demand by ever-hovering 'helicopter parents', truly Little Emperors (*xiao huangdi*). Of course there is another side to them; parents have poured all their hopes and aspirations into their one child, placing great pressure on them to succeed academically, pushing them to excel through a punishing education and examination system. Sure, there are treats and snacks, but only after hours of homework and after-school classes have been done and satisfactory exam scores and teachers reports received. It would be wrong to think the Little Emperors of China's middle class have it all easy, but it would be right to think that child rearing and familial relations in China have significantly changed.

Cases of excessively obese children have been regular features of the domestic media and international coverage of China for a decade now. Of course, there are extremely obese children and they do sometimes get sent to fat-reduction centres ('Fat Camps') for daily army-style regimens of exercise, diet counselling, acupuncture and, if the pictures on Chinese TV are representative of life at a Fat Camp, plenty of verbal abuse about their weight, all for a reported six weeks costing RMB10,000 (US$1,234). We have resisted discussing Fat Camps in any detail, as they are the sensationalistic exception and not the general rule. Most children are not so overweight as to require such drastic intervention and most families cannot afford the camps, anyway (the majority are privately run and prohibitively expensive even for middle-class parents). They appear to be a temporary fad (after a brief media flurry, most appear to have shut their doors, but old stories regularly get recycled in the domestic and international media) and their success rate was always highly dubious, anyway. Fat Camps popped up in the Chinese media for a select (unlucky) few the way camps to solve the supposed problem of Internet addiction have appeared more recently. They involve only a fraction of children with either a weight problem or a tendency to want to stay on their computers all night. Admittedly, though, these 'camps' do make good and noisy media, and journalists have been unable to resist them and continue to find new and more bizarre 'camps', including one called the 'devil eating programme' that reportedly allowed overweight children to eat only fruit and drink only water.[3]

Similarly, the media has liked to link the growth in child obesity cases with the rise of fast-food – an invasion from the West – but this is not necessarily the case (as Chapter 6 illustrates), though more fast-food has not been helpful. More important, and as shown overall in Chapter 4, it is the wider changing diet combined with increased consumption. This increased consumption of food – fast-food, traditional food, nontraditional food – is the key to understanding why more Chinese urban children are being diagnosed as obese. More of everything is a problem when children cannot be expected to differentiate between types of food or drink, but simply accept all they are given. In this sense the problem lies with the givers, not the receivers.

In part, the rising obesity rate among children in China is a problem of the combination of rising disposable incomes, easy availability of a wider variety of foods and drinks and the One-Child Policy. Wealthy countries have all seen rising rates of child obesity; including Hong Kong, where concerns over excessive coddling and spoiling as well as pressures on kids leading to obesity and other problems (stress, depression, etc.) has led the government's Education and Manpower Bureau to run TV adverts since 2005 encouraging parents to 'let children grow and explore' and calling on them to stop putting so much pressure on kids over examinations. However, on the mainland, the pressures to succeed are getting heavier rather than lighter.

The Six-Pocket Syndrome and Loaded Teens

When you have money or credit cards in your pocket, ceding control of responsibility becomes easier. A whining child, who you dote on anyway, demanding a McDonald's Happy Meal, a can of Coke or an ice cream, can be dealt with much more easily if you can, without thinking, buy the product and let them have it. No hassle, no tantrums, and you feel you are providing for your child in a way that most parents, and certainly most grandparents, in China never thought they would and were never able to enjoy it themselves as children. As diet has changed in China, it is children's diets that have changed the most. Older Chinese may be able to afford more, but they don't always want fast-food or Western food or snacks. Children do – their metabolisms tell them that as well as peer group pressure, doting parents and advertisers.

Grandparents are extremely helpful in lightening the child-rearing burden and allow for a couple to both remain working (stay-at-home mums are still rare in China), but can also be a major part of the problem.[4] With more and more parents working long hours, grandparents, usually quite willingly, are taking care of more and more children. This generation generally knows what it means to be hungry, not have a lot of choices and be deprived. Naturally, they are delighted that their grandchildren probably will not know any of these deprivations and will grow up in a country so radically different than anything their grandparents could have visualized in the 1970s, 1980s or even 1990s.

The desire of Chinese parents, grandparents, uncles and aunts to provide well for their children is natural enough, although sometimes the attention can be lavished a little too thickly. Chinese researchers believe that parents and grandparents, many of whom have themselves endured famine, are regularly overfeeding their children, both to express love and to flaunt their new wealth.

Researchers have drawn parallels to 1940s America and also admit that the One-Child Policy has led to excessive coddling and spoiling by parents and grandparents, who outnumber the kids six to one in what is referred to as the 'six-pockets syndrome' or the '4-2-1 indulgence factor': i.e., where an only child is spoiled not only by his parents but also by both sets of grandparents, who are living longer and are wealthier than ever.

The six-pockets syndrome allows for additional spending per child above and beyond the means of the parents, and for all spending to be lavished on the one child rather than spread across several. It not only means more spending per child, but also allows for the purchasing of items that might otherwise severely stretch the two parents' budget. This is especially true of higher-priced items deemed essential by many parents, such as infant formula, fresh milk, as well as regularly eating out. Of course, a wide array of products also becomes available to the child via the six-pockets syndrome, from more cans or coke or chocolate bars to PlayStations and branded clothing. China's One-Child Policy has now been in place long enough that a generation of children are growing up without aunts and uncles, but thanks to increased longevity, grandparents are now finding that they are helping their grandchildren get on

Table 25: **One Kid, Multiple Costs – The Parental Cost in China**

According to Shanghai Academy of Social Science estimates, the average cost of bringing up a child in Beijing and Shanghai, from pregnancy to the child finding their own place to live, breaks down as follows:

– Pregnancy (US$800)
– Delivery (US$400)
– Pre-kindergarten (US$5,900)
– Kindergarten (US$8,500)
– Primary school (US$12,400)
– Junior high school (US$6,500)
– Senior high school (US$7,600)
– College (US$14,400)
– First three years after college (US$5,800)
– Wedding (US$6,500)
– 30% down payment for a house (US$26,000)

This adds up to US$94,800, over what is likely to be a 30-year period. At 2006 currency exchange rates, this works out as about RMB752,000, or RMB25,000 a year (on average). Consider that in 2006 the average income in Beijing and Shanghai was between RMB35,000 and RMB36,000, you are looking at 70 per cent of the average annual wage in these cities going toward the expenses related to child rearing. It is therefore no surprise that both parents tend to work, or that they have high expectations in regard to careers and getting a good income.

the property ladder and are purchasing big ticket items (college fees, cars, etc.), just as they previously helped their own children.

Also important, but far harder to quantify with statistics, is the role children play in influencing wider family decisions. The importance of 'pester power' and the 'nag factor' are, of course, well known by both parents and advertising professionals. Eat at Pizza Hut rather than mum's favourite Sichuanese restaurant round the corner? Stop off for ice cream on the way home? Allow that extra packet of sweets at the supermarket checkout? These, and a host of other decisions affecting diet and lifestyle, result in purchases by adults that have been influenced by children. The combination of the elevated role of the Little Emperors in One-Child Policy China, rising wealth and greater access to a wider range of products in a now highly developed retail market means that China's urban consumer society can now be termed a 'filiarchy' – where children are in charge of a wide range of consumption decisionmaking. This can even extend to expensive electronics, where the children simply know more than their parents about the products and become advisors in making decisions about the relative merits of technological features.

Grandparents and the six-pockets syndrome is also playing a role in determining the relatively high amounts of disposable income pre-teens ('tweens' in marketing speak), teenagers and young adults have to spend. According to Chinese statistics, the total population of China between 14 and 24 years of age (they don't officially actually have a 'teens' category) in the country's major cities is around 50 million – equal to the total populations of Canada and Australia combined. Most urban teens are not working (Saturday jobs and part-time work for younger people is virtually nonexistent in urban China) and have a per capita disposable income of approximately RMB4,995 (US$720) a year. Not much perhaps, but they are also increasingly able to tap into their parent's pockets, too. Living at home, enjoying the six-pockets syndrome and with cash in their pocket.

Teenage disposable income was expected to rise to about RMB6,500 (US$936) by 2007 with an average annual increase of 9.2 per cent. This gives urban teens a total disposable income of RMB230 billion (US$33 billion) – or over 8 per cent of total urban disposable income available. That's approximately RMB525 (US$76) per month, not including what their families spend on them. By 2007 teens were arguably accounting for as much as 15 per cent of total urban expenditure – no wonder advertisers and brands are paying attention to them.[5]

A recent survey by the China Mainland Information Group found that for most urban teens, price wasn't that much of a factor – they prefer quality to price. They may take money from their parents or aunts, grandparents and other family members, but they insist on deciding how the money is spent. Over 50 per cent of Chinese teens believe that determining what they buy themselves is the most important thing about shopping. (Conclusion? Teenagers are in many senses a very universal category!) However, just how much they are truly making independent decisions is questionable, given that 50 per cent also agreed with the statement that they were greatly influenced by advertising.

Food is a major expenditure for teens, given the generally low cost of eating in China. Nearly 30 per cent of all food spending now goes to fast-food (with McDonald's and KFC relatively evenly pegged in terms of teens' favourite) and around 12 per cent on drinks. Most of the drinks spending is on non-alcoholic beverages, with Coca-Cola preferred by nearly 50 per cent of teens and Pepsi by only 20 per cent. Snacks, which many Western manufacturers had hoped would emerge as a bigger segment, still only accounts for just over 5 per cent of spending.

This reflects the social hub that eating out represents in Chinese society, only transcribed onto a generation that has been brought up under a constant barrage of fast and processed convenience food and soft drinks advertising, where the social gathering hubs are now fast-food outlets in shopping malls. The change in social patterns and eating patterns have certainly had an effect, and what that means for Chinese society and its youth can already be seen in an economically advanced Chinese society, especially just over the border in Hong Kong.

Hong Kong Offers an Example

When it comes to fat and children, China need look no further than Hong Kong for some idea of the future. Fat and obese children are a major problem in Hong Kong. Childhood obesity was first raised as an issue in the then British colony in 1962, with major policy discussions around the issues in the early 1970s and late 1980s. It hasn't gone away, and now 16.7 per cent of Hong Kong children are thought to be overweight or obese, a 5.1 per cent increase since 1993,[6] according to one source, or according to the Hong Kong Department of Health, almost one in five primary school kids are overweight and the mean weight of 18-year-old boys had risen 16 per cent in five years, and for girls, 11 per cent.

Certainly, the likes of McDonald's and KFC have found Hong Kong a great market and their restaurants proliferate across the Special Administrative Region (SAR). McDonald's has made major inroads in Hong Kong. As well as a number of 24-hour stores, delivery is also a major business in Hong

Kong. Additionally, Hong Kong has been one market where the Big Mac has successfully penetrated the schools system. As of mid-2004 over 100 McDonald's outlets were providing a daily service to schools. Admittedly, this privatization of Hong Kong's school meals service is nothing new; nutritionists had long bemoaned the rather poor quality, MSG-laden and fatty lunch boxes of rice and meat delivered to schools.

Hong Kong is a fast-food lover's paradise, probably second only to the Philippines in terms of per capita fast-food consumption in Asia – and the Philippines has its own obesity and weight issues. A staggering 98 per cent of Hong Kong customers visit McDonald's at least once a week compared with an international average of 60 per cent. There are a number of reasons for this, including the fact that Hong Kong is a very compact place – McDonald's has managed to be on nearly every corner – as well as the fact that many older people also visit branches, if only for coffee and gossip in the early morning. However, McDonald's has traditionally been a very heavy advertiser in Hong Kong and the compact nature of the territory means legislation requiring branches to not be located near schools is virtually impossible.

Additionally, the company has introduced a lot of locally specific products to their stores over the years. McDonald's, at least in the eyes of many Hong Kong children, remains 'cool' and eating habits begun in childhood often follow the individual through their adult years. Hence, McDonald's has no problem attracting the twenty- and thirty-something office workers of Hong Kong – they are used to it. Indeed, it seems, in Hong Kong at least, that McDonald's cool image also lingers into adulthood. Local Hong Kong newspaper columnist Allison Jones commented that 'It [McDonald's] occupies such a hallowed place in our culture that one of my friends was treated to dinner under the golden arches by her boyfriend on their first date. He thought it was romantic. I can't believe she married him.'[7]

Hong Kong is an example close to home, but many other Asian countries have reported rising obesity rates in children. In Japan, obesity in nine-year-old children has tripled while approximately 20 per cent of Australian children and adolescents are overweight or obese, according to the WHO, while in Thailand the prevalence of obesity in 5- to 12-year-old children rose from 12.2 per cent to 15–16 per cent in just two years. Children's changing eating habits obviously have a lot to do with it.

The Most Important Meal of the Day

Children's eating habits are changing as much as their office-working parents'. For instance, a nutrition survey carried out in 1992 showed that it was quite common for school pupils to have a breakfast lacking in important nutrients or to have no breakfast at all. In fact, 6.4 per cent of the primary and middle school students surveyed seldom ate breakfast. In 1994, another survey of eight Beijing urban primary and middle schools found that 5.3 per cent of the primary school pupils and 16 per cent of the middle school pupils seldom, if ever, ate breakfast. Then in 1998 another survey of more than 2,000 Beijing primary and middle school pupils showed that the incidence of skipping breakfast had increased again, to 16.1 per cent of primary pupils and 32.8 per cent of middle school pupils. The survey also showed that of those who did eat breakfast, 9.5 per cent of the primary school pupils and 10 per cent of the middle school pupils ate their breakfast at a vendor's stand, or while walking. The reasons for this seem to be mostly related to the early start of the school day as well as the high incidence of both parents working.

In the same study, it was found that the improper nutritional content of what the Chinese kids ate for breakfast was also a cause for concern. The survey found that 66 per cent of urban primary and middle school pupils did not have milk at breakfast, 60 per cent of them did not have soybean milk, 17.9 per cent of them did not have eggs. Skipping breakfast and/or eating an unhealthy or low-protein breakfast, has been proven to harm children's physical development and interfere with their ability to study. Of course, shifting to Western-style cereal-based breakfasts would not be a total cure for the problem, despite the current push on these courtesy of advertisers in China – America's independent and nonprofit Consumers Union (CU) tested a range of the most popular breakfast cereals available in the USA (and now being launched in China) and declared many of them to simply be the equivalent of a 'doughnut in a bowl' due to their high sugar and fat content.[8]

Many children, armed with pocket money, were acquiring their own breakfast at c-stores or street stalls with all the attendant bad choices that would naturally involve. In recent years the number of street stalls and vendors has been reduced on China's urban streets, and so children are increasingly likely to derive their away-from-home breakfast in c-stores or (as the authors have regularly observed while taking their own unhealthy breakfast) in McDonald's, KFC or other fast-food outlets, which open at 7 a.m. and provide a relatively cheap breakfast menu within the spending power of middle-class urban school children.

School Lunches

Meanwhile, in Hong Kong, much of the debate around children and obesity has centred on the question of school lunches. Of course, children's diet and school lunches have been issues wherever childhood obesity has become an issue – for instance, celebrity chef Jamie Oliver and his school dinners programmes in the UK. The school lunch is important it seems – research in China's Jiangsu province among children from high socio-economic status (HSES) families (official Chinese code for middle class) by the Jiangsu Provincial Centre for Disease Control and Prevention, and Norway's University of Oslo, found that 76 per cent of the school students had three meals a day regularly, but 8.1 per cent of urban students, as opposed to 3.4 per cent of rural students, had breakfast only one to three times per week or less frequently. The report also noted that 'More than half of the students reported a liking for Western-style fast foods including hamburgers, soft drinks and chocolate. Among high SES boys, 21.5 per cent consumed soft drinks on a daily basis; however, as many as 72.3 per cent wanted to drink soft drinks more often if they could afford it.' The report's authors concluded, 'SES and urban location were positively associated with frequency of intake of high-energy foods. Reported food preferences may enforce this trend. Nutrition education for adolescents and parents is needed to promote healthy eating. Health Authorities should strengthen the monitoring of food intake and its association with overweight/obesity.'[9]

Hong Kong school lunches have raised concerns on a number of issues, staple dishes such as fried rice and noodles being high in fat, cholesterol and sodium. In 2006 Hong Kong launched a campaign entitled EatSmart@school. hk to promote territory-wide healthy eating. The campaign included issuing new Nutritional Guidelines on School Lunch for Primary School Students to guide caterers to provide balanced diets to 300,000 students in some 600 whole-day primary schools. At the time, the Assistant Director of Health, Dr. Regina Ching, told the press that 'the campaign would promote healthy lunches and snacks at schools and cultivate healthy eating practices among children.'[10]

But it hasn't been easy, as anyone visiting a fast-food restaurant in Hong Kong around lunchtime or just after school can testify. School meals can be improved, but children still have their own disposable income to spend. Schools can ban fatty foods, and have, both in Hong Kong and elsewhere; the Bangkok government, for instance, banned sweets, carbonated drinks, sweetened milk and fatty foods from 433 schools across the Thai capital following a report that 25 per cent of pupils were obese.

School lunches in China have also been a subject of debate regarding quality and the ability of kids to skip out and visit fast-food and other outside catering establishments during their lunch hour, as well as before and after school. As we've seen, many of them also have the disposable income to afford to do this regularly. Some schools, invariably the more privileged ones, often private or semi-private, have made changes. Schools have tried to introduce more vegetables and less deep-fried food and pre-packaged food. Interestingly the results appear to mirror those in other countries, including the UK. Like Jamie Oliver, Chinese teachers and school nutritionists have found themselves up against kids who have the spending power to simply eat what they want outside the school, parents who have insisted their children have what they like rather than what the school nutritionist has devised, and parents sending their children to school with packed lunches featuring HFSS foods that undermine the school lunch programme. For less privileged urban schools, principals complain that their budgets are already too stretched without additional spending or time devoted to lunch menus.

Perhaps the kids need more exercise?

Sport for All?

And it seems few if any really do get exercise. According to a survey by the Chinese Centre for Disease Control and Prevention (CDC), 94.1 per cent of obese Chinese kids engage in no physical activity whatsoever.[11]

As China has reformed, so the media and sports business have become more professional, brands have sought domestic sponsors and the roster of China's elite athletes has grown significantly. Yao Ming stands tall (literally) as a representative of Chinese sporting prowess, as do several other Chinese basketball players who have made it to the NBA, a number of Chinese footballers who have made it to the top European leagues and those who have excelled internationally in their chosen sports, from Liu Xiang, the world record breaking hurdler, Fu Mingxia and China's other award-winning divers, the national volleyball, hockey, table tennis and other teams. All have become adopted national heroes, major celebrity endorsers and have agents, wealth and fame. All of this, of course, reached a massive crescendo in the summer of 2008 at the Beijing Olympics.

But, so much for professional and elite sports and elite athletes. Unfortunately, nobody ever got fit or lost weight simply watching other people win medals on TV. Unless this growth and success at the high performance end of the sports spectrum can be matched by the dissemination of a broad-based mass sports culture – one that emphasizes sport for all, from childhood into adulthood, for general exercise, health and other positives (such as teamwork, participation, etc.), then all the gold medals in the world won't shift one inch from urban China's collectively bulging waistline.

Many in China would agree (off the record) that sport in China has become over professionalized and fixated on medals and performance, with a disproportionate amount of money funnelled into the training of elite athletes capable of competing on the world stage. Under Chairman Mao, sports became firmly established as political in China. From the start of the New China, Mao exhorted the masses to take up sport and physical fitness. Sport became another vehicle to channel people's energies, promote the collective spirit and fuel a resurgent nationalism. The Great Helmsman set the tone personally with his Yangtze swim in 1966, and it seemed little of the resurgent nationalism had changed by the opening ceremony of the Beijing Games.

However, the concept of 'sport for all' quickly gave way to a system designed to turn out top-class athletes rather than a healthy population. By the mid-1980s, by the government's own estimate, there was just one gymnasium for every 3.5 million people and many of these were off limits to ordinary people, being controlled by schools, the army or other institutions for their own private use. The State Commission for Sport didn't seem to care much and continued – at the insistence of the highest levels of the political system – to funnel the vast bulk of funds made available for sport and recreation into elite sports schools designed to train gold medal athletes in a sort of medals sausage factory that selected kids at a young age, took them away from home and drilled them mercilessly in both their sport and national pride. By the mid-1980s, when most people could only dream of going to a gym, China had 3,200 elite sports schools with 500,000 students enrolled.

Still, despite the central government's sports thrust, some educationalists and sports officials did make attempts to promote a sport for all ethos and encourage grassroots sporting activity in the 1980s. Football was promoted at both primary and secondary levels with all manner of programmes, cups and championships initiated. However, while recognizing the importance of the inculcation of a sporting and exercise culture at a young age, there was an overwhelming emphasis still on 'elite' and 'excellence' rather than 'participation'. Ultimately, rather than disseminating involvement in sports horizontally, it ended up becoming increasingly vertical and fixated on seeking trophies and prestige. Various other initiatives around sports such as tennis were slightly more broadly based, at least in terms of facilities, and may have yielded more participation. At the same time, it is worth noting the rise of golf in China, but this remains a sport for a tiny minority of people (despite the vast amount of land it takes up). Most golf clubs are technically bankrupt in China due to overcapacity; many Chinese officials dropped the game after a senior leader declared it a major source of corrupt deals. And few overweight teens or white collars will ever get out on the greens to work of their spare tyre.

Crucially, school sports have dropped off dramatically in recent years due to a range of factors, including the loss of many school sports fields and areas, due to property development and urban land grabs, parental pressure to emphasise academic studies over seemingly 'unimportant' sports and physical exercise and the rise of a litigious society in which schools are often wary of organizing sports where children could be injured and the school potentially sued by parents. Perhaps the best and most imaginative excuse offered by many school principals, when encouraged by sports-for-all-activists to offer more school sports activities, was the rather odd reason that using their sports grounds would lead to higher maintenance bills!

A similar situation has occurred in Hong Kong, which in this sense, gives some indication of how little exercise Chinese school children may now be getting. The indication came from three surveys undertaken by Professor Albert Lee, Director of the Centre for Health Education and Health Promotion at the Chinese University of Hong Kong and attached to the Department of Community and Family Medicine. In Hong Kong, a cross-sectional study conducted in 2004 of 26,111 students aged 10 to 19 found that less than one-third reportedly participated in vigorous exercise regularly, approximately one-third of the students frequently consumed an unhealthy diet, and 2 per cent of the students were frequent smokers.[12] Another survey of 3,516 junior secondary Hong Kong students in 2001 revealed that 64.9 per cent took no regular exercise.[13] Similar surveys across the border in southern China in the city of Guangzhou, revealed similar findings as early as 2003, with 60 per cent of adolescents not undertaking any regular exercise.[14]

Yet, there were people in the sports promotion field who really wanted to encourage sports and exercise participation across the wider society. Perhaps ironically, many of these 'grass roots' projects came to an almost total halt in July 2001 when China was officially awarded the 2008 Olympiad. From that point on, the Beijing Olympics – and by extension – sport in China, became a nationalistic tool of the government. What mattered was winning, and winning publicly, at the world's most prominent sporting event. Funds for programmes, facilities, personnel and schools were almost immediately diverted away from the community into the sports-medal sausage factories; sport, in the form of the Olympics, was to become something the vast majority of the Chinese people would watch, consume and take pride in, but not participate in. Though they could not speak out publicly, many involved at the ground level of sport in communities across China were depressed and felt a golden opportunity to create a sport for all had been missed with the intense focus on winning and medals tallies. Rowan Simons, a British sports entrepreneur who launched the Club Football grass-roots soccer initiative in Beijing, recalled the problem of local sports organizers once the Olympics deal was sealed, in his book *Bamboo Goalposts*:

'Sadly, the one area that was likely to remain immune to criticism and closed to change would be the sports system itself. Over at the glorious

Sports Ministry, officials were being tasked with making sure China won as many gold medals as possible. The first order from on high was to CONCENTRATE ON THE ELITE.'[15]

At a high level conference, held prior to the Games and organized by Beijing's prestigious Tsinghua University around the subject of 'Post-Olympics Sport', some emboldened and unusually outspoken Chinese academics argued that hosting the Games had retarded China's sports reforms by at least ten years. Any last hope that in the run-up to the Games, the Chinese public's heightened awareness of and interest in sports was dashed finally, when after having announced in 2006 that all Beijing schools should keep their sports facilities open to all as a sporting remit of the Olympics, the government changed its mind, declaring instead that all sports facilities had to close to outside use under the 'public safety' remit of the Olympics. Any Beijing kids feeling encouraged by the endless sports-related TV and media coverage and feeling encouraged to emulate their sporting heroes and their fitness, found themselves with literally nowhere to go. They could, of course, see their sporting heroes on adverts for McDonald's, Coca-Cola and a host of other HFSS products in any shop.

Not that grass roots sport went away entirely. Instead, it took to the streets as determined kids continued to find spaces to play sports. Urban Chinese teenagers took to basketball, attracted by the style and image of the game as much as by Yao Ming's success in America. Where interest in football had briefly soared following China's qualification for the 2002 FIFA World Cup held jointly in South Korea and Japan, China's poor performance at the tournament and subsequent failure to qualify for the FIFA World Cup 2006 in Germany, dampened enthusiasm. Football, though still massively popular, became a sport to be watched on TV with up to 20 million people tuning in for English Premier League Games (while they were widely available on free-to-air channels) as well as other European and regional leagues. At the same time, crowds grew for the Chinese football league despite a rash of scandals. Yet, despite the huge viewing figures for football, it had become largely a spectator sport either at grounds or on TV. David Beckham was mobbed at Chinese airports, as he was everywhere else from Kuala Lumpur to Los Angeles. Former England manager Sven-Goran Erikson was paid to promote a property development in China while Michael Owen and a host of European and Latin American soccer stars (as well as, of course, the ubiquitous Becks) were prominent faces on TV advertising, billboards and magazine pages – again often for HFSS foods. However, it has been America's National Basketball Association (NBA) that has best capitalized on grass-roots sport in China, with local leagues and other initiatives encouraging kids to play basketball (and, of course, watch and buy related merchandise).

Other sports also appeared and appealed to younger people, sports that seemed partially to have escaped the Communist medals fixation and combined exercise with fashion and lifestyle – X-sports. Back in the 1990s a demonstration of skateboarding or BMX biking in Beijing or Shanghai would draw an excited, intrigued and sometimes puzzled crowd; a few years later, similar scenes were witnessed in tier-two and tier-three cities. A skateboard and BMX demonstration in the central shopping district of Shenyang in 2002 led to a scrum that had to be controlled by the police, such was the fascination with these new sports.

China's elite sports schools continue to take very young children and groom them for glory as medal winners. At the same time, hundreds of thousands of less-naturally gifted or selected kids are getting less sport, less exercise and are suffering for it.

It's Tough Being a Kid

China's children find themselves faced with a confusing and conflicting image of what they should look like. Plump and larger children and babies still feature widely in many adverts and political propaganda posters, particularly in the countryside. On television, big kids often feature in programming, but they are also surrounded by advertisements showing teenagers and young adults as almost universally slim and thin. Increasingly, they are seeing magazine articles, newspaper features and advertising for diets and slimming aids. They can often be understandably confused by the mixed messages given by their parents concerning their weight when they are children and pre-teens, and then when they become older. In this sense, they are perhaps caught in a similar dilemma to kids the world over in developed urban societies. For many young people, especially women, this mixed message of body shape is causing problems.

Chapter 9

THE FAT AND THE THIN – CHINA'S BODY IMAGE

To Get Thin is Glorious

When discussing the issue of weight and obesity in this book, so far we have attempted to limit ourselves to the question of what happens when an individual's weight, or body mass, impinges upon their good health. We have identified weight gain as symptomatic of rising personal wealth in a fast-developing Chinese society that has led to a rise in obesity as has happened in many other nations, notably North America and Western Europe, and is also occurring in other rapidly developing societies such as India.

All societies have historically had changing notions of what is a desirable weight and body image for its members. Perceptions of what is desirable shift. 'Rubenesque' is still used to describe a certain sort of 'full bodied' figure in women, and refers of course to the art of the seventeenth century Flemish painter Peter Paul Rubens, best known for portraying full-bodied women. China is no different in this sense and Chinese art, literature, advertising and media all reflect the changing notions of desirable body shape over the generations.

Indeed, debates over the most desirable body shape have formed part of the overall discussion of beauty among the urban Chinese elite for generations. This was particularly so during the Republican period (1911–1949) when the urban elites were experimenting with new ideas and philosophies and encountering Western ideas of body shape and beauty, particularly in Shanghai, and particularly when it came to women. Following the 1911 Republican revolution, unbound feet became common, and according to one historian of Chinese fashion, clothing and style, Antonia Finnane, quickly accepted, while the 1920s saw vociferous debates among the urban elite about short hair as well as breast binding – a prohibition against breast binding had been introduced in 1927 in Guangdong province leading to much debate in the newspapers regarding the superiority or desirable preference for bound versus 'natural' breasts. This in turn led to a debate about the suitability of the brassiere (invented only a few years previously in New York, but not introduced into China until 1927). At the time, Chinese women preferred what was variously known as the *xiaomajia* (little vest), *xiaoshan* (little shirt) or *doudu* (an apron for the upper body), none of which provided support for the breasts. As Finnane writes, 'The little vest was designed to constrain the breasts and streamline the body.'[1] Exposure of the body was considered immodest, but streamlining was seen as fashionable. The well-known *qipao*, invariably worn with a little vest underneath, would only accentuate this trend in streamlining. Later, in the 1930s, *qipao* lengths would move from full length to shorter, meaning that those arbiters of body image would pay more attention to legs.

Aside from the obvious body-shape-changing tradition of foot binding, it could be argued that traditionally, Chinese did less to change the appearance of their shape than European cultures. Chinese fashion developed nothing to rival the contraptions of tightly laced corsets that ultimately pushed up the breasts creating cleavage, frames for skirts, steel stays, etc., that forced waists in and everything else out. Chinese clothing was often more functional, even at an elite level, and certainly less revealing and more modest compared to the European fashions. Until the 1930s at least, clothing was largely designed to obscure the body shape except for the urban elite, where accentuating aspects of the body occurred.

Certainly, in the Republican period there had been concern over obesity that mirrored much of that seen in Europe and America, obesity being reflective in some way of a weakness at the heart of society and so, by extension, of the state. However, of course, the defining fears of famine throughout the Second World War, the subsequent civil war and then the great famines under Mao (1958–1961) and the hardship endured during the Cultural Revolution meant that when greater security and prosperity arrived, people would eat more to make up for the privations of the preceding era – literally, famine to feast.

But that was then and this is now. In China, in this current period, thin is seen as preferable to a fuller-bodied figure in the vast majority of advertising and in public figures offering themselves (whether they like it or not) as role models, such as actresses and pop stars. The perception of the 'correct' body shape being tall and thin is reinforced in the vast majority of advertising aimed particularly at girls and women. Anything less than skinny has become, in many people's eyes, synonymous with ugly and also increasingly with a bad 'lifestyle'. As Sander Gilman, who has written on the cultural history of obesity and also on China has observed, 'Fat is now a sign of the deleterious effect of the modern (read American) influence on the body.'[2] 'Lifestyle' is a major buzzword at the end of the first decade of the twenty-first century in China; lifestyle, how to have one and what one to have (invariably 'aspirational') appears everywhere from glossy magazines to TV chat shows, and a key component of the generally accepted desirable lifestyle (apart from wealth and the acquisition of assets from property and cars to travel and luxury brands) is thinness. Thin is beautiful, thin gets you the perfect partner, perfect job and all the material wealth you could want – according to the advertisers and magazine editors.

The Fat/Thin Contradiction

There's a contradiction when it comes to body image in China that is affected by the rising rates of obesity. Urban China is getting fatter while its personal body image is getting thinner. And despite a rash of articles in Chinese magazines and fashion press about the arrival of the 'S-shape' in China, from everyone including superstar actress Gong Li to celebrity blogger Sister Furong, reports indicate that many girls still preferred the 'I-shape'.

Body image and, subsequently, weight loss have become major topics and often obsessions for the Chinese media and consumers, from leading Chinese Internet portal Sina.com reporting that the most asked 'How to' query their search engine received was 'How to lose weight?' (followed closely by 'how to invest in the stock market?'), to pride that in 2007 a 23-year-old secretary from Beijing was crowned Miss World at the ridiculous tournament's now permanent home on China's Hainan Island.

In 2001 the Chinese branch of the International Life Sciences Institute surveyed overweight people in Beijing, Shanghai and Guangzhou. The survey revealed that most respondents were attempting to lose weight primarily to improve their appearance, while less than a quarter saw losing weight as primarily a way to improve their health. The institute conducted the survey to highlight that weight loss could help people avoid chronic disease, but the truly revealing part of the survey was that over 95 per cent of the respondents had tried a weight-loss product, though just over 50 per cent reported that they had never continued with a single weight-loss product for more than two months.

China's economy, its urbanization and consumption growth are all moving at what feels like warp speed. In this hyper-fast China, 'slimming' pills and surgery appeal to many, rather than the apparently harder slog of the gym, as providing a short cut to weight loss. In many cases, these 'instant remedies' are themselves causes of deteriorating health and can be, in extreme cases, killers. And at the same time the expanding media and advertising industries, in their broadest sense, have elevated the concept of the thin and the beautiful as the most successful, further pushing people, especially women, to find 'get thin quick' solutions, while the same media and advertising industry 'pushes' unhealthy and obesity-creating foods and drinks at them just as remorselessly.

But it's all a bit contradictory and confusing for people. Magazine adverts, TV advertising, pop and movie stars as well as the endless parade of model

Table 26: **Asian Women Considering Cosmetic Surgery**

South Korea – 53%
Taiwan – 40%
Japan – 39%
Thailand – 37%
Vietnam – 30%
Philippines – 17%
Singapore – 10%
India – 4%
Malaysia – 4%

Women Considering Themselves Overweight
Japan – 69%
Taiwan – 63%
Hong Kong – 49%
South Korea – 47%
Thailand – 47%
Vietnam – 44%
China – 43%
Malaysia – 39%
Singapore – 39%
Philippines – 33%
India – 31%

Source: Unilever Real Beauty Survey – 2005.

shows and beauty pageants on Chinese TV, all suggest the ideal body image is thin. At the same time, a raft of advertising pushes the idea that chubby babies and fat children are symbols of health and, probably, later success. However, for a child who has grown to adulthood overweight or obese suddenly becoming model-thin – 'size zero' – is impossible without binge dieting or surgery. Gyms and exercise work, but take time. A changed diet works, but requires information and dedication. Perhaps it would be OK if it was just a question of a few celebrities, but the effects of this mismatch between heavier youngsters (usually through the fault of their parents rather than themselves) feeling they need to be stick-thin teens is widespread and affects people's lives directly – especially women.

Wanted: Only the Pretty Need Apply

Time Magazine recently reported the comments of the owner of a 'beauty centre' in Shenzen's Jiulong City Mall: 'China has too many people. How do you make yourself stand out from 1.3 billion? Imagine [that] your boss sees two people of similar ability. He will definitely pick the person with the better appearance.' The growing number of overweight people does not appear to be leading to a greater acceptance of overweight members of the community. Lax job discrimination regulations and enforcement mean that people, women in particular again, are regularly denied jobs for being not just considered overweight, but also for being 'ugly'. Discrimination due to weight in China is technically illegal, but rarely enforced, and cases of discrimination seldom if ever brought before the courts.

For job applicants, fat is clearly not something many prospective employers in China want. According to a report in the *China Youth Daily*, Li Ya, a 24-year-old Beijing woman who weighs 90 kgs (198 lb), was turned down or quickly dismissed seven times in only ten months following her college graduation:

> Land developers, department stores, and trading companies all either rejected her applications or quickly gave her the push. No matter how well she performed, her waistline, she lamented, was a permanent stigma.[3]

Other examples have appeared frequently in the Chinese press, and continue to appear. For instance, one of Beijing's largest electrical appliance retail chains demanded its staff keep their weight within a range dictated by senior management (who's own weight was not noted). Reportedly, two months after the directive was issued, staff whose weight remained above the 'preferred range' were to be fined half a month's wages. Anyone whose 'fat situation' remained unchanged after a further two months would be fired. Height requirements are also still regularly stated for both women and men in job adverts (the seemingly arbitrary cut of point of 5' 8" seems to apply for men in many jobs adverts – below that and many jobs with a public interface appear to be impossible to get).

It's not just in China's private sector either. In June 2004 policemen in the northeast Chinese city of Harbin were officially warned that they might lose their jobs if they became too fat. The Patrol Police branch of the Public Security Bureau of Harbin passed a new regulation stating that policemen with waistlines more than 0.90 m would be laid off. Overweight cops had till the end of the year to lose the excess, with those cops under 30 years of age required to keep their weight under 70 kg and their waistlines within 0.83 m while those between 30 and 40 required to keep their weight below 75 kg and waistlines under 0.90 m.[4]

China's top legislators in the National People's Congress (NPC) met in 2005 for their annual session and once again discussed the introduction of a national equal opportunities law governing all types of job-related discrimination. Such an all-encompassing law is yet to make it formally to the statute books, though new labour rights legislation has been passed in recent years tightening up hiring and firing practices. However, as a party to the UN International Covenant on Economic, Social and Cultural Rights, China is technically obliged to eliminate all forms of discrimination in economic, social and cultural spheres and prevent discriminatory practices in both the public and the private sectors. This requires the elimination of discrimination on the grounds of gender, age and appearance, or requirements that arbitrarily exclude individuals from jobs for which they are professionally qualified constitutes discrimination.

Yet adverts calling for applicants to be 'beautiful', 'pretty' or 'slim' continue to appear. The 2008 Beijing Olympics saw this tendency rise to a new height as a rash of adverts appeared for Olympics-related jobs calling for these qualifications and little else, once again indicating how engrained notions of beauty and slimness are in many employers' minds right up to the central government. Zhao Dongming, Director of the Cultural Activities Department at Beijing's Organizing Committee for the Games (BOCOG), commenting on the hiring of staff for the Olympics told the Chinese press:

> We have certain requirements for their height, since they are to present the medals to our athletes. They need to be of a height between 1.68 m (5' 6") and 1.78 m (5' 10"). That's above average.

While there were no specific weight requirements, Zhao added, 'Generally speaking, they can't be too fat. Their figure should be good. They shouldn't be too heavy.'[5] Presumably being overweight too would be an insurmountable problem to giving an athlete a medal!

Diets and Dieting

Dieting, of course, has a long tradition in societies where excess weight, either real or imagined, has occurred. China has not traditionally been a country susceptible to the hordes of diet 'fads', as weight was simply not an issue for the vast majority of the population until recently. While there is a long and ancient tradition of deriving medical benefits from adopting certain dietary practices and eating certain foods to cure or prevent illness, specific diets for weight loss were not widely offered. Dieting, in the sense of fasting, is also not traditionally part of most Chinese people's belief system, historically or previously (excepting those of the Muslim faith in China, and converts to Christianity observing Lent, etc.). Buddhism, in its

Chinese forms, has rarely prioritized fasting for its practitioners (though the rules can and have been different for monks and nuns), and fasting is not intrinsic to Daoism particularly, or as a component of the more recent revival of a somewhat selective Confucianism in China. Again, it has been the shortage of food that has been more of a problem in more recent Chinese history, rather than abstaining for any particular reason, religious, social or medical.

This is now changing. Of course, doctors can use dieting as one of the tools (along with the injunctions to stop smoking and take more exercise) they can prescribe for patients concerned about their weight, or whom doctors believe could improve their health through weight loss. But diets and dieting is also a business, and the diet business has come to China in response to people's concerns about their weight.

So far, there has been some resistance to diet plans in China as noted by observers. A combination of the inability of an offered diet regimen to 'guarantee' weight loss combined with a now widespread and growing distrust of advertising and product claims in the wake of various scandals and repeated exposures of products offering false claims, has led an increasing number of the Chinese public to distrust such offerings. Weight Watchers International opened its first China outlet in Shanghai in 2008, as Weight Watchers Danone (China) Weight Loss Consultation Company, owned by a joint venture between Weight Watchers International and Danone, the French water-to-biscuits conglomerate that is highly active in China's food and beverage market. Weight Watchers' plan is to spread across China opening branches. Whether or not the venture will be successful remains to be seen.

China's rapid rise and the desire to get rich quick has meant that many people seek rapid gratification – instant weight loss – and this, combined with the rise of cosmetic surgery outlets, both private and in state hospitals (not to mention completely unlicensed 'clinics') and its relative low cost by international standards, has meant that the knife and the pill have often become the preferred weight loss method over the diet plan or exercise.

Body Beautiful, Courtesy of the Surgeon

Across China, countless women, and some men, are undergoing cosmetic surgery as a route to fame and fortune – be it an office job or a modelling career, or perhaps just a job in a retail store. As China becomes obsessed with beauty, levels of perfection get costlier and harder to attain. A 29-year-old Beijing-based actress and singer, Shadow Zhang, claimed in the *South*

China Morning Post that she couldn't find a boyfriend. 'I think it's partly my looks; I'm too strong. My mother said once maybe I should have a job done on my lips. They are too big. It's not the Chinese beauty ideal.'[6] This kind of story is common now in China as cosmetic surgery becomes a must-have accessory. Indeed, the industry is raking in over US$2.4 billion a year, according to *Xinhua*.

Shanghai's Ren'ai Hospital advertises its newly imported South Korean plastic surgeons in the city's taxis. Across Shanghai there are now over 250 private cosmetic surgery clinics alone, an increase from 130 in 2002, with the number of operations leaping by 20 per cent a year. Each Chinese Lunar New Year holiday sees a rush in demand for larger eyes and bigger noses at Shanghai clinics, which perform over 30 operations a day. Over the summer, another rush occurs as women take advantage of the holidays to have surgery and recuperate while the swelling goes down before returning to work.

A great deal of the pressure comes from the perceived need to be beautiful to get a good job as well as conforming to traditional ideas of beauty and parental pressure – in one reported instance, a six-year-old child asked for double eyelids. Another mother insisted a doctor plant two dimples in her three-year-old daughter to cultivate her sense of being a 'model'. Recently, a retailer in Nanjing placed a recruitment ad for salesgirls stating that they would be paid according to their beauty – those deemed most beautiful would get a higher commission rate than those deemed not so beautiful. This is the downside of China's 'beauty economy'.

Artificially enhancing beauty to get a job is now big business in China. Chen Qi, 21, a performing arts student in Shanghai, recently had an eyelash transplant in the city's No.9 People's Hospital.

> My eyelashes were thin and dull. I felt less attractive than the other girls in my class. Even with mascara, my eyes didn't shine. And on hot days mascara just melts, making you look like a panda. My goal is to become a professional performer, so the way I look really counts. And I am not alone. Some of my classmates have also had plastic surgery, fixing eyes and noses.

It's nothing new. The *Chengdu Evening News* reported in 2004 that a girl persuaded her father to sell one of his kidneys to raise money for her plastic surgery operation:

> Zhang Fang, 18, left her hometown in Anyue County for Chengdu, capital of Sichuan Province, to find a job there. Learning that having an

attractive appearance would help her find a good job, Zhang persuaded her father to sell his kidney to fund an operation. The father went to Xi'an to sell the kidney, but reporters there persuaded him to give up the idea and send his daughter back to school.[7]

School children demanding plastic surgery became something of a media sensation in 2004 – *China Information Times* reported that Chinese teenagers were being given cosmetic surgery by their parents as a reward for their hard work in school. Three hospitals in Guangzhou reported that 90 per cent of their plastic surgery patients were middle school pupils. Parents were paying for the surgery to reward children for passing university entrance exams and also in the hope that better looks would lead to a better future. Doctors say the girls generally favoured nose jobs or work around their eyes, while most of the boys wanted liposuction.[8] These extreme examples made the news because they were extreme, though the vast majority of those going under the knife in the name of beauty are just regular people who've saved for the operation.

For some, surgical enhancement has become a fixation. One woman in western China has reportedly had 48 cosmetic surgery operations, including 18 on her nose, in an attempt to make herself more beautiful. The 30-year-old from Kunming, Yunnan Province, reportedly spent RMB200,000 (US$28,811) over five years.[9] As the demand for cosmetic surgery has boomed in popularity in China in recent years, worryingly unlicensed clinics have been springing up all too frequently, leading to a rash of legal cases after operations went wrong, sometimes with permanent disfigurement the result and some with fatal and tragic results. According to the *China Quality Daily*, an official consumer protection newspaper, over 200,000 lawsuits have been filed in the past decade against cosmetic surgery practitioners.[10] And it's become a long-running media obsession; in 2005, TV stations across the country followed the case of 24-year-old Hao Lulu, who had four rounds of 'all over' plastic surgery to make herself more attractive after a friend called her 'plain'.

One offshoot of the plastic surgery fashion is the number of instant celebrities that have been created by people who have apparently turned their life around after cosmetic surgery. One young woman called Yang Yuan became a national star after a beauty contest refused her admission because she had had extensive cosmetic surgery. She had already made it through the first rounds of the Miss Intercontinental Beijing contest before she was disqualified.

The national press coverage that Yang Yuan received led to the launch of a series of 'Cinderella Pageants', more unkindly dubbed 'Ugly Contests' by the

Table 27: **Most Popular Cosmetic Surgery Operations in China**

Liposuction – surgery in which localized areas of fat are removed from beneath the skin using a suction-pump device inserted through a small incision

Double Eyelids – making the eye rounder and more 'Western' through the addition of an extra fold or the removal of the double ellipse (blepharoplasty)

Higher Nose bridges – to slim the nostrils and turn down the nose creating a generally more 'Western appearance' (rhinoplasty)

Eyelash transplants – approximate cost: US$1,200

Chin tuck – effectively having your jaw line shaved (mentoplasty)

Lips – either fuller or thinner augmentation

Breast – invariably enhancement and also breast lifting (mastopexy)

Source: *Xtribes China* from interviews with cosmetic surgery clinics in Shanghai.

press, that have become popular with those who want cosmetic surgery but can't afford it. The rules of this (somewhat humiliating) contest dictate that the ugliest woman wins and is then rewarded with enough plastic surgery to transform her into a beauty. She then returns to the show to reveal her transformation and, she hopes, pick up a bunch of lucrative product endorsement deals. One young woman, Zhang Di, who won a pageant and had a month of intensive surgery, told the press that she felt like '…the luckiest girl on the planet'. Most of these competitions are actually advertising promotions for one or other of the new private cosmetic surgery clinics.

Yang Yuan is just one of a number of 'artificial beauties' that have become celebrities in China. Apparently, the public loves them and have criticized the beauty show organizers who demanded only natural beauties on blogs and bulletin boards. Yang Yuan told the Chinese press after being ousted from the pageant, 'Is it not good to make society full of beautiful people?' Yang claims she undertook the extensive and expensive surgery because she wanted 'to be equal to beautiful women'.

The aforementioned 'artificial beauty' who has achieved national recognition, Hao Lulu, spent RMB208,251 (US$30,000) on 14 different procedures in a Beijing clinic. The Chinese press printed her diary of the operations where she wrote, 'Everybody wants natural beauty, but nobody is perfect, everybody has flaws, but now we have shortcuts to beauty.' The problem reached a height of media frenzy when Chen Lili, a transsexual, was disqualified from the provincial heats of China's Miss Universe competition even though, according to the *Shanghai Morning Post*, she '…seemed to outshine all the beauty queens onstage.' Chen, a successful model, was known as Chen Yongjin, or Brave Soldier, before she had a sex change operation in 2003.

Men have not proved immune to the instant beauty cult, either. In 2004, 30 men competed in what the organizers claimed was China's first male pageant for the chance to receive RMB45,000 (US$6,483) in free plastic surgery, courtesy of sponsor Shanghai Kinway Plastic & Cosmetic Surgery Centre. Cosmetic surgery clinics have begun attracting men through their advertising, offering a range of popular procedures including stomach reduction, male breast reduction (gynecomastia) and pectoral muscle implants.

The downside to all this is that the industry's growth has come with very little regulation, hence, the more than 200,000 malpractice lawsuits that have been filed in the last ten years concerning botched operations. Among 4,000 people who had plastic surgery in the 2004 summer holidays, a reported 10 per cent came back to make up for the flaws left from previous operations. Jiang Hua, a spokesman for the Changzheng Hospital, said most of the patients went to unqualified hospitals that used inappropriate materials that even caused rotten noses or breasts.[11]

Hao Lulu, Yang Yuan and a raft of other 'artificial beauties' all cite as reasons behind their desire for surgery: the plethora of beautiful women used in advertising in China that have created impossible markers for many women. With beauty raised to the level of an academic qualification or skill, life for the ugly, or those who perceive themselves or are perceived by an interviewing manager to be ugly, is tough.

Chinese TV has played a major role through its seemingly saturated coverage of beauty pageants and model shows which can be seen on multiple channels nightly. Until the last few years, beauty pageants were a novelty in China. Mao dismissed them as bourgeois nonsense, declaring that their participants were 'lacking in self- respect'. Not any more. Chinese women now stand in line to enter beauty shows run by TV stations with prize money that often reaches RMB1 million (US$146,000) or more. As elsewhere in the world many young Chinese women see beauty pageants as springboards to 'instant celebrity' and careers in show business or fashion.

The turnaround in opinion is so fast that even though in 2002 police raided the qualification heats of Miss China, less than a year later, the government had announced that the country would host the finals of Miss World – every year. They were dutifully held in a specially built pavilion on Hainan Island and won by Ireland's Rosanna Davison, much to the bemusement of many Chinese viewers who believed Miss China to be the obvious choice and declared Ms Davison 'fat'.

Most of the pageants are televised, and paid for by advertising, largely from cosmetics firms. China's cosmetics market is worth over RMB14 billion (US$2.05 billion) a year, according to the China Association of Fragrance, Flavour and Cosmetics Industry. The state-run body estimates that the Chinese spent RMB46 billion (US$6.73 billion) on cosmetics in 2007, and it predicts that the market will grow by between 9–11 per cent over the next five years. Beauty pageants are also a central theme of many adverts with the winners being the girls who used the featured product – shampoo, soap, skin cream, toothpaste, etc.

Though the government has shown some wariness about these sorts of advertising-sponsored pageants, it appears the trend will continue. *The People's Daily*, the official mouthpiece of the Communist Party, recently stated, 'Governments and enterprises should learn more about and improve the operation system of pageants for a healthy, orderly development of pageants and beauty economy in China.' Miss Globe, Miss International and Miss Universe have all been staged in China over the last few years, and the Miss China franchise has signed a sponsorship deal with Rupert Murdoch's Hong-Kong based Phoenix TV. Somewhat lesser known contests such as China World Model Competition and International Advertising Model have all signed lucrative local sponsorship and marketing deals.

Suck Out the Fat

Though the press has concentrated on facial cosmetic surgery, the most frequently performed cosmetic operation in China is liposuction to remove fat from both men and women. In China, clinics are offering a range of liposuction (also known as lipoplasty, liposculpture or suction lipectomy) techniques including solution injections, in which a special solution is injected into the fat tissue. The solution usually consists of a local anaesthetic (usually Lidocaine) to reduce pain and adrenalin (usually epinephrine) to contract the blood vessels to reduce bleeding, and fluids to help separate the fat from the tissue with the help of a salt solution. Also available is the tumescent technique whereby much larger amounts of solution are injected and the so-called super-wet technique in which the amount of solution injected equals the amount of fat tissue removed. Ultrasound-assisted lipoplasty is another technique where sound waves are targeted at fat tissue. The idea is that the waves break the connection between the fat cells, which are then removed by suction. The fat is usually removed via a cannula (a hollow tube) and an aspirator (a suction device).

In Europe and North America liposuction is not usually promoted as a weight loss method, but instead, as a body contouring procedure, though people looking to lose weight know what liposuction is. However, in China it is regularly advertised as a one stop, quickly done weight loss solution. Most liposuction operations in China target the abdomen and thighs in women and the abdomen and flanks in men.

Liposuction has not been without problems for some patients in China – just as the number of court cases claiming negligent cosmetic surgery have risen in recent years, so the number of people reporting unusual 'lumpiness' or 'dents' in the skin following liposuction procedures has risen. Such conditions are usually attributed to 'over-suctioning' and the attempt to remove more weight than the procedure is really designed for; the American Society of Plastic Surgeons, for instance, defines a 'large' amount as being more than five litres of fat. The China Consumer Association reports a growing number of liposuction-related complaints from scarring and inflammation to skin hardening. Other countries where governments have become concerned about the rise of liposuction as a weight loss technique have instituted new safeguards – for instance, Singapore insists patients seeking liposuction wait 15 days to make sure they want to undergo the surgery.

Surgeons are also reportedly fitting more adjustable plastic bands as a form of gastric surgery around the top of patient's stomachs designed to restrict food intake and create a sensation of fullness – effectively sealing off most of the stomach to limit food intake. The most popular gastric banding method is to create a small pouch in the upper part of the stomach with an adjustable stoma so as to limit food intake. Though that sounds rather invasive, many experts consider gastric banding to be one of the simplest and safest obesity surgery methods. It can lead to a 30–40 per cent weight loss one year after the operation, and 50–60 per cent after three years.

At present, the China Medical Association considers 'banding' a cosmetic procedure rather than a treatment, which means that patients cannot claim the procedure on their medical insurance and must pay privately, with the treatment costing approximately RMB40,000 (US$5,762). Naturally, cosmetic surgeons, who perform the vast majority of banding procedures, are lobbying for a change. This might well happen; the US Medicare system added banding as an approved treatment in 2006 with some insurers following, and approximately 178,000 Americans had some form of bariatric procedure in 2006, according to the Society for Bariatric Surgery. Notably in China, cosmetic surgeons report a growing number of parents bringing in young children, as young as ten, for banding. Though most doctors stipulate a minimum age of 16, the pressure is on them, both in the form of parental pressure and 'gifts', to perform the procedure on younger children.

And so, for the moment, banding and liposuction remain growth industries.

Pill Popping – Slimming Pills, Laxatives and Anorectics

So-called 'slimming pills' are widely available and advertised heavily on TV and in the wider media across China. They are mostly essentially laxatives and so, either through design, or through a misunderstanding of the true nature of these products, misuse has become prevalent. Despite some scandals in recent years with women becoming seriously ill, and in several highly publicized cases, dying, there have been no effective limits placed on the sale of these erroneous products, particularly when they claim 'herbal' (and now, 'organic') properties. Women, and it invariably is women that are targeted by these pills and consume these products, find that their potassium gets dangerously low and can result in cardiac arrest or arrhythmia problems.

In 2007 Canadian health authorities advised consumers not to use two herbal weight loss products from China – Super Fat Burning and LiDa Daidaihua Slimming Capsules – when they were found to contain sibutramine, a prescription drug that should only be taken under medical supervision. Sibutramine, a common ingredient found in many easily available 'slimming' products in China, is a medication that suppresses the appetite, though if used improperly, can have serious health consequences, including increased heart rate and blood pressure as well as increased pressure in the eyes (ocular hypertension) which can lead to a variety of problems including glaucoma. Other 'slimming' pills have been found to contain amfepramone and phentermine, both sympathomimetic stimulant drugs (i.e., that mimic the effects of the hormone epinephrine, or adrenaline, and the hormone/neurotransmitter norepinephrine) marketed as appetite suppressants that were previously in use in Europe and North America, but where medical authorities have since withdrawn them from circulation due to problematic side effects, including the onset of serious heart and lung problems, as well as triggering severe mental illness in some users.

Again, this problem is nothing new in China. Back in 2001 the Chinese media reported that the anti-obesity medication (anorectic) Fenfluramine, also known as Pondimin, phentermine and dexfenfluramine (all three were often generically called Fen-phen and enhanced the brain's release of serotonin to help people lose weight) were widely available over the counter in Chinese pharmacies, despite having been withdrawn from the North American market in 1997 after reports of heart valve disease and pulmonary hypertension (a condition known as cardiac fibrosis).[12] As well as the concern that uninformed Chinese consumers could be consuming these and other anorectics that could harm or kill them, there is also a question of liability; a Fen-phen mass tort crisis has occurred in the US where more than 50,000 product liability lawsuits have been filed by alleged Fen-phen victims and estimates of total liability run as high as US$14 billion.

As well as a consumer, China is also a major producer of anorectics, diuretics and a whole host of 'slimming' pills. For instance, Sibutramine (whose trade name is Meridia in the USA and Reductil in Europe and other countries) is an anorectic and a centrally acting serotonin inhibitor. Despite some attempts to get the drug banned in the US, it remains classified as a Schedule IV controlled substance in America.[13] This is despite a petition raised by consumer activist Ralph Nader's non-governmental organization (NGO), Public Citizen, and comments from the epidimeologist and FDA 'whistleblower' Dr David Graham, who testified before a Senate Finance Committee hearing that sibutramine may be more dangerous than the conditions it is used for. Yet, a quick Google search on sibutramine will locate any number of manufacturers in China.

While problems with 'slimming' pills have occasionally appeared in the Chinese media, it has been abroad that the scandals have really occurred. Made-in-China 'slimming' pills, with brand names such as 'Slim 10', have been linked to deaths in countries where they are available and popular, such as Hong Kong, Japan, Malaysia, India and Singapore since the 1990s. Most of these pills have been found to cause liver or thyroid problems, and in extreme cases, complete liver or kidney failure, and the banned appetite suppressant fenfluramine has been detected in many people. The Beijing authorities have stepped in to ban these products; indeed, fenfluramine was banned in China in 2000, yet they continue to appear both in China and globally, usually purchased via numerous websites and spam e-mail advertising anti-obesity and weight loss 'miracle cures'. Indeed, Slim 10 (marketed as Yuzhitang in China) became the most notorious of these weight-cut drugs, appearing for sale in Singapore without a listing of its ingredients, ingredients that were found to contain both fenfluramine and nicotinamide (a water-soluble vitamin that is part of the vitamin B group). Singapore authorities banned the product, but not before several hundred thousand bottles had entered the market and been sold to unsuspecting customers. Deaths from Yuzhitang/Slim 10 were reported or suspected in places as far apart as Guangdong Province, Singapore and Japan, while also damaging the health of at least 20 more people, including the prominent Singaporean TV personality, Andrea De Cruz, who needed a liver transplant from her boyfriend, well known local actor Pierre Png, to survive.

Scares and tragedies over slimming pills, either bought and consumed in China or made in China and consumed elsewhere, continue, and online buying is a major problem. Recently, it was alleged that the death from heart failure of a female teenage college student in Tokyo may have been linked to her intake of slimming capsules labelled Tiantiansu Qingzhi Jiaonang. Other women in Japan who took the product, labelled as produced in Guangzhou, reported diarrhoea, headache and diminished appetite. All had purchased the tablets online and did lose weight, but became severely dehydrated. The tablets contained Sibutramine, which is not authorized as a medical ingredient in Japan.

It is also still relatively common in China to see diuretics (drugs that elevate the rate of urination) and laxatives (drugs taken to induce bowel movements) for sale, marketed as slimming and weight loss aids. In a sense, this use of diuretics is explained in some instances by interpretations of traditional Chinese medicine (TCM), which sees fat as *yin*, and therefore an accumulation of substance. TCM holds that fat, or adipose tissue, is mostly phlegm and dampness and considers the spleen to be charged with transportation and transformation of this dampness, and so diuretics and laxatives are often prescribed by TCM practitioners. However, overuse or excessive use of diuretics for rapid weight loss can cause severe dehydration and loss of potassium, which can result in heart arrhythmia (irregular heartbeat), weakening of the kidneys, depression, fatigue, high blood pressure, hyperglycaemia (high blood sugar), impaired growth, mood swings, unhealthy changes in the nervous system and can, in extreme cases, cause heart failure.

Similarly, the 'get slim quick' culture in China, combined with the easy availability of relatively strong laxatives and enemas has meant that those seeking rapid weight loss have turned to these products, often advertised as slimming and weight loss aids. Overuse of laxatives can cause repeated vomiting and muscle weakness, and when a strong desire for weight loss leads to a serious eating disorder, laxatives can become far more dangerous. Again, as with diuretics, dehydration is a problem, with all the attendant problems of blurry vision, kidney damage, fainting spells, etc., as well as loss of vital electrolytes such as potassium and sodium if vitamin and mineral supplements are not taken. And again, the risk of heart attacks is increased as is the risk of bowel cancer due to irritable bowel syndrome and bowel tumours forming which can be both benign and cancerous.

Despite the dangers of using dubious slimming pills, laxatives and anorectics as weight loss methods, all three remain readily available, widely advertised and easily accessible and continue to be used by many, many people.

Eating Disorders – Still a Taboo

While obesity and weight gain have become open subjects of discussion in China – reported on in the press, discussed on radio and TV and constantly featuring in newspapers and magazines – and the problems around 'slimming pills' and diuretics have now also been discussed openly, the opposite is true of eating disorders such as bulimia and anorexia nervosa. Eating disorders are rarely if ever mentioned, and no official statistics on the problem exist. Yet anecdotal evidence suggests that an increasing number of urban Chinese, predominately young women, are suffering from eating disorders ranging from, at the extreme, bulimia nervosa and anorexia nervosa to the time-honoured method of eating and then retreating to the toilet to stick your fingers down your throat and regurgitate the food before the body has had a chance to absorb it.

Bulimia nervosa, characterized by episodes of excessive eating (binge-eating) followed by inappropriate methods of weight control, such as self-induced vomiting, abuse of laxatives and diuretics has been reported, while anorexia nervosa, a more psychologically grounded disorder characterized by markedly reduced appetite or total aversion to food, is also apparent and has been reported in the press, including the tragic consequences and the deaths of several young women.[14] In one sense, the appearance of these disorders is no surprise in a society where thinness is accentuated so constantly through the media and in advertising. However, in China, a major problem that has arguably encouraged the increase of bulimia in particular, is the easy availability, mis-labelling and blatant mis-selling of laxatives.

Some have pointed once again to the One-Child Policy, a policy, it seems, that can cause both greater obesity and greater anorexia – in short, more eating disorders. Several surveys in eastern China have indicated that (to the surprise of many) among young people diagnosed with anorexia, the majority were boys rather than girls. The researchers concluded that this was due to 'non-fat phobic anorexia', where children developed unhealthy eating habits after being spoiled by their parents and ultimately became undernourished.[15]

Eating disorders remain taboo in China, which will ultimately lead to more sufferers. The obvious irony, of course, is that as more people have more wealth and are able to afford to eat anything they like, they are then puking it all up. But the truth is that at the moment, we simply do not have data on the extent and prevalence of eating disorders in China. There have been attempts to extrapolate data from surveys in other Asian countries that may provide some guidance. For instance, Dr Chen Kuan-yu at Taipei City Hospital in Taiwan, who refers to anorexia as a 'hidden problem' and has estimated that anorexia and bulimia may affect 0.2 per cent of women in Taiwan, while other studies have indicated that eating disorders are affecting perhaps as many as 1 per cent of the female population in Japan, South Korea and Singapore. Extrapolating those numbers for China, based on a population of approximately 1.3 billion, indicates that upwards of 24 million people may be suffering some kind of eating disorder in the PRC. However, these numbers are extremely rough – guesstimates – and clearly, eating disorders, like obesity, will be overwhelmingly an urban rather than rural problem in China, perhaps significantly reducing the overall number. The point is, we just don't have a handle on this issue in China.[16]

What we do know is that both obesity and severe weight loss are leading to more Chinese people having to go into hospital to be treated for a range of ailments related to their weight and lifestyle. As Chinese society continues to get wealthier, the middle class, with high rates of disposable income, so even more will enter China's healthcare system seeking treatment. So, finally, it is necessary to see what obesity is costing China's healthcare services and ultimately its government and people, and whether or not the system can cope with the inevitable additional strains in the coming years from weight and lifestyle illnesses.

Chapter 10

CHINA'S FAT CLINIC – THE IMPACT OF OBESITY ON CHINA'S HEALTHCARE SYSTEM

The Pressures on the Healthcare System

Obesity is just one lifestyle problem that is affecting China as it modernizes; increasing rates of stress are accentuating incidences of cardiovascular disease, and pollution is leading to higher rates of asthma and other respiratory diseases, and one downside of greater car ownership is a steep rise in traffic accidents. In short, non-communicable diseases have become leading killers, even while the lifespan of an urban Chinese citizen rose by 2.8 years on average since 1990. Great strides have been made; famine is a thing of the past and China has all but totally eradicated small pox, diphtheria and polio; the child mortality rate has been slashed with deaths of children under five years of age dropping from 12 per cent to 8.5 per cent since 1990.

However, today's overweight and obese in China can look forward to a mixed future of bright economic hopes for their country, but all too often, poor and deteriorating health for themselves. Along with the explosion of HIV/ AIDS, pollution-related illness, smoking-related diseases and the lack of long-term care for the increasing number of elderly, the overweight and obese are part of China's predictable 'healthcare time bomb'. Among the unpredictable factors lurk more SARS-type outbreaks that have the ability, when combined with rising pressures on the already strained healthcare system, to cause an acute crisis that could tip China's healthcare system into a state of chaos and collapse. China's healthcare system remains in a perpetual state of crisis – a situation recognized by both the government and the people and reflected regularly in the media and pretty openly discussed on the streets.

The rise of obesity and a host of other non-communicable lifestyle-related diseases that are growing are creating new challenges for the Chinese healthcare system. Increased rates of high blood pressure, diabetes and hyperlipidemia seem inevitable, as does a rise in heart attacks, coronary artery disease, strokes, respiratory diseases and cancers associated with obesity (especially the hormonally related and large-bowel cancers, and gallbladder disease), as well as vitamin deficiencies (particularly vitamin-A) and the host of problems associated with this, from failing eyesight to musculoskeletal disorders (MSDs). Other weight-related health problems will also probably rise in prominence and occurrence including arthritis, gallstones, cirrhosis, osteoarthritis (degenerative arthritis) and other MSDs such as slipped discs and hips, which are often accentuated and more common in the overweight and obese. The clinically obese are more likely to suffer from a range of ailments from simple back pain, poor circulation, breathing difficulties, knee joint disorders and skin disease to hypertension and infertility, and recovery rates from major surgery are lower than average among the overweight. At best the overweight and obese will occupy much-needed hospital beds for longer and cost more in recuperation; at worst, they will die with more regularity on the operating table.

Healthcare for women will face new challenges. Obese and overweight women can suffer a range of problems specific to their gender. Obesity is a major cause of early puberty among girls under ten years of age, as well as causing erratic menstruation and increased hirsuteness, and, more seriously, overweight women can be more susceptible to polycystic ovary syndrome (a condition in which cysts in the ovary interfere with normal ovulation and menstruation) and *pseudotumor cerebri*, a brain tumour-like condition usually occurring in obese women. Obese females who become pregnant also face the possibility of, at best, greater discomfort during their term and, at worst, fatal complications – stillbirths are reportedly more frequent when the mother is obese.

As has been shown in previous chapters, children are suffering disproportionately from overweight and obesity and this will increasingly throw up new challenges for paediatrics. The range of illnesses listed previously, notably diabetes in ever-younger obese children (MODY, Maturity-Onset Diabetes of the Young), will place greater strains on the system.

There is also a knock-on effect with obesity that means that a range of other illnesses and conditions not always directly related to weight will probably grow in incidence. Being overweight and obese can add to problems that affect people's quality of life including a reduced libido, impotence, acne, rashes, fainting spells, weight-induced sleep apnea (where excess fat literally presses on the lungs during sleep, causing discomfort), bowed legs, asthma, restlessness, profuse sweating and just plain being out of breath. All of this is added to by the psychological problems that affect some overweight and obese people: poor self esteem, raised incidence of snoring, feelings of rejection as well as problems for young children from bullying, taunting, social isolation and general low levels of self-confidence and, in the extreme, eating disorders, self-harming and suicidal tendencies. Psychological problems and counselling, as with issues around eating disorders such as bulimia and anorexia, are subjects that have not been fully tackled in Chinese society or the country's medical establishment as yet, due to traditional prejudices and lack of funding.

All in all, China is now being hit with a rash of new demands on its healthcare system from lifestyle diseases, those diseases that appear to increase in frequency as countries become more industrialized, wealthier and people live longer. However, China's government appears to have finally grasped the nettle of healthcare reform after having largely ignored it for so long, despite innumerable problems with the system. The question of whether or not the government's healthcare reforms will go far enough and be enacted in time with sufficient funding to recognize the startling rise of lifestyle diseases is a major question affecting the future of Chinese society and the ruling Communist Party's stated aim of ensuring a harmonious society.

Confucian Notions of Protection

We have seen that even at the poorer, more disparate margins of Chinese society, citizens will go to great lengths, for long periods of time, to protect and defend their loved ones and families. They will engage the state in any means they can: talking to journalists, using the Internet, petitioning Beijing and the court system. They will 'reach out' to their local representatives and call in favours; they increasingly know how to play the game to shame the government into making concessions to save face and maintain stability. All this is, of course, not without personal risk (experience has shown people that in China even the tallest poppies can be quickly cut down), but increasingly the obesity debate revolves around children – an emotive subject in any country. This makes obesity and obesity-related illness and care a subtly different and more politically explosive phenomenon than previous disease issues.

With the breakup of traditional extended-family networks, both in urban and rural regions, due to the need for workers to migrate in order to obtain work, the whole fabric of the welfare support system that used to maintain the elderly, the young and the sick has disappeared, leaving the state with an even greater 'paternal' role in having to provide such welfare support, extending its influence even further into people's private lives. Besides the cost of the additional expenditure required to provide such government services, both nationally and regionally, there is the mounting strain on the resources of China's huge bureaucracy. For China's government system to continue to cope with the effects of increased poor health requires balancing the changes in policy and administration with local government priorities, often at odds with those of the central government.

Not only are the mounting healthcare issues creating the potential for huge costs, as well as possible strains on the fabric of Chinese society, they are also creating a new source of potential friction in the sphere of politics. For this reason, if no other, the Chinese government is attempting to grapple with the healthcare crisis.

China's Healthcare System

The ruling Communist Party knows that healthcare is in crisis. That is why they are planning to overhaul the system. The benefits of successfully managing this overhaul will be multiple, and they realize this; the goal of a 'harmonious society' will be close to achievement, their position as the ruling party delivering improvements solidified and perhaps they can convince Chinese families to stop saving at such high rates out of fear of illness and the associated costs and start consuming more with all the knock-on benefits to the economy that would entail.

The problems in the current system are myriad and include the wide discrepancy in service and availability levels between China's rural and urban areas. However, this book is really about urban China, and there the problems are somewhat different. In China's cities the fear is not that treatment won't be available – it usually is, but at a price. The small social security net provided (the Basic Medical Insurance (BMI) programme, available in all Chinese cities since 1998) rarely extends to anything beyond minor ailments and this has led to notorious press reports and TV investigations into massive bills run up by sick people in hospital – bills that at best, have sent them and their families digging deep into their savings, and at worst, bankrupting them completely.

Ill health is Chinese society's greatest fear and accounts for the importance, saturation marketing and sales of supposedly preventative medicines, including everything from vitamins to tonics to traditional medicines. Keeping healthy in China is literally keeping wealthy.

Despite these fears, the system has improved in some areas; government funding increased significantly between 2002 and 2004, largely to help improve the system of countering epidemics in the wake of the SARS crisis. Between 2002 and 2005, the average time it took for a report of a new case of one of China's 37 major communicable diseases to go from the county level to the central government fell from 29 days to just one day. 'Collapse' is too strong a word for what has happened to China's healthcare system – 'collapse' is what happened to post-Soviet Russia, for instance. Average Chinese life expectancy remains higher than in Brazil, India or Russia, while detection of communicable diseases such as tuberculosis (TB) are far higher in China than other developing countries.

Indeed, China's success in tackling TB reveals exactly why the system has not collapsed due to planning in the past, but now needs to be radically overhauled. As China's leading infectious disease, TB was a real killer, but between 2002 and 2005 the detection rate for TB shot up from 30 per cent to 80 per cent, thanks in part to government guidelines to healthcare workers and a massive increase in anti-TB programme funding. The detection rate is now in excess of 80 per cent and the treatment rate approximately 95 per cent. TB is not the scourge of China it once was. However, what the fight against TB showed was that the Chinese healthcare system could gear up and tackle a major communicable disease. Arguably, that is what the healthcare system has been able to do since 1949, identifying and tackling communicable diseases such as malaria (with mosquito eradication campaigns), schistosomiasis (snail fever) and syphilis with mass campaigns, as well as outbreaks of infectious and epidemic diseases. Despite this, to date, the system has not shown itself similarly capable of tackling non-communicable and lifestyle diseases as successfully. As the *China Economic Quarterly* noted in a 2007 survey of China's healthcare landscape:

> Citizens do not receive, on average, objectively worse health care than they did in the past. It is more accurate to say that the health care system has failed to keep up with rapid changes in the nature of demand.[1]

It is also worth noting that many of these successfully tackled diseases were concentrated in China's rural areas or poorer urban communities. As diseases such as TB and malaria become ever rarer in China, so the growing areas of healthcare demand will be non-communicable and lifestyle diseases affecting a more affluent, urbanized society – heart disease, cancer and diabetes, for instance. And as these patients enter the system, they will demand far higher levels of care and treatment than previous heavy users of the system, while their ailments will increasingly be chronic, i.e., diseases of long duration and generally slow progression, and therefore, invariably costing more to treat in terms of both medicines and healthcare worker time and facilities.

Nobody to Tell You You're Obese

While people can ignore media campaigns and school campaigns, not so many people ignore their doctor. So far, government- and media-led campaigns against obesity have not been noticeably successful; changing parents' perceptions of weight and the damage it can do to their offspring is proving hard to achieve. A major problem is the lack of a primary care system. People in China do not visit their general practitioner (GP) or family doctor; they go to the hospital, whatever their condition. This also naturally means they tend only to go to the hospital when sick or injured and rarely for checkups. Clinics, when they exist, tend to be highly specialized and as we have seen, tend to specialize in areas that make money, such as cosmetic surgery or orthodontics.

China's problem is not so much a lack of doctors, nurses or hospitals, but that people only encounter these personnel and facilities once they are sick and require treatment. With few GPs or primary care physicians there are few opportunities for doctors to examine children and assess their weight and urge their parents to do something about it. Adults, too, suffer from the same problem – they arrive at the hospital once they are sick.

Put simply, the current system's lack of primary care means that all too often, people know they have hypertension only when they have a stroke. The only way to successfully contain and deal with lifestyle, chronic and non-communicable diseases like hypertension, diabetes and heart disease is through primary care that can sound alarm bells and recommend preventive treatment. The mere act of a child and parent visiting a doctor in a primary care setting to talk about that child's weight and to do something about it could be crucial in reducing later illnesses. Without that primary care, the overweight child and the parents will all too often be unaware that there is a problem until they are in a hospital bed in serious condition. That this process ultimately adds costs, misery and early death to the system is obvious.

Additionally, this lack of primary care is inefficient and causes further inefficiencies throughout the system. It also causes overloads and strains on hospitals, as patients arrive with everything from severe symptoms to headaches and colds. Additionally, many people do not trust clinics, believing them to be staffed by second-rate doctors unable to get a job with a hospital and more interested in charging than treatment – neither of these assumptions is by any means wholly incorrect.

'Basically a Failure' – The Need to Rethink

By the turn of the century, it was clear that China's healthcare system had become a slightly bewildering patchwork. The vast majority of the system was state-owned and controlled, either by provincial-level health bureaus or by the Ministry of Health. Large state-owned enterprises (SOEs) ran a portion of the system (though were supposed to be shedding such old-style welfare responsibilities), as did university-linked hospitals under the Ministry of Education or military hospitals. The private sector remains small scale and niche (mostly cosmetic surgery, etc.), and private or group practices are not allowed. There is a small level of foreign involvement, mainly catering to ex-patriots and the very rich. This will surely grow in coming decades, but remain expensive and exclusive, by and large.

In 2005 following an influential report from the Development Research Centre (DRC), the State Council's think tank, who declared the system 'basically a failure', the central government finally decided that the system needed overhauling. The report advocated introducing primary care as a top priority and criticized what it perceived as the failure of competition in the market. To a significant extent, the government had tried to offload healthcare to the market and the result had been growing levels of costs and public disgruntlement.

The fact was – and everyone in China knew it, from the leadership down to the villages – that healthcare had become a profit-generating machine looking for economies of scale, profitable niches and wealthy patients. This had led to all manner of imbalances in the system, from an orgy of purchasing of medical equipment such as ever-more complicated scanners in the hope of impressing would-be high paying patients, to setting aside space for coffee shops and fast-food joints on hospital grounds. However, it was not a true market. The government still capped fees and drug prices, which, over the years, had led to a massive growth in overprescription, recommending of wasteful and unnecessary (but expensive and profitable) procedures such as MRI scans, and flat-out bribery, with cash-filled envelopes going to doctors to ensure faster and better treatment and care. In this, Big Pharma also played a role by incentivizing doctors with everything from free gifts to holidays, while the hospital administrators effectively condoned the practices by awarding bonuses to doctors based on how much they increased hospital revenues.

What the high charges and costs of visiting hospitals have done is to discourage people from going, often despite being advised by a healthcare professional to attend a hospital. Additionally, patients are discharging themselves early more often. Every time, the major reason given is fear of costs. Eventually, this self-avoidance of the healthcare system will start to show up in the healthcare statistics impacting negatively on the nation's health.

The Dilemma of Reform – Between a Rock and a Hard Place

As the *China Economic Quarterly's* 2007 survey of China's healthcare system indicated:

> The biggest problem with health care in China today is how it is paid for: mainly, cash on the barrelhead by patients. The state share of national

health care spending plunged from over 80 per cent in 1980 to 36 per cent in 2001. It has since crept back up to 39 per cent, but is still easily the lowest in the world. Judged by who pays the bills, communist China runs a more privatized health care system than the United States.[2]

This system of ever-higher cash payments for healthcare is impacting everything from retail sales growth, the high savings rate, to urban levels of disposable income. Staying in a Chinese hospital, judged by the relation between average earnings, is among the most expensive in the world. What is required, and what the central government is grappling with, is a health insurance system that both provides cover and is trusted to deliver.

Herein lies the dilemma for China's healthcare planners. China's economy and the success of its urban middle class, as well as those just about to be – or not quite yet – raised out of poverty, is predicated on investment and job creation. To achieve this, the country needs to remain competitive and maintain the so-called 'China Price'. The options for healthcare reform fall broadly into two categories and both, if mishandled, could cause far wider systemic problems in the Chinese economy:

1) **A healthcare system based on insurance paid by individuals and company schemes – i.e., a similar system to that operating in the US.** Putting aside the problem of what to do about people who can't or won't pay for medical insurance and then require treatment, it is clear that without significant government infusions of cash, the insurance premiums for such a system would be high and extremely burdensome on people. The inevitable result would be a demand for higher wages to meet these additional costs. That demand, if not met, would leave impossible numbers of people outside the system, but if met, would mean rising wages and the 'blowing' of the China Price, leading to a drop in investment and job creation. Additionally, requiring people to pay high insurance premiums for a healthcare system would, at best, just divert money currently being saved in bank accounts into premium payments and do nothing to achieve the government's avowed intention of freeing up personal savings to drive up consumption.

2) **A socialized, or comprehensive service, healthcare system – i.e., one paid primarily through taxation, similar to the UK's National Health Service (NHS), other European models and those operating in Canada, etc.** A similar problem would occur here in that requiring people to pay high levels of personal taxation would again lead to wage demands adversely affecting the China Price. Additionally, a

core problem would be whether or not people felt they were indeed getting a fully socialized treatment-on-demand system, and if they were not, would probably still save for private health treatment at current rates, thereby not delivering the much desired consumption boom of released savings.

Ultimately, both broad forms of financing could have disastrous knock-on effects within the wider economy. There are the problems that currently exist with the Basic Medical Insurance (BMI) system of those who lack coverage, such as workers in short-term or irregular employment, many migrants, the nonworking members of families and those firms that don't enroll employees, claiming they can't afford it. A more fully privatized insurance system would inevitably involve higher costs than the current BMI (which is a system that, by and large, requires the patient to pay and then seek reimbursement later) and presumably more companies would avoid the scheme while the low-paid, marginal and migrant workers would potentially find themselves even further away from healthcare than is currently the case. For those covered by BMI but unable to pay the upfront charge before being reimbursed, the system is next to worthless anyway; hence, once again, China's high savings rate is the coping mechanism to get around this flaw in the system.

It is also worth noting that most Chinese hospitals are busy places at the moment, and a socialized system, while good at encouraging people to seek treatment free of financial fears, could soon overburden the existing healthcare infrastructure and both systems would presumably see people starting to object vociferously to the system of bribes and under-the-table payments that form so much of doctors' and hospitals' income currently.

Insuring the Obese

The suggestion that a more inclusive American-style insurance system could be introduced, regardless of its impact on wage demands, savings and incomes, inevitably raises issues for China's insurance business. Indeed, China's rising obesity crisis is likely to have ramifications for the country's nascent insurance industry. As health, critical illness and other forms of insurance are introduced, promoted and sold across China, so obesity is likely to become a factor. It has been already in countries such as the US, where the policy journal *Health Affairs* reported in 2007 that obesity-related illnesses represented just 2 per cent of spending by health insurers in 1987, a figure that rose sharply to 11. 6 per cent by 2002 and continues to trend upwards.[3] Factor in that overweight adolescents have a 70 per cent chance of becoming overweight or obese adults, and insurers start to get nervous. Some American insurers have already started to offer discounts and rebates for gym memberships and weight loss programmes, but increasingly, the spotlight is shifting to the statistics.

The largest target market for all the new health and medical insurance policies in China is naturally the urban middle class – that same group that are suffering disproportionately in the obesity crisis. At the moment, the new middle class is the primary target market for insurers, but if they become obese, this may change due to the assertion, according to Jay Bhattacharya of Stanford University and Neeraj Sood of the RAND Corporation, that in the US, 'The lifetime medical costs related to diabetes, heart disease, high cholesterol, hypertension, and stroke among the obese are US$10,000 higher than among the non-obese.'[4] Naturally, costs in China are different, but then so are insurance premiums and so the basic premise holds – obesity leads to higher medical costs. It is also the case, following Bhattacharya and Sood's argument, that as insurance premiums do not depend on weight, non-obese people in the same pool are paying for the food/exercise decisions of the obese (of course, in countries with socialized medicine this additional cost is borne by the taxpayer, be they fat or thin).

It is clear that obesity is becoming an increasingly important cost driver and exposure issue for insurers in many countries. Given that it is generally accepted that the lifespan of an obese person is shortened, on average, by seven years, life insurers must account for the difference in their underwriting. In some countries, including the USA, life insurance for overweight and obese people generally costs more than for normal-weight people. However, in group life insurance plans, obesity is so far generally not a factor used to rate individuals, whereas smoking, age and gender usually are. Similarly, as obese people tend to miss more workdays through chronic ill health the same problem applies for disability insurers, and as recovery times from conditions are longer, so the issue affects Workers Compensation-type schemes.

For medical insurance, so far, the obese have not been widely punished in the way smokers and people with HIV/AIDS and other illnesses allowing for opt-outs have been. However, this may be different in China. Indeed, the core thrust of the medical insurance market to date has been to simply get more people insured. According to Chinese government data, between 2003 and 2008, the number of people covered by some form of medical insurance grew by just under 500 per cent, rising from 15 per cent of the population in 2003 to over 85 per cent by 2008.

This massive rise in coverage has been based on a range of different medical care schemes targeting different social groups within the population. The first of these is the Urban Employees' Medical Insurance (UEMI) programme. This scheme is aimed at all urban employees working in government institutions, commercial enterprises, social groups and non-profit organizations. For those

Table 28: **China Medical Insurance Coverage, 2003–2008**

	2003	2004	2005	2006	2007	2008
Covered persons (mns)	189.42	231.04	317.83	567.32	953.11	1,133.22
% of population	14.66	17.77	24.31	43.16	72.13	85.33

Source: 2003–2007 data from China Ministry of Human Resources and Social Security; 2008 figures from National Bureau of Statistics.

not employed, it's the Urban Residents Basic Medical Insurance scheme (URBMI), paid for by government subsidies and covering, for example, elderly people, the medically incapacitated and children. In rural areas, the New Rural Cooperative Medical Scheme (NRCMS) provides coverage for all rural residential families, paid for through government subsidies. For those in particularly hard circumstances in both urban and rural settings, there are also tax-financed medical assistance programmes.

The UEMI scheme is financed through contributions paid by both employees and employers, with employees paying 2 per cent of salary into an individual account, while employers pay 6 per cent into a fund. The individual account is meant to be used to pay medical expenses for up to 10 per cent of the local average annual wage income, while the employer contribution fund is meant to cover amounts ranging from 10 to 400 per cent of the average annual income. By 2008, per capita annual contributions into the URBMI scheme ranged from RMB150 (US$22) to RMB300 (US$44), at a national average of RMB236 US$34.50). In the same year, annual contributions into the NRCMS scheme were a per capita average of RMB96 (US$14). Unlike the UEMI scheme, the URBMI and NRCMS schemes are meant for covering higher-cost medical expenses, such as the treatment of major diseases and hospitalization fees.

The two programmes that have contributed the most to the massive extension of healthcare coverage in China are the NRCMS and URBMI schemes. By the end of 2008, according to the official data, the rural scheme covered 815 million people, or 91.5 per cent of the rural population, with the number of people covered by the scheme having risen by 662 per cent since 2003. Meanwhile, the urban scheme was only piloted in 2007 in 88 cities. By 2008, the coverage in these cities was said to be about 50 per cent, with a projected coverage of 80 per cent by the end of 2009. While the rural scheme is heavily subsidized by the government, covering up to 80 per cent of premiums, in the rural scheme, government subsidy covers 36 per cent for adults and 56 per cent for children, the rest being financed by individuals themselves, or their parents.

Table 29: **China's New Rural Cooperative Medical Scheme Coverage, 2004–2008**

	2004	2005	2006	2007	2008
Covered persons (mns)	107	180	410	730	815
% of population	11.6	23.7	50.7	86.0	91.5

Source: 2004–2006 data from the Report on Implementation of China's National Economic Plan for 2006; 2007 and 2008 figures from the Xinhua News Agency.

As well as trying to raise overall healthcare spending, especially since the beginning of 2009, prior to this, the government had been attempting to reduce spending on healthcare by individuals as a proportion of the total. Looking at the official data, individual spending on healthcare reached a high of 60 per cent by 2001, but successive government spending injections have gradually been reducing this, with the effect that individual spending as a proportion of the total fell below the 50 per cent mark by 2006.

Based on the statistics in the table above, in terms of growth rates since 1998, total nominal healthcare spending grew by 198.9 per cent between 1998 and 2007, while government spending grew 291.2 per cent, social spending by 287.1 per cent and individual spending by 133.5 per cent. Government and social healthcare spending have therefore grown ahead of the rate of total GDP (1998–2007), which rose by 212 per cent. This means that over this period, total healthcare spending has grown slightly as a percentage of total GDP, but still remains low, at less than 5 per cent. The latest available year's data for government health spending was, at time of writing, said to be about RMB1,129 billion (US$165 billion), of which RMB229.7 billion (US$34 billion) came directly from government budget, which represented only 4.35 per cent of GDP in 2007.

Then in January 2009 the government publicized its new medical reform plan. Aware that personal incomes were becoming mired in savings to cover future healthcare needs, thus inhibiting the true potential of China's domestic consumer economy, Beijing released its plans to throw some some RMB850 billion (US$124 billion) at establishing a modern healthcare service in China, spread across the 2009–2011 period, with an aim to achieve a minimum coverage of 90 per cent of the population by the end of the period. The government's Guidelines on Deepening the Reform of Health Care System, published in April 2009, sets out a blueprint for the establishment of a basic healthcare system by 2020 that can provide 'safe, effective, convenient and affordable' health services to all urban and rural residents.

Under this new plan, two-thirds of the government money will go to low-income consumers via medical insurance premium subsidies (as summarized

Table 30: **China's Total Healthcare spending 1998–2007**

(RMB bn)	Total Nominal	Government Budgetary	Social Expenditure	Resident Individual	% Government	% social expenditure	% Individual
1998	377.65	58.72	100.60	218.33	15.55	26.64	57.81
1999	417.86	64.09	106.46	247.31	15.34	25.48	59.18
2000	458.66	70.95	117.19	270.52	15.47	25.55	58.98
2001	502.59	80.06	121.14	301.39	15.93	24.10	59.97
2002	579.00	90.85	153.94	334.21	15.69	26.59	57.72
2003	658.41	111.69	178.85	367.87	16.96	27.16	55.87
2004	759.03	129.36	222.54	407.14	17.04	29.32	53.64
2005	865.99	155.25	258.64	452.10	17.93	29.87	52.21
2006	984.33	177.89	321.09	485.36	18.07	32.62	49.31
2007	1128.95	229.71	389.37	509.87	20.35	34.49	45.16

Source: China Statistical Yearbook, 2009, Table 21–48.

Table 31: **China's Healthcare Spending as a Proportion of GDP
1998–2007**

(RMB bn)	GDP	Total Healthcare Spending	Healthcare % of GDP
1998	8,302.43	377.65	4.55
1999	8,847.92	417.86	4.72
2000	9,800.05	458.66	4.68
2001	10,806.82	502.59	4.65
2002	11,909.57	579.00	4.86
2003	13,517.40	658.41	4.87
2004	15,958.67	759.03	4.76
2005	18,408.86	865.99	4.70
2006	21,313.17	984.33	4.62
2007	25,925.89	1128.95	4.35

Source: China Statistical Yearbook, 2009, Table 2–1 and Table 21–48.

in the schemes above), while the other third will be invested in community-level service providers, especially in rural healthcare facilities. Effectively, this latter third is an investment in healthcare infrastructure, mainly the construction of 29,000 rural township healthcare centres, and renovation and expansion of 5,000 or so larger rural township healthcare centres, during 2009. Over three years, the government will support the construction of 2,000 county-level hospitals and ensure that every administrative village has at least one clinic. In urban areas, 3,700 community healthcare centres and 11,000 community healthcare stations are to be newly built or renovated, and 2,400 urban community healthcare centres will be built in underdeveloped regions.

The two-thirds of the government money targeted for health insurance premium subsidy will be used to gradually increase the reimbursement ceiling from between three and four times the average per capita income, to six times. At the same time, the money will fund an increase in the hospitalization expense reimbursement rate under the UEMI, URBMI and NRCMS health insurance schemes, which will grow from 70, 50 and 38 per cent, respectively, to 75, 60 and 50 per cent. The stark difference between the level of services between richer urban areas and poorer rural areas is a key feature of the new plan.

However, this spending is being made to cover the gaps in the basic healthcare needs of the nation as it is already, and does not yet address the likely mounting costs associated with the conditions that are expected to see increased prevalence due to a direct link with growing obesity in the population. In order to begin to calculate what these conditions might add to the healthcare costs of China, we need to know what are the prime suspect conditions, and what are the healthcare costs associated with those conditions. First, the conditions themselves.

The Core Conditions

Diabetes

Type1 diabetes remains a problem, though is not largely thought to be obesity related. It accounts for only 5–10 per cent of cases and usually appears in childhood. Type 1 results when the immune system kills off the person's own beta cells (the cells of the pancreas which are responsible for making insulin). Type 2 diabetes results when the body's muscle and liver tissue becomes progressively unable to properly use insulin (insulin resistance); the beta cells try to compensate by producing higher levels of insulin and eventually exhaust themselves. Type 2 diabetes accounted for 90–95 per cent of known cases globally. Type 2 diabetes is potentially crippling, blinding, lifelong, and can lead to debilitating amputations and hypertension. Diabetes sharply raises the risk of heart disease, kidney failure and blindness. Diabetics suffer heart disease at twice the normal rate, and about two-thirds of diabetics ultimately die from cardiovascular problems.

Diabetes is particularly concerning to health professionals as it has traditionally been seen as an adult disease in China, but is now appearing with increasing frequency in pre-pubescent children and being encountered increasingly often by paediatricians in China's major cities due to MODY. In the US, the appearance of increasing incidences of type 2 diabetes in children in the 1990s was a major wake-up call that obesity was starting to cause significant health problems – type 2 diabetes usually appeared in patients after age 35 or 40. Globally, approximately 85 per cent of people with diabetes are type 2, and of these, 90 per cent are obese or overweight. The WHO predicts far higher rates of type 2 diabetes in China between now and 2050. Almost 3 per cent of Chinese adults have diabetes today, compared with less than 1 per cent in 1979, before China's economic reform process began. The situation is far worse in the cities than in the rural areas; in China's big cities, the diabetes rate is over 6 per cent, but in the poorer rural areas, the incidence of diabetes and obesity is much less. The obvious reason for this discrepancy between town and country appears to be the rural preponderance for physical labour, a more traditional diet and fewer private cars.

By way of comparison, 17 million Americans have diabetes with rates rising fastest among young adults. If current trends continue, the percentage of Americans with diabetes could rise from about 6 per cent currently to more than 10 per cent by 2050. Globally, the prevalence of diabetes is expected to swell from around 190 million people today to 360 million by the year 2030, with major growth occurring in the twin most-populous nations of China and India. This link between development and rising incidences of diabetes has led Western healthcare professionals to label type 2 diabetes as a 'lifestyle disease'.

Obesity also appears to be a factor in Maturity-Onset Diabetes of the Young (MODY). In 2005 Hong Kong University conducted a survey of MODY patients in Hong Kong's Chinese community. In Caucasians, MODY is mostly caused by mutations in the DNA binding agent hepatocyte nuclear factor 1 alpha (HNF 1 alpha) (MODY3) and glucokinase (MODY2) genes, a regulator of carbohydrate metabolism. However, most Japanese MODY patients are not linked to known MODY genes. The Hong Kong researchers studied ethnic-Chinese patients with MODY of unknown cause (known as MODYX). In subjects with MODYX, 3 per cent were glutamic acid decarboxylase (GAD-Ab) positive and 60 per cent were overweight.[5] The Chinese MODYX patients tended to have a higher BMI, higher insulin resistance and higher triglyceride levels (that is the storage form of fat consisting of three fatty acids and glycerol) as well as lower HDL (high-density lipoprotein) levels and more hypertension – all obesity related issues. The conclusion was that though a majority of Chinese MODY cases are due to defects in unknown genes and appear to be characterized by insulin resistance, the instances rose dramatically in the obese and overweight.[6]

It also seems that the shift to a more Western diet may be raising the incidence of diabetes. Studies of Japanese–Americans and Chinese–Americans have shown that the prevalence of diabetes is two to seven times higher than in those who actually live in Japan and China, according to Dr George King, Research Director of the Joslin Diabetes Center at the University of California, Irvine Medical Center in Orange, California. Dr. King believes that Asian–Americans living in the United States adopt the same unhealthy behaviour that contribute to diabetes in other racial groups: lack of physical activity and a diet high in calories, fat, sodium and refined sugars.[7]

Diabetes will clearly be a major drain on resources in the Chinese healthcare system in the future. In the US, diabetes-related treatments incur 20 per cent of the nation's total medical costs. With the US diabetic population forecast to exceed 30 million in a couple of decades, the annual cost to society could approach US$200 billion (double the estimates for 1999). Some estimates have found that sales of diabetes prevention and treatment pharmaceuticals could double to US$11 trillion by 2011 globally. Most of the major drug companies have diabetes-related product lines including Merck, Eli Lilly, GlaxoSmithKline and Novartis, as well as many smaller specialist pharmaceutical producers such as Amylin Pharmaceuticals, Alkermes and Nektar Therapeutics. The global insulin market, the major treatment for diabetes, is dominated by Lilly, Sanofi and Novo Nordisk, while the market for oral drugs that make cells more receptive to insulin are big sellers for Glaxo and Eli Lilly. New products, such as Byetta, from Amylin and Eli Lilly, that mimics a naturally produced hormone and helps control glucose levels, are next-generation diabetes drugs.

While most insulin is injected, a number of companies are working on inhaled insulin products. It should be remembered that while insulin obviously helps, life as an insulin-dependent patient is not always pleasant, and more targeted or inhaled drugs may improve both the condition and the patient's lifestyle. Primary among these new products is expected to be DPP-IV inhibitors, which boost natural levels of glucose-controlling hormones. Both Novartis and Merck are working on these treatments and pharmaceutical industry analysts believe that if ultimately successful and approved, they could add billions in annual sales for these companies.

Whatever the future costs, present costs are already high. In October 2009 for instance, the International Diabetes Federation (IDF) released new data through its IDF atlas, which indicates that the situation is already 'worse than we thought... ', according to Dr. Stephen Colagiuri, chair of the IDF task force on clinical guidelines and professor of metabolic health at the University of Sydney in Australia, noting that an estimated 285 million people around the world have diabetes, a figure that's predicted to soar to 435 million within 20 years. 'And unfortunately, diabetes is responsible for four million deaths a year and this is at a cost globally of US$376 billion.' Diabetes is fast becoming an Asian disease. The continent is home to four of the world's ten largest diabetic populations – India, China, Japan and Pakistan. In India alone, more than 35 million people are estimated to have diabetes, more than in any other country in the world.

As well as treatment, preventive education is important, to make people more aware of what healthcare professionals call the problems associated with a 'diabetigenic lifestyle' – that is to say, that treatment should begin long before blood glucose reaches levels considered diabetic. Spotting potential diabetics may not be that difficult; for instance, 'big belly syndrome' is a major sign. Some researchers suspect that big-bellied people develop insulin resistance as a result of biochemicals spewed out by large fat deposits in the liver and abdomen. Additionally, several North American studies have shown that patients who lose just 5 per cent of their body weight and exercise five times a week can reduce their chance of developing diabetes by 50 per cent.

Cancer

Similarly, for the obese, higher rates of cancer of the breast, colon, ovary, prostrate, endometrium (the layer of tissue that lines the uterus), kidney and gallbladder are all expected, and in younger patients than previously observed.

Cancers are a particular concern that will impact the cost of healthcare in China over the longer term. Clearly, obesity, as well as smoking and high levels of pollution, will add to the cancer problem. In April 2005 *Xinhua* reported that cancer rates in Shanghai were approaching a level equal to those seen in North America and Western Europe, with the disease affecting 300 out of every 100,000 people nationwide, and Shanghai having 110,000 cancer patients undergoing treatment along with 40,000 new patients being identified annually. Lung and breast were the major forms of cancer in the city and the second leading cause of death after cardiovascular disease.[8]

Heart Disease

The WHO has declared that by 2020 angiocardiopathy (diseases affecting the heart and the blood vessels) will be the main cause of death in China. According to data from the Asia Pacific cohort studies collaboration, the incidence of stroke in China is four times that of Western countries, and cardiovascular disease tends to strike Asians ten years earlier than it does their Western counterparts.

Smoking is obviously a factor in China, which, along with South Korea, has Asia's highest percentage of smokers; approximately 60 per cent of Chinese men smoke. Smoking, of course, is integrally linked to the obesity issue. The 5 January 2002 issue of the *British Medical Journal* reported that babies whose mothers smoked during pregnancy had almost a 40 per cent increased chance of being obese, and more than a 300 per cent increased chance of having developed type 2 diabetes at an early age.[9] Shanghai's Social Medical and Health Management Research Centre has reported smoking rates among the city's women to be 6 per cent of the total – up from 2 per cent in the mid-1990s. Shen Yifei, a women's issues expert at Shanghai's Fudan University has stated that, 'Women smokers were first seen at some social venues, such as bars and disco halls, but now it is fairly common among educated women, including white-collar workers and local university students'.[10]

Additionally, many believe that overweight and obese people tend to take up smoking more prevalently as a result of low self-esteem, a craving for acceptance or to reduce appetite. Of course, in a nation where 60 per cent of males smoke and some women, too, and where antismoking regulations are lax, passive smoking is a major factor.

Hypertension

According to the WHO, over 100 million Chinese suffer from hypertension, with their blood pressure above the normal range. The number of hypertension patients is thought to be increasing by 3 million annually.

A Chinese Ministry of Health survey in 1999 revealed that knowledge and awareness of hypertension among Chinese people, especially those between 35 and 44 years old, was significantly lacking. This lack of awareness was subsequently affecting the treatment and control of the disease. A national programme – 'Physicians and Patients, Heart by Heart' – to educate doctors and patients more extensively about hypertension was launched by the Ministry to try and improve the situation in October 2000, during China's third National Hypertension Day. Subsequent campaigns have concentrated on the link between hypertension and smoking. National Hypertension Day has continued in China annually, supported by the government as well as the WHO and Pfizer Pharmaceuticals who have jointly published a manual, *Instructions on Hypertension Prevention*, aimed at young and middle-aged workers.[11]

The Cost of Obesity – The Available Evidence

Being fat will cost in China's new healthcare system. According to the WHO, obesity accounts for between 2 per cent and 6 per cent of total healthcare costs in developed countries, though some researchers (such as Christopher Wanjek in *Food at Work*, a review report commissioned by the United Nations' International Labour Office) have estimated that the figure could be as high as 7 per cent.[12] The true costs are undoubtedly much greater as not all obesity-related conditions are included in the calculations.

There has been some work done already to calculate the financial cost of obesity, with most work having been done, perhaps predictably, in the US. In 1999 the American Obesity Association commissioned a cost study by the Lewin Group, a leading healthcare consulting firm.[13] The key finding was that the direct health care costs of obesity in the US were a total of US$102.2 billion in 1999. According to the Washington, DC-based Worldwatch Institute, the cost is about 12 per cent of the US healthcare budget.[14] By whatever measure, the cost is financially high. The Lewin Group, rather usefully, tried to calculate the percentage cost of each disease, based on the available scientific literature

at the time, and then calculated how much of the total cost of each disease
was attributable to obesity. This calculation does not include the related costs
of indirect health and social issues, but could also contain some degree of
double counting. Table 32 shows how those figures break down.

The same study also looked at results from other studies that linked the
direct correlation between the raised prevalence of conditions, such as type 2
diabetes, hypertension, heart disease, stroke and arthritis, with a raised BMI.
Those figures are detailed in Table 33.

Other studies have looked less at the cost of treating the diseases related
to obesity, but rather at the indirect costs. One, again in America, looked at
the cost of obesity to US business in 1994, found that US business was out of
pocket to the tune of US$12.7 billion in that year. Of this, US$2.6 billion was
attributed to mild obesity, the rest of the loss to 'moderate to severe' obesity. In
terms of how that money was spent, US$7.7 billion (60.6 per cent of the total)
went to health insurance expenditure. The costs of obesity-related paid sick
leave, life insurance and disability insurance totalled US$2.4 billion, US$1.8
billion and US$800 million respectively.[15]

Table 32: **US Obesity Costs in Relation to the Co-Morbidities**

Disease	Direct Cost of Obesity (US$bn)	Direct Cost of Disease (US$bn)	Direct Cost of Obesity as a % of Total Direct Cost of Disease
Arthritis	7.4	23.1	32%
Breast Cancer	2.1	10.2	21%
Heart Disease	30.6	101.8	30%
Colorectal Cancer	2.0	10.0	20%
Diabetes (Type 2)	20.5	47.2	43%
Endometrial Cancer	0.6	2.5	24%
ESRD	3.0	14.9	20%
Gallstones	3.5	7.7	45%
Hypertension	9.6	24.5	39%
Liver Disease	3.4	9.7	35%
Low Back Pain	3.5	19.2	18%
Renal Cell Cancer	0.5	1.6	31%
Obstructive Sleep Apnea	0.2	0.4	50%
Stroke	8.1	29.5	27%
Urinary Incontinence	7.6	29.2	26%
Total Direct Cost	102.2	331.4	31%

Source: The Lewin Group, 1999.

Table 33: **Factor of Increased Risk of Obesity Related-Diseases with Higher BMI**

Disease	BMI of 25 or Less	BMI Between 25 and 30	BMI Between 30 and 35	BMI of 35 or More
Arthritis	1.00	1.56	1.87	2.39
Heart Disease	1.00	1.39	1.86	1.67
Diabetes (Type 2)	1.00	2.42	3.35	6.16
Gallstones	1.00	1.97	3.30	5.48
Hypertension	1.00	1.92	2.82	3.77
Stroke	1.00	1.53	1.59	1.75

Source: Centers for Disease Control. Third National Health and Nutrition Examination Survey.

Adding the direct disease-treatment costs to the costs to business cited above provides a good rough working total for the US, US$114.9 billion, for the mid- to late-1990s. WHO figures for the year 2000 put the bill in that year at a total of US$122 billion, of which US$64.1 billion was attributed to direct costs, and US$58.8 billion to indirect costs. Of the total, type 2 diabetes represented US$98 billion. This was when, according to the Organisation for Economic Co-operation and Development (OECD), the US percentage of obese and overweight population was 64.5 per cent, out of a population of about 281 million in 2000, according to the census that year. That gives us a working overweight and obese population of 181 million. According to yet another study, obesity and smoking each account for about 9.1 per cent of total US health spending, that healthcare costs for overweight and obese people are on average 37 per cent more than for people of normal weight, and that this additional cost adds an average of US$732 to the annual medical bills of each American.[16]

In the UK, similar calculations have been worked on by various National Health Service agencies, as detailed in January 2006 in the report by the National Diabetes Strategic Programme Board in its report *The economics of diabetes: a structure for discussion by SPB members*, written by Professor Brian Ferguson.[17] In this report, Ferguson mentions previous work done in the UK on calculating the cost of diabetes to the health service budget:

For example, the 1996 King's Fund report estimated that all diabetes expenditure accounted for over 8 per cent of the acute hospital budget in the UK. More recent estimates (Diabetes UK, 2004) suggest that this may now be 10 per cent, with diabetes accounting for at least 5 per cent of all UK health care expenditure. The first Wanless report (2002) estimated the total annual cost of diabetes to the NHS to be £1.3 billion.

Ferguson then goes on to list some specific per annum cost estimates for the various treatments for diabetes, based on various sources, chiefly the previous Wanless Report, which, summarized, are:

Primary Prevention

Lifestyle interventions in high-risk groups: around £11,600 to £22,100
　Prescription of Metformin: around £15,000 to £42,400.

Secondary prevention

Blood glucose control: around £1,200
　Intensive blood pressure control: around £400
　Control of blood lipids: around £22,000

Complications

Retinopathy screening: around £1,400
　Foot complications: if targeted, around £4,000
　Professor Ferguson suggested a useful cost-effective figure for annual treatment as being about £20,000. He also states in his report that the estimated diabetes population of England (including both diagnosed and undiagnosed) was some 2.35 million people, or 4.67 per cent of the total population. Based on a total cost estimate of £1.6 billion (as per the Wanless report), per capita cost would be about £680 per diabetic per annum.

Given the age of the above research, and the rise in the cost of living, it can be estimated that the current cost per person in the US would by now be about US$900 a year. The UK cost is probably higher, the UK generally having a higher cost of living. The cost of living in China is, of course, less than in the US or the UK, and so, therefore, the costs associated with the same treatments for obesity would generally be less, based on Purchasing Power Parity (PPP). The Chinese government also caps the price of many drugs, keeping them significantly below market prices.

Take the Evidence, and Multiply That by China

To recap some of the statistics we noted at the start of this book: across China, 7.1 per cent of adults are obese and 22.8 per cent (more than one-fifth) are overweight, and throughout the country, an estimated 200 million people out of a total population of around 1.3 billion are overweight (over 15 per cent), and that this rate rises to nearly 20 per cent in China's major cities. In the past decade, the number of Chinese defined as overweight increased 39 per cent and the number deemed clinically obese by 97 per cent. The adverse effects on health in China were already starting to show:

- Hypertension rates among adults had reached 18.8 per cent, increasing by 31 per cent or 70 million cases since 1991;
- 160 million people were suffering from high blood pressure;
- Over 20 million people were suffering from diabetes, fully 2.6 per cent of the population.

Compared with the data collected in a 1996 survey, the prevalence of diabetes among adults over the age of 20 in China's major cities had increased from 4.6 per cent to 6.4 per cent. China's growth rates in obesity and associated illness have outstripped all other countries, and the number of overweight is growing at 8 per cent per annum.

We know that China is cheaper to live in than the US. If the US PPP is the benchmark index of 1, then in 2006 China was 1.79, according to the World Bank. A crude measure, perhaps, for the costs associated with healthcare, but the best one available to us. This means that if we assume that the average cost per capita of obesity treatment in the US has now risen to about US$900, then in China the cost will be about US$500 per capita.

There are about 1,028.95 million adults in China. If 7.1 per cent are obese, this represents about 75 million people. If 22.8 per cent are overweight, this is another 235 million people. Add them together, and you have 310 million people. Cost each of these people at US$500 per annum, and the annual additional cost to China created by the problems of its overweight and obese population reaches US$155 billion. In 2005 total healthcare spending in China was RMB866 billion. In that year, the average US$/RMB exchange rate was about 1:8. This means that the above total healthcare budget of China was about US$108 billion.

Clearly, US$108 billion is less than US$155 billion. This means that either the cost of treatment in China is much less than in the US, or that many Chinese are simply falling through the net. It is arguably most likely that both are true. Government caps on drugs are going to significantly reduce the amount spent on treatment of obesity issues. Likewise, many obese people will simply not get treatment, either because they avoid seeking treatment, or because they are just outside the social security safety net in China – a net that has very large holes in it.

What are the Potential Costs of Obesity to China?

To try to estimate the potential costs of obesity to the Chinese economy, it is necessary to make some very broad-stroke assumptions. The following is not meant to be a very detailed forecast, but is an attempt to illustrate the possible implications to China's healthcare costs over the next 10 years. Trending data on the skeletal historical data makes these assumptions more likely to be off the real mark, but we attempt this simply to give a hint as to the scale of the problem facing China, should things not improve.

The first task we must face is estimating the number of obese and overweight people in China. This we have done by evening out the growth rate in the estimated numbers across the surveys conducted in China, and trended that data forward. This we have also combined with trending forward the total population figures.

Based on projecting the historical estimates forward, both the overweight population and the obese population, given a continuation of historical trends (although gradually slowing as a natural trend within the population as China's economy matures and economic growth slows), are likely to increase as a proportion of the total population. Our broad-stroke estimate takes the overweight up to 29.3 per cent of the population by 2020, the obese to 15.9 per cent. This population of overweight and obese combined will see annual growth rates decline from over 5 per cent per annum now, to about 3.3 per cent in 2020. The total combined overweight and obese population in 2020 could be as high as 45 per cent of total population in China.

Let us assume that we are only able to cost for the obese population. We have elsewhere in this book used an average cost per person for treatment of obesity related illness, adjusted for purchasing power parity, of US$500 per capita per annum. If we use this as the cost in 2009, and assume a constant price for the period, i.e., no inflation of that price (although in the real world inflation is bound to increase the price), and multiply the number of obese people by that per capita price, we get the following set of figures.

These figures, it should be noted, are based on a constant 2009 year-end average exchange rate between the US$ and the RMB. Given recent economic events, China's currency is likely to increase in value, and this will most likely reduce the forecast RMB figure, but as we are unable to forecast future exchange rates, we have to use the constant figure.

To put the figure of RMB827.5 billion into perspective, we have also forecasted growth in Chinese government healthcare spending, based on recent historical growth rates.

Table 34: **Projected Costs of Obesity to China's Healthcare System, 2009–2020**

	Total Population	% Annual Growth	Total Overweight	Total Obese	% Overweight	% Obese
2009	1,369.58	1.03	309.63	136.65	22.61	9.98
2010	1,383.56	1.02	322.05	146.27	23.28	10.57
2011	1,397.53	1.01	334.46	155.88	23.93	11.15
2012	1,411.50	1.00	346.87	165.49	24.57	11.72
2013	1,425.47	0.99	359.28	175.10	25.20	12.28
2014	1,439.44	0.98	371.69	184.72	25.82	12.83
2015	1,453.41	0.97	384.10	194.33	26.43	13.37
2016	1,467.38	0.96	396.51	203.94	27.02	13.90
2017	1,481.35	0.95	408.92	213.55	27.60	14.42
2018	1,495.32	0.94	421.33	223.16	28.18	14.92
2019	1,509.29	0.93	433.74	232.78	28.74	15.42
2020	1,523.26	0.93	446.16	242.39	29.29	15.91

Source: authors' own estimates.

Table 35: **Average Projected Costs for Treatment of Obesity in Per Capita Terms, 2009–2020**

	US$ bn	RMB bn
2009	68.33	466.54
2010	73.13	499.35
2011	77.94	532.17
2012	82.75	564.99
2013	87.55	597.80
2014	92.36	630.62
2015	97.16	663.44
2016	101.97	696.25
2017	106.78	729.07
2018	111.58	761.88
2019	116.39	794.70
2020	121.19	827.52

Source: Authors' own estimates.

Table 36: **Projected Growth in Government Healthcare Spending and Costs of Obesity Treatment, 2009–2020**

RMB bn	Government Healthcare Spending	Cost of Obesity	% Cost of Obesity
2009	1,387.53	466.54	33.62
2010	1,519.01	499.35	32.87
2011	1,650.49	532.17	32.24
2012	1,781.97	564.99	31.71
2013	1,913.45	597.80	31.24
2014	2,044.93	630.62	30.84
2015	2,176.41	663.44	30.48
2016	2,307.89	696.25	30.17
2017	2,439.37	729.07	29.89
2018	2,570.85	761.88	29.64
2019	2,702.33	794.70	29.41
2020	2,833.81	827.52	29.20

Source: Authors' own estimates.

In Table 35, we have attempted to show that healthcare spending will keep ahead of the growth in cost of the obesity problem, assuming that any sane government will increase spending in order to stem the problem. Given this, we would estimate that the Chinese government will need to increase its annual spending on healthcare by an average of 6.7 per cent every year for the next 10 years (at constant prices) in order to be able to pay JUST for the illness related to the obese population and not including those associated with people who are classed as overweight.

A thumbnail sketch indeed, but one that illustrates the huge potential costs facing the Chinese government in order to pay for remedial treatment for obese people's lifestyles, on top of the already mounting costs of healthcare issues created by people living longer, facing more environmental pollution-related health issues, facing more stress-related health issues created by busier lifestyles, the mounting cost of drugs and treatments in themselves, and not including anything related to those overweight but not obese. Clearly, doing nothing but treat the symptoms rather than the causes of obesity is not going to be viable, even for a government that is as cash rich as that in China.

Can the Cost be Reduced?

Most surveys on obesity conducted around the world have found that as BMI increases, so do the numbers of sick days, medical claims and healthcare costs. One report concluded that the mean annual healthcare costs were US$2,274 for individuals above a BMI of 27 and US$1,499 for workers below that level. The researchers suggest, 'Employers may benefit from helping employees achieve a healthier weight.'[18]

However, Thompson, Edelsberg, Kinsey and Oster have developed an encouraging model based on the relationship between BMI and the risks and costs of five obesity-related diseases.[19] They then calculated the lifetime health and economic benefits of a sustained 10 per cent reduction in body weight of men and women, aged 35 to 64 with mild, moderate and severe obesity. They found that a sustained 10 per cent weight reduction would:

- Reduce the expected number of years of life with hypertension by 1.2 to 2.9 years, with hypercholesterolemia by 0.3 to 0.8 year, and with type 2 diabetes by 0.5 to 1.7 years;
- Reduce the expected lifetime incidence of coronary heart diseases by 12 to 38 cases per 1,000;
- Reduce stroke by 1 to 13 cases per 1,000;
- Increase life expectancy by 2 to 7 months;
- Reduce expected lifetime medical care costs of these five diseases by between US$2,200–US$5,300.

Meanwhile, back in China, and according to Gong Xiaodong, in a study entitled '*Firm ownership, satisfaction with working environment and absenteeism in urban China*', published by the Australian National University, of some 7,000 sampled employees aged between 16 and 60, on average, in 1995 workers took off 16 days from work, and while 12.5 per cent did not take any time off, about 91 per cent took between 1 and 30 days off, which means that some 78.5 per cent took at least one day off. There were 190.4 million urban workers in China in 1995, with an annual average wage of RMB5,500 (US$805.5), the daily rate of pay being about RMB22.80 (US$3.33). Even if all 78.5 per cent only took off one day, the loss of such workers due to sick leave in 1995 was at least RMB3.4 billion (US$450 million).[20]

In the ten or more years since 1995, obesity rates have increased dramatically. Due to the lack of available statistics, the cost to companies in loss of earnings because of obesity-related health issues, can only be guessed at. This does not include factors such as inflation. A dollars-and-cents analysis, or rather a yuan-and-fen analysis, of the costs to the Chinese healthcare system of obesity is only part of the story. At the same time, productivity is threatened as obese and overweight people miss work due to weight-related illness. This, too, costs in terms of time away from work, in bed, resting, recuperating, seeing doctors or just getting up late for work due to a restless night. Similarly, in the education system, children are losing days of school for the same reasons, not to mention the possible traumatic and depressing effects of bullying the fat kid. Lack of sleep and concentration affect knowledge retention and examination scores.

But there has to be some kind of reckoning for the cost of the obesity problem. In 2006, China's GDP was RMB21,180.8 billion (US$2,708.5 billion) and total healthcare spending was RMB984.33 billion (US$125.9 billion), or 4.64 per cent. If you take government spending on healthcare as a percentage of GDP in the same year, then this drops to 0.84 per cent. However, based on our previous calculations of the possible cost of obesity reaching as much as 17.5 per cent of GDP, the current spending of only under 5 per cent of GDP on healthcare is still not enough to cover the possible costs of obesity-related diseases. Or, if you base the costs of such treatments in China on GDP per capita, compared with the US, which is (US$37,000 in the US, as opposed to US$5,000 in China in 2003), then the total cost could be around US$61.5 billion, and with China's GDP in 2006 being about US$2,600 billion, even at a reduced price rate, the cost of obesity could still be 2.4 per cent of GDP. But if you consider an article posted on the *British Medical Journal* in March 2005, this estimated figure based on per capita GDP must be too small:

China has 160 million people with hypertension and another 160 million with hyperlipidaemia. Assuming the daily cost to be RMB1 (£0.06; $0.12; €0.09) for antihypertensive drugs and RMB2 for cholesterol lowering drugs, a conservative estimate of the total drug cost would be RMB175 billion (£11 billion; $21 billion; €16 billion) a year if all these patients were given drug treatment. This alone would consume almost a third of the total healthcare expenditure in the country.[21]

But spending will now rise more rapidly since the National Party Congresses in 2007 and 2009. Realizing the risks of disease (such as avian flu) spreading and going unchecked due to bad infrastructure, Beijing knows it has to step up to a new level of investment intensity, particularly in rural areas, and is beginning to put that investment in place. However, obesity is a predominantly urban problem, and the new healthcare spending plan is aimed at raising basic levels of healthcare provision in rural areas, which means urban Chinese are still going to be expected to foot most of the health costs created by their obesity problem.

The healthcare spending plans also have to cope with an increasingly aged Chinese population, with the related illnesses and cost of long-term treatments of degenerative disorders that comes with increased age in the population. The old used to be cared for by their extended families in traditional Chinese society, but China's new economy has seen declines in the extended family network, and economic migration means that many workers now live in nuclear families, often a long distance from their place of origin, and from their elderly parents.

But, back to obesity. It is not clinics and hospitals that create improvements in people's eating and living habits and ultimately improve people's understanding of the obesity issue; it is the healthcare professionals within those institutions who impart their advice and knowledge that are the key to changing the increasingly entrenched eating habits that have emerged to create the obesity problems.

Beijing and Big Pharma

The cost of paying for obesity-related treatments, especially drugs, is also likely to get more expensive because pharmaceutical companies are finding it increasingly hard to agree with the Chinese government's capping of drugs prices in China.

In late 2000, hoping to reign back the rapidly rising costs of drugs within the healthcare budget, and with pharmaceuticals representing almost half of the total budget, Beijing switched its drug pricing policy from trying to control drugs prices at each stage, which was becoming increasingly complicated and unwieldy, to simply capping the retail prices. The idea was to make drugs cheaper for the citizenry of China, leaving the drug companies and healthcare providers to fight over the remaining profits on the drugs. Inevitably, this led to over-prescription, prescription of nonessential drugs and the prescribing of more expensive drugs where cheaper alternatives existed, in order to improve incomes. The drug companies also found it was in their interest to 'work with' healthcare providers to ensure that their drugs were given 'shelf space' in the healthcare market place. By 2001 the retail prices of most drugs were slashed by 15 per cent.

Then, in October 2006, China's government announced further pricing controls through the National Development and Reform Commission's (NDRC) introduction of centralized control over all drug prices, not only to unify the pricing of drugs, but also to further cap the profit margins of the pharmaceutical industry in China. This capping was extended from 1,500 items to 2,400. However, these price controls depended on the type of drug, and key within the policy was the introduction of a tiered pricing system providing differential pricing for generic, original, patented and first-line drugs. The NDRC also capped the price markup at retail outlets at 15 per cent, and a series of pricing incentives was introduced to help prop up the flagging, profit-starved domestic drugs manufacturers.

Drugs prices took a further pounding as recently as October 2009, when the NDRC again introduced new price caps on 1,057 pharmaceutical products, further lowering prices by an average of 12 per cent, although the prices of another 1,300 or so drugs remained static. Meanwhile, a few drugs considered to be in short supply were given a price rise in order to encourage greater production.

The problem for domestic drug companies is that the price capping is making them very lean, with little or no profit to invest back into new product R&D. The problem for the foreign companies is that they are simply selling way below their international prices in a market that is supposed to be market led. Foreign and domestic, the pharmaceutical industry is finding it hard going in China. It also means that when acute or chronic healthcare issues arise, such as those mentioned above, and the demand for treatment suddenly or significantly increases, market forces would indicate a rise in prices due to increased demand, but what is more likely to happen is that prices will be artificially forced down.

Obesity and its related diseases are clearly a case where this kind of rise in treatment demand would normally create rising costs. However, longer-terms illnesses, such as those associated with obesity, cannot see justification for short-term, shock-averting price caps, and the pharmaceutical industry will have to negotiate hard for more advantageous pricing with a Chinese government that will be looking for hard discounts on proprietary drugs that are always facing the ticking explosive of time limits to their proprietary nature and their potential as cash creators for the drug companies.

Clearly the drug companies and the Chinese government could find that they are at loggerheads in the future, and a rise in obesity-related illnesses could be a key catalyst in a rise in tensions between Beijing and Big Pharma.

Balancing the cost of treatment is one problem, but helping to reduce the problem in the first place is surely the better option. For drug manufacturers, it might seem like anathema to be promoting good health, as they make their money from bad health. However, promoting good health is not only more humane, but it also creates good PR, and that can be crucial when negotiating favours from political commanders. Many drug and healthcare products and services companies like to show that they 'care', both in China and elsewhere. One case of direct relevance to the key theme of this book is that since at least 2005 the China subsidiary of leading diabetes care group Novo Nordisk, based in Denmark, has been running diabetes prevention and awareness programmes with the Beijing Diabetes Prevention Office at schools in the capital.

All well and good, but without the same primary prevention programmes being carried out wholesale across the country by local health authorities and (still too few) nutritionists, the obesity problem (and its related clinical issues) is not going to go away. Nor are the costs associated with the treatment of those issues, as described above, even if the government tries even harder to prune back drug prices.

Unless the Chinese government takes significant and direct action very quickly, specifically targeting the overweight/obesity issue that is growing, the problem will continue to grow and get ever more expensive to deal with. It is clearly a complex matter, putting an exact price tag on the consequences of this issue, and therefore, the wider economic and government budgetary constraints around it. However, the consequences are less difficult to predict.

Nutrition and Nutritionists

If the number of specialists in bariatric medicine are few in China, outside those claiming to be such and working for privately run cosmetic surgery clinics, then nutritionists are also in short supply. Though there are no official statistics and certification is problematic – most estimates, including those from the China Nutrition Society, indicate that there are somewhere between 2,000 and 4,000 qualified nutritionists in the whole country. Based on the premise that there should be one nutritionist for every 300 people, that means a shortfall of qualified nutritionists of about four million. Of course, arguably, there is a need even greater than the international norm, as China now suffers from two distinct nutritional problems requiring radically different solutions:

nutrition deficiency among those in poverty and among those in the urban areas whose diet has changed. Shanghai, where there are more nutritionists than in any other Chinese city with several hundred qualified nutritionists, still claims a shortfall of more than 6,000. Additionally, those that are qualified are mostly working within medical institutions (often on research) rather than in communities, schools or nursing homes. Additionally, some are being hired by large companies to work in-house.

It was only in 2006 that the Ministry of Labour and Social Security listed nutritionists serving at public food venues as a new profession. For several years now it has been rumoured that the national authorities are evaluating a draft of a regulation that requires all major hospitals, kindergartens, schools, communities and other public food sites to have their own nutritionists. In light of this, the number of people enrolling in nutritionist courses and the number of institutions offering certification courses has grown in the last two years, though, perhaps predictably, there have been calls that these courses (normally only four to five months in length) are inadequate and are turning out only marginally qualified professionals.

Despite the multiplying plethora of courses, many still believe that China is not seriously investing in professional nutritionists. Yu Xiaodong, Director of the National Development and Reform Commission's Public Nutrition and Development Centre, has noted that the US government spends US$60 billion a year on improving nutrition, while the figure in China is negligible. Yu also pointed out that China had indeed tackled comparable problems before with a high degree of success, noting the state's enforcement of iodized salt in 1978, which did much to reduce the incidence of endemic goitres (enlargement of the thyroid gland) along with other health benefits, and was widely praised internationally. At the same time, Peng Jiarou, a member of the National Committee of the Chinese People's Political Consultative Conference (CPPCC) and a doctor at Peking University's Medical School, contrasted China with Japan, where the government has introduced nutrition laws.[22] These public criticisms from prominent members of the medical community did appear to lead somewhere, and in 2005/2006 nutritional elements were included in the Eleventh Five-Year Plan, the first time nutrition had ever appeared in China's overarching national development guidelines.

The Cost of Failure

Some China analysts dismiss the idea that the longer-term effects of being overweight and obese will lead to either a crisis in the Chinese healthcare system or any potential collapse. They point to the fact that at other times of chronic strain on the system, most notably SARS, problems in the system were simply covered up, pushed under the carpet and blocked from the press or public discussion. However, obesity is different.

In the past, inadequate healthcare has been hidden due to the fact that problems have, by and large, affected the rural population or those on the edges of society. SARS, outbreaks of encephalitis, avian influenza flu H5N1, even hepatitis B have largely been outbreaks affecting either rural populations or migrant worker concentrations, i.e., those at the margins of Chinese power and society and largely unable to claim their rights or protest effectively. To an extent, other notable outbreaks such as the Hunan AIDS crisis (due largely to mixed blood) and various outbreaks linked to pollution and toxic spills have overwhelmingly affected people in less developed rural or semi-rural areas.

However, a buildup of untreated problems from obesity affects a different constituency – one the Chinese government is far more mindful of. Obesity is an urban disease, largely an affliction of the relatively wealthy – obese children destined for college educations, and successful white-collar, urbanite, professional parents. In many cases they are the children of party cadres – one of the two sectors supposed to benefit most from the system.

Additionally, the problem is accentuated by the fact that unlike most previous chronic strains on the healthcare system, they are not short-lived 'one-off' shocks to the system, but are ailments and diseases that develop and increase in frequency more slowly, and once evident, require long-term care. In many cases the ailments will be identified at a relatively young age and require lifelong treatment while not necessarily significantly reducing the life span of the patient. This means long-term, intensive and expensive care involving large amounts of time for doctors, nurses, hospital administrations and other healthcare professionals. It also means longer-term provision of expensive pharmaceuticals and other medical treatments and longer stays in hospitals for treatment and post-operative/treatment care. Which all adds up to massive costs, and these are costs that are growing as connected and informed diabetics or parents of diabetics follow the growing practice elsewhere in the world, use the Internet and demand more targeted and more expensive pharmaceutical products, rather than just insulin shots. The expenses are also getting more costly, thanks to rising prices and spending power.

If these costs are not met and adequate treatment and medication not provided, then parents, grandparents, uncles, aunts and friends of the sick will become annoyed. These people are not poor peasants, nor are they, by and large, uneducated, remote from the centres of power or financially without means. They are professionals with university educations who own homes, cars, businesses and other assets, while also having access to a wide range of media, including overseas media and the Internet, and know how to use them to their advantage. Additionally, they are increasingly emboldened by their position in society to call for their rights, understand the legal and petitioning system, the party structure and where to apply influence.

Conclusion

THE FUTURE OF FAT CHINA – VICTIMS OF THEIR OWN SUCCESS?

Lifestyle – The New Threat

Obesity is a bullet that the Chinese government, society and their healthcare system cannot dodge. It's happened already, is continuing and will filter out across China's rapidly growing hinterland cities and impact the creaking healthcare system over the coming years. Beijing realizes this. Wang Longde, China's former Deputy Health Minister, has stated that 'Lifestyles, eating habits and the healthcare system have changed, and so have diseases and death rates…chronic diseases don't only affect people's health they undermine the working strength of society….'[1]

For most of China's urban residents, their lifestyle, and consequently their diet, have changed radically over the last 30 years and obesity is just one important consequence. The urgency of this became evident in a major study published in 2005 examining the leading causes of death among Chinese adults over 40 years of age: the conclusion was that vascular disease and cancers had become the leading causes of death. The report found that control of hypertension, smoking cessation, increased physical activity and improved nutrition were all crucial factors in reducing premature death. While noting that China has made incredible strides in reducing infant mortality and deaths from infectious diseases (such as tuberculosis) and significantly extending life expectancy, at the same time, adverse changes in lifestyle, notably a rapidly increasing intake of dietary fats and decreased levels of physical activity typical of industrialization and urbanization, were increasing the risk and incidence of chronic diseases, including vascular disease and cancer.[2] Put simply – Chinese people's new lifestyles were in some cases killing them.

We should, of course, never forget that according to China's Health Ministry, approximately 24 million Chinese still suffer from malnutrition, while some NGOs put this number still higher. Malnutrition and poverty are, like smoking, preventable risk factors if tackled seriously. In this sense, the obesity issue is merely one extreme of a whole host of healthcare issues facing the Chinese nation, with poverty and malnutrition at the other extreme – further proof of the complications and multiplicity of issues which reflects the complexity and wide range of extremes within China as a nation, a crucial facet of the country that is often ignored or glossed over.

In a report entitled *Future Consumption Patterns in Developing Countries: From Rural to Urban, Malnutrition to Obesity, Sorghum to McDonald's*, International Food Policy Research Institute (*IFPRI*) researchers argued succinctly that:

> Obesity is increasing in developing countries among both the rich and the poor. However, there will be a lag period before developing countries see the current increase in obesity rates translate into higher rates of chronic disease. It is important for developing countries to change eating habits now before obesity leads to diseases down the road.[3]

Exactly how the debate on obesity in China will shape up in the coming years is not altogether clear. Any numbers of facts, assumptions, stereotypes, deeply ingrained beliefs and visual messages are simultaneously at play. It is not altogether likely that any clear consensus on weight and obesity will develop, and any developments that do occur may well be (as it is, effectively, now) contradictory. The belief that excess weight indicates prosperity, even health, will likely persist in a portion of the popular imagination; the notion of additional weight as evidence of the triumph over famine in previous decades will be shared by some; that weight equals status and success will persist in other minds, while instant gratification and conspicuous consumption will override longer-term health concerns for many. Single children will undoubtedly continue to be spoiled by many doting and, ultimately, well-meaning parents, grandparents, uncles and aunts. This issue is as much about lifestyle choices and social enlightenment as is it about menu choices and awareness of ingredients.

On the other hand, the new urban middle class of a later generation can already be seen to be embracing concepts of lifestyle and leisure in a way previous generations simply could not, or chose not to. Health education along with healthcare services and choice of diet, through both increased access and availability as well as greater disposable income, are also generally increasing for a significant portion of the population. China is globalized in many ways – its emerging middle class especially so – and at the forefront of awareness of international trends, and this knowledge may increasingly grow to encompass a heightened awareness of weight, obesity and diet ('globesity' has already popped up as a buzzword, courtesy of the WHO in 2001). Food producers, food brands and food retailers are also likewise increasingly globalized and may start to add more 'healthy options' to their product ranges in China. China is shifting from being the market where foreign companies sell their products to being the place foreign and domestic companies develop new products and services, not just for China, but for the rest of the world, too. Labelling and regulation should improve, allowing concerned consumers more choice and education about their diet; restaurants, fast-food joints and others may also respond to consumer pressure, both internationally and in China, to improve the healthy options and alternatives on their menus. A new generation of more educated, urbanized, globalized Chinese youth may demand better and healthier foods to improve their diets, and food manufacturers and retailers will have to respond to stay in business.

However, it is impossible to ignore the massive importance of the state as an agent capable of promoting rapid and widespread change in a society such as the modern People's Republic of China. State intervention in the weight, obesity and diet issue will be crucial. Health, and consequently the eradication of obesity, can become government campaigns – a healthy non-obese China is a strong China; an overweight, obese China is a weak China, as Wang Longde, quoted above, and others have noted. There are, of course, inherent dangers in such categorizations that play to the worst aspects of national chauvinism sometimes displayed in China. The reintroduction of the state into people's private lives may not be appreciated or deemed desirable; 'demonizing' the overweight is, ultimately, never helpful.

Also, obesity in China is not simply about McDonald's, KFC or other Western fast-food joints expanding across the country (though these share a portion of the blame) or the range of new food and beverage products available to consumers, but really about volume. While in the West volume has been a problem since the end of the Second World War in North America and after the austerity years in Europe, fast-food and all the new food products have just added to the problem, and in many cases tipped the scales in the wrong direction for many people. As Dr Henk Bekedam, the WHO's Chief China Representative in Beijing at a time when obesity first became a media issue in the country, commented, 'People are eating more, but unfortunately they're not eating better.'[4] And so, we'll give the last word to Professor Philip James, a former Chair of the London-based International Obesity Task Force (IOTF) who commented that '…political will and increased public awareness will decide whether obesity is here to stay or go…'[5]

NOTES

Introduction

1 The debate on obesity as a disease has progressed in recent years with the 2008 publication of a paper claiming that differences in BMI and waist were 77 per cent governed by genetics. See Jane Wardle, Susan Carnell, Claire Haworth and Robert Plomin, 'Evidence for a strong genetic influence on childhood adiposity despite the force of the obesogenic environment', *American Journal of Clinical Nutrition*, 87 (2008): 398–404.

2 It is worth making the point early on that the authors do not consider obesity to be a 'disease' in the classic sense, but rather a condition, and that individuals do not actually die from obesity but from pathologies that may arise from being extremely overweight.

3 'Satcher: Obesity almost as bad as smoking', CNN.com, 16 July, 2002, available at http://edition.cnn.com/2001/HEALTH/conditions/12/13/satcher.obesity/index.html.

4 Greg Critser, Fatland: How Americans Became the Fattest People in the World (New York: Penguin, 2004); Eric Schlosser, Fast Food Nation: What the All-American Meal is Doing to the World (New York: Penguin 2002).

5 Mireille Guiliano, *French Women Don't Get Fat: The Secret of Eating For Pleasure*, (New York: Knopf 2004).

6 As a point of clarification, the authors are limiting themselves to discussing obesity as due to various economic circumstances and not other possible factors causing weight gain or obesity, such as and including overeating as a psychological condition or addiction (clinical rather than any moral weakness) and as a result of changes to the endocrine system through pathological changes, hormonal imbalances (such as hypothyroidism or hypopituitarism) or genetic predisposition to extreme weight gain.

7 Frank Dikötter, *The Age of Openness: China Before Mao* (Hong Kong: Hong Kong University Press 2008), p. 92.

8 Carl Crow, *Four Hundred Million Customers* (New York: Harper & Bros, 1937), p. 1.

9 Stephen L. Morgan, 'Biological indicators of change in the standard of living in China during the twentieth century', in 'The Biological Standard of Living in Comparative Perspective: Contributions to the Conference held in Munich, January 18–22, 1997, XIIth Congress of the International Economic History Association' (Stuttgart: Franz Steiner Verlag 1998).

Chapter 1: China Gets on the Scales

1 Charlotte Ikels, *The Return of the God of Wealth* (Palo Alto: Stanford University Press 1996).

2 'China Revises Body Weight Index Which Shows 50 per cent Overweight', *Asian Economic News*, 9 July 2001.

3 mmHG = millimetres of mercury.

4 *Shenzhen Daily*, 13 October 2004.

5 'Overindulging in Sichuan cuisine may harm your health', *China Daily*, 3 November, 2007.

6 Stephen Green, 'China Years: How Many are you Living?', *Standard Chartered*, 19 September 2007.

7 Rachel DeWoskin, *Foreign Babes in Beijing – Behind the Scenes of a New China* (New York: W. W. Norton & Company 2005).

8 'Obesity weighs down Shanghai's children', *China Daily*, 9 November 2004.

9 As a point of clarification, while the use of the term 'epidemic' to describe the rise of obesity in China (or globally) has been used in sensational ways by the media, the authors feel its use justified when qualified. Though the term 'epidemic' inherently suggests contagion, the term can be applied to a sudden rise in many phenomena including obesity as well as deaths from firearms, cigarette smoking, gang culture, etc. While many definitions of epidemic do specifically mention contagion or the spread of infectious diseases (and obesity is obviously not contagious) the OED gives a nontechnical definition of an epidemic as 'a widespread occurrence of a disease in a community at a particular time.'

10 Barry M. Popkin, 'Will China's Nutrition Transition Overwhelm Its Health Care System And Slow Economic Growth?', *Health Affairs* 27, no. 4 (2008): 1064–1076.

11 'Healthy lifestyle to tackle obesity', Centre for Health Protection, Department of Health, Hong Kong SAR Government, 15 September 2005.

12 China National Diabetes and Metabolic Disorders Study Group, 'Prevalence of Diabetes Among Men and Women in China', *The New England Journal of Medicine*, 362, No.12 (25 March 2010):1090–1101.

Chapter 2: China's Fat Class

1 'Consuming China: pretty fictions, hard facts', *China Economic Quarterly*, Q4, December 2006, Dragonomics Ltd.

2 Dawn Gilpin and Priscilla Murphy, *Crisis Management in a Complex World*, (Oxford: Oxford University Press 2008), p. 105.

Chapter 3: Fat City – Obesity and Urbanisation

1 Though several other cities in China's northeast (*dongbei*) give Beijing a run for its money, the statistics from those cities are nowhere near as complete as the surveys conducted in the capital.

2 '60% Adult Beijingers Are Overweight', *China Daily*, 12 October 2004.

3 'Complete Kitchen Living' (2005), Survey for IKEA Services AB, by ISOPUBLIC, Market and Opinion Research.

4 Paula M. Miller, 'IKEA with Chinese Characteristics', *China Business Review*, July–August, 2004.

5 Ken Too Wing-tak, 'A study of private/public space in Hong Kong', University of Hong Kong, 2007.

6 www.xintiandi.com

7 'Report on Longevity and Mortality in Beijing', National System Reform Committee (NSRC), 2003 (in Chinese).

Chapter 4: Mega-Wok – China's Diet from Cabbage to Cuisine

1 China Statistical Yearbook 2007, food price index.
2 'Chinese People's "Face" vs. Restaurant Food Waste', *People's Daily*, 4 September 2001.
3 Carl Crow, *Foreign Devils in the Flowery Kingdom*, (New York: Harper & Bros. 1940).
4 See, for instance, Jikun Huang and Howarth Bouis, 'A 2020 Vision initiative study of China, the Philippines, and Taiwan', IFPRI.
5 Qingbin Wang and Wei Zhang, 'China's Potato Industry and Potential Impacts on the Global Market', *American Journal of Potato Research*, March–April 2004.
6 *China Daily*, 6 July 2005.
7 'Food police needed to fight gluttony and paucity', *Xinhua*, 26 May 2005.
8 'Foundation warns over hidden salt', *Taipei Times*, 25 July 2009.
9 Kazuteru Yokose and Hossein Janshekar, 'Monosodium Glutamate (MSG)', *SRI Consulting*, January 2007.
10 M. Hermanussen et al. (2006) 'Obesity, voracity and short stature: The impact of glutamate on the regulation of appetite', *European Journal of Clinical Nutrition* (August 2005) 60:25–31, 31.
11 Ka He et al., 'Association of Monosodium Glutamate Intake With Overweight in Chinese Adults: The INTERMAP Study', *Obesity* 16: 8 (2008): 1875–1880.
12 Robert Ho Man Kwok (1968), 'Chinese restaurant syndrome', *New England Journal of Medicine* 18 (178), 796.
13 Alex Renton, 'If MSG is so bad for you, why doesn't everyone in Asia have a headache?', *The Observer*, 10 July 2005.

Chapter 5: Shelves of Fat – Food Retailing in China

1 'Chindia Leads The Way Shape Of Things To Come', *CLSA Quarterly*, October 2008.
2 'Distribution and Logistics in China', *Access Asia*, March 2009.

Chapter 6: Fast Fat – The Impact of Fast-Food in China

1 Warren Liu, *KFC in China: Secret Recipe for Success* (Singapore: John Wiley & Sons 2008).
2 Paul French, 'Retail Markets: Tough Times for the Colonel', *China Economic Quarterly* Vol. 13, No. 3, September 2009.
3 'Hidden danger in half term "treats"', *Consensus Action on Salt and Health* 19 October 2007, available at http://www.actiononsalt.org.uk/media/press_releases/fast%20foods%20 2007/fast_food_release_october_2007.doc
4 Katherine M. Flegal et al., 'Excess Deaths Associated With Underweight, Overweight, and Obesity', *Journal of the American Medical Association* Vol. 293, No. 15, 20 April 2005.
5 *The Economist*, 25 August 2009.

Chapter 7: Selling Fat – Promoting Fat in China

1 Paul Kingsnorth, One No, Many Yeses: A Journey to the Heart of the Global Resistance Movement (London: Free Press 2004), p. 150.

2 'Children's food choices, parents' understanding and influence, and the role of food promotions', Ofcom, available at http://www.ofcom.org.uk/research/tv/reports/food_ads/

Chapter 8: Little Fat Emperors – Obesity Among China's Children

1 Sander Gilman, *Fat: A Cultural History of Obesity* (Cambridge: Polity 2008).
2 Guo Nei, 'Child obesity a bigger problem', *China Daily*, 10 July 2006.
3 Indeed, stories about fat people are generally run as amusing features in Chinese newspapers. For instance, a dozen Chinese newspapers including *TBN*, the *China Times* and the *Beijing Times* all prominently covered the launch of the Beijing Fat Person's Club in 2006, the only event that seemingly was able to push the ongoing soccer World Cup in Germany off the front page at the time. Most also covered the story of '1000-pound Dancing Troupe,' a group of four women from Nanjing.
4 The pros and cons of stay-at-home vs. working mums is a whole other debate and a continually raging one, with some arguing that the diets of children reared by stay-at-home mums are better and healthier and others, that it leads to excessive coddling and spoiling in a culture where both are already a problem for single children. The only point we wish to make here is that stay-at-home mums are a distinct minority in China, meaning that grandparents have become widely involved in raising children.
5 *Access Asia* from Chinese national statistics and household consumer survey data.
6 D. F. Y. Chan et al., 'New Skinfold-thickness Equation for Predicting Percentage Body Fat in Chinese Obese Children', *Hong Kong Journal of Paediatrics* Vol 14. No. 2, 2009.
7 Allison Jones, 'Let's Hope McDonald's Deliveries Trigger a Backlash', *South China Morning Post*, 10 April, 2005.
8 *Consumer Reports*, November 2008.
9 Zumin Shiet et al., 'The sociodemographic correlates of nutritional status of school adolescents in Jiangsu Province, China', *Journal of Adolescent Health* Volume 37, No. 4, (October 2005), pp. 313–322.
10 '1 in 5 primary school kids overweight', *Hong Kong Government News*, 3 April 2006, available at http://news.gov.hk/en/category/healthandcommunity/060403/html/060403en05002.htm
11 'Kids Discover Joys of Sport with "Happy Ten"', *China Daily*, 2 June 2006.
12 A. Lee and K. K. Tsang, 'Healthy Schools Research Support Group. Youth Risk Behaviour in a Chinese Population: A territory wide Youth Risk Behavioural Surveillance in Hong Kong', *Public Health* 118 (2) (2004): 88–95.
13 A. Lee et al., 'Health Crisis of Our New Generation: Surveillance on Youth Risk Behaviours', Centre for Health Education and Health Promotion, School of Public Health, The Chinese University of Hong Kong, 2002.
14 A. Lee et al., 'Multi-centre youth risk behaviours survey in southern part of China'. Symposium Paper presented at the 18th World Conference in Health Promotion, International Union for Health Promotion and Education April 26–30 April 2004, Melbourne, Australia.
15 Rowan Simons, *Bamboo Goalposts: One Man's Quest to Teach the People's Republic of China to Love Football* (London: MacMillan 2008).

Chapter 9: The Fat and the Thin – China's Body Image

1 Antonia Finnane, *Changing Clothes in China: Fashion, History, Nation* (New York: Columbia University Press 2008), pp. 161–167. Of course, now the brassiere is commonplace in China, though it is perhaps interesting to note that variations on the traditional *xiaomajia* and *doudu* became fashionable items worn outwardly by many urban women in the late 1990s and early 2000s, akin to a localized take on the 'spaghetti strap' tops then popular in the West.

2 Sander Gilman, *Fat: A Cultural History of Obesity*, (Cambridge: Polity 2008).

3 'Heavy People From All Walks of Life Unite', *China Daily*, 26 March 2005.

4 'Fat Cops to be Laid Off', *China Daily*, 16 June 2004.

5 'Wanted: tall, thin women to present Olympic medals', *Reuters*, 20 November 2007.

6 *South China Morning Post*, 16 February 2004.

7 *Chengdu Evening News*, 7 June 2004 (in Chinese).

8 *Information Times*, 22 June 2004 (in Chinese).

9 *South China Morning Post*, 19 February 2004.

10 'Cosmetic Surgery Lawsuits', *China Quality Daily*, 5 November 2005 (in Chinese).

11 *Oriental Morning Post*, 4 August 2004 (in Chinese).

12 'Weight Worries Create a Market', *Xinhua*, 4 April 2001.

13 Which still places it in the same class as benzodiazepines such as Xanax, Librium and Valium, as well as a host of long-acting barbiturates such as Phenobarbital.

14 *Xinhua*, 26 March 2007, available at http://news.xinhuanet.com/newscenter/2005-08/24/content_3394533.htm (in Chinese).

15 D. G. Chen, X. F. Cheng and L. L. Wang, 'Clinical analysis of 200 cases of child anorexia', *Chinese Mental Health Journal* 7 (1993): 5–6 (in Chinese).

16 See *The China Beat*, 'When Skinny is Too Thin', 24 March 2010, available at (http://www.thechinabeat.org/?s=eating); Diana Freundl, 'Bingeing, purging, starving in the dark', Taipei Times, 2 January 2005.

Chapter 10: China's Fat Clinic – The Impact of Obesity on China's Healthcare System

1 'Healthcare: Time for a Check-Up', *China Economic Quarterly*, Q3, 2007.

2 ibid.

3 Charles Homer and Lisa A. Simpson, 'Childhood Obesity: What's Health Care Policy Got To Do With It?', *Health Affairs* 26, no. 2 (2007): 441–444.

4 Jay Bhattacharya and Neeraj Sood, 'Health Insurance, Obesity, and Its Economic Costs', *Economic Research Service/USDA* (E-FAN-04–00).

5 GAD is an enzyme necessary for the synthesis of the inhibitory neurotransmitter GABA in GABAergic nerve endings.

6 'Genetic and clinical characteristics of maturity-onset diabetes of the young in Chinese patients', *European Journal of Human Genetics* 13(4) (2005),422–427).

7 Lisa Liddane, 'Asian Americans Face Higher Diabetes Risk', *Orange County Register*, 24 May 2005.

8 'Xinhua, Cancer Becomes Second Leading Killer in Port City', *South China Morning Post*, 16 April 2005. Shanghai's official population at the time was 17.4 million.

9 Scott M. Montgomery and Anders Ekbom, 'Smoking during pregnancy and diabetes mellitus in a British longitudinal birth cohort', *British Medical Journal* 324 (5 January 2002), 26–27.

10 'Shanghai young women reaching for the fag', *People's Daily*, 5 November 2003.

11 'China Sees 3 Million More Hypertension Patients A Year', *People's Daily*, 8 October 2000.

12 Christopher Wanjek, *Food at Work: Workplace Solutions for Malnutrition, Obesity and Chronic Diseases* (Geneva: International Labour Office 2005).

13 'The Lewin Group Study—What Does It Tell Us and Why Does It Matter?', *Journal of the American Dietetic Association* 99: 4, pp. 426–427.

14 'Chronic Hunger and Obesity Epidemic Eroding Global Progress', The Worldwatch Institute, 4 March 2000.

15 D. Thompson, J. Edelsberg, K. L. Kinsey and G. Oster, 'Estimated economic costs of obesity to US business', *American Journal of Health Promotion*, 13:2 (November–December 1998), 120–7.

16 Eric Finkelstein, Ian Fiebelkorn and Guijing Wang, 'National Medical Spending Attributable To Overweight And Obesity: How Much, And Who's Paying?', *Health Affairs*, 10.1377/hlthaff.w3.219, May 2003.

17 'The economics of diabetes: a structure for discussion by Strategic Programme Board members', available at http://www.diabetes.nhs.uk/downloads/economics_%20of_%20diabetes_%20Jan06.doc

18 W. N. Burton et al.,'The costs of body mass index levels in an employed population', *Statistical Bulletin of the Metropolitan Insurance Corporation* 80:3 (July–September 1999), 8–14.

19 D. Thompson et al., 'G. Estimated economic costs of obesity to U.S. business', *Am Journal of Health Promotion* 13 (1998),120–7

20 http://econrsss.anu.edu.au/pdf/china-abstract-pdf/Gong.pdf

21 Jin Ling Tang and Yong Hua Hu, 'Drugs for preventing cardiovascular disease in China' (Editorial), *British Medical Journal* 330 (19 March 2005), 610–611.

22 Vivien Cui, 'Diet standards urged to avoid wrong sort of China rising', *South China Morning Post*, 4 August 2006.

Conclusion

1 Clifford Coonan, 'China's new wealth threatens to take heavy toll on health', *The Independent*, 10 May 2006.

2 Jiang He et al., 'Major Causes of Death among Men and Women in China', *The New England Journal of Medicine* 353: 11 (15 September 2005), pp. 1124–1134.

3 Barbara Rose, 'Future Consumption Patterns in Developing Countries: From Rural to Urban, Malnutrition to Obesity, Sorghum to McDonald's', International Food Policy Research Institute, available at http://www.ifpri.cgiar.org/2020/backgrnd/consump.htm.

4 John Liu, 'China's Wealth Breeds Obesity, Sparking Boom in Stomach Surgery', *Bloomberg*, 10 January 2007.

5 Roger Tatoud, 'French fries and fat kids – Asia's next epidemic', *China Dialogue*, 18 August 2006, available at http://www.chinadialogue.net/article/show/single/en/295-French-fries-and-fat-kids-Asia-s-next-epidemic.

ACKNOWLEDGEMENTS

This book is, in many ways, an extension of the work Access Asia has undertaken in China for over a decade, watching the growth of China's consumer markets – particularly the food, beverage, retail and catering sectors of the economy. Naturally, developments have often matched those seen in developed nations a generation or two previously and those currently ongoing in other developing nations – though invariably at a faster pace. Additionally, these changes have always come with a certain set of specific Chinese characteristics that made them and the outcomes of their arrival in China different. That's what makes China endlessly fascinating.

This project would not have happened without the support of CLSA Emerging Markets who kindly invited us to present to their clients on the subject of the growing rates of obesity in China. This book is the culmination of a research process that began with that initial presentation and also includes ideas from both CLSA and their clients who suggested useful avenues of exploration.

Thanks must also go to several useful sources including Hen Hong at Access Asia; Arthur Kroeber and the *China Economic Quarterly* team at Dragonomics in Beijing; Dr Richard Wellford of Hong Kong University and his *CSR-Asia* project (www.csr-asia.com); Stephen Green at Standard Chartered in Shanghai; Rowan Simons and the team at *China Media Monitor* in Beijing; Jeremy Goldkorn at Danwei.org; Grace Hung, Andy Rothman, David Murphy and Paul McKenzie of CLSA Emerging Markets. Others who gave us a chance to work out these ideas to an audience include Dr Kerry Brown and the China Discussion Group at Chatham House, the Great Britain-China Centre in London, the British Chamber of Commerce in Shanghai, Toby Webb and John Russell of *Ethical Corporation* magazine and Jonathan Fenby of Trusted Sources in London. Georgia Malden, Paul Kemp-Robertson and Matthew Carlton at Xtreme Information in London allowed us to work out many of the ideas in this book through their publication *Insight China*. For comments on the manuscript, many thanks to Tim Clissold, John Van Fleet, Dr Alison Hardie and Duncan Hewitt.

Also thanks to Tej Sood, Janka Romero and the team at Anthem Press for adopting this project so wholeheartedly from the start and seeing it through to fruition.

Cover Image

The cover image of this book is an example of the traditional Chinese New Year (*nianhua*) posters that invariably feature plump babies or well-fed children. They are still published every lunar year in China and distributed around the country. They have been an important influence on the propaganda posters produced by the Chinese Communist Party, combining various elements of folk art and symbolism – including the idea of fat as prosperous.

INDEX